篮球规则解释 2024

OBRI-OFFICIAL INTERPRETATIONS 2024

中国篮球协会 审定

本书"防伪码"使用说明

第一步　刮开右侧"防伪码"涂层。

第二步　微信扫一扫右侧二维码。

第三步　验证成功后，点击查看本书电子版。

注：本书"防伪码"支持两个微信号进行验证，验证成功后，再次扫描右侧二维码，即可查看相应内容。

资源获取入口

防伪码

扫码验证并激活

刮开涂层

北京体育大学出版社

策划编辑：曾　莉
责任编辑：王泓滢
责任校对：陈　颖
版式设计：高文函

图书在版编目（CIP）数据

篮球规则解释. 2024 : 英汉对照 / 中国篮球协会审定. -- 北京 : 北京体育大学出版社, 2025. 1. -- ISBN 978-7-5644-4240-8

Ⅰ. G841.4

中国国家版本馆 CIP 数据核字第 2024AL7302 号

篮球规则解释 2024　LANQIU GUIZE JIESHI 2024　中国篮球协会　审定

出版发行：北京体育大学出版社
地　　址：北京市海淀区农大南路 1 号院 2 号楼 2 层办公 B-212
邮　　编：100084
网　　址：http: //cbs.bsu.edu.cn
发 行 部：010-62989320
邮 购 部：北京体育大学出版社读者服务部 010-62989432
印　　刷：河北盛世彩捷印刷有限公司
开　　本：880mm × 1230mm　1/32
成品尺寸：145mm × 210mm
印　　张：12.75
字　　数：386 千字
版　　次：2025 年 1 月第 1 版
印　　次：2025 年 1 月第 1 次印刷
定　　价：85.00 元

出版说明

- 《篮球规则解释2024》是国际篮球联合会（简称“国际篮联”）对《篮球规则2024》的官方解释，自2024年10月1日开始生效执行。本文件取代所有以前公布的国际篮联《篮球规则解释》。

- 整本《篮球规则解释2024》内容对所有性别均适用，并应以同样方式予以解读。

- 本书英文部分是在上一版《篮球规则解释》的基础上修订而成的，所有的改动都用标黄的方式突出显示，方便读者对照；中文部分由英文部分翻译而来，不再一一标出。

TABLE OF CONTENTS

目录

TABLE OF DIAGRAMS

图例

Introduction

The FIBA *Official Basketball Rules* are approved by the FIBA Central Board and are periodically revised by the FIBA Technical Commission.

The rules are kept as clear and comprehensive as possible, but they express principles rather than play situations. They cannot cover the rich variety of specific cases that could happen during a basketball game.

The aim of this document is to convert the principles and concepts of the FIBA *Official Basketball Rules* into practical and specific situations as they might arise during a basketball game.

The interpretations of the different situations can stimulate the referees' minds and shall complement a detailed study of the rules.

The FIBA *Official Basketball Rules* shall remain the principal document governing FIBA basketball. However, the referees shall have the full power and authority to make decisions on any point not specifically covered in the FIBA *Official Basketball Rules* or in these FIBA *Official Interpretations*.

For the sake of consistency of these Interpretations, 'team A' is the (initial) offensive team, 'team B' is the defensive team. A1 – A5 and B1 – B5 are players; A6 – A12 and B6 – B12 are substitutes.

引言

国际篮联《篮球规则》由国际篮联中央局批准，并由国际篮联技术委员会定期修订。

规则力求清晰、全面，但规则表述的是原则，而不是比赛情况，规则无法囊括一场篮球比赛中所有可能发生的丰富的具体案例。

本文件的目的，是将国际篮联《篮球规则》文本中的原则和概念转换到在一场篮球比赛中可能出现的实际和具体的情况下。

对各种情况的解释可激发裁判员的思维，并能辅助裁判员对规则进行详细的学习。

国际篮联《篮球规则》是国际篮联关于篮球运动的纲领性文件，但在实际情况下，主裁判员应有充分的权力对国际篮联《篮球规则》或《篮球规则解释》未涉及的特殊情况作出决定。

为了规则解释的一致性，“A 队”是指（最初的）进攻队，“B 队”是指防守队。A1—A5、B1—B5 是指队员；A6—A12、B6—B12 是指替补队员。

Article 4 Teams

4-1 Statement: All players on the team must have all their arm and leg compression garments, including undershirts and undershorts, headgear, wristbands, headbands and tapings of the same solid colour.

4-2 Example: A1 wears a white headband and A2 wears a red headband on the court.

Interpretation: A1 and A2 wearing different colour headbands is not permitted.

4-3 Example: A1 wears a white headband and A2 wears a red wristband on the court.

Interpretation: A1 wearing a white headband and A2 wearing a red wristband is not permitted.

4-4 Statement: Wearing of scarf-style headbands is not permitted.

Diagram 1 Examples of scarf-style headbands

4-5 Example: A1 wears a scarf-style headband of the same solid colour as any other additional permitted equipment of the team-mates.

Interpretation: A1 wearing a scarf-style headband is not permitted. The headband shall not have opening/closing elements around the head and shall not have any parts extruding from its surface.

4-6 Example: A6 requests a substitution. The referees recognise that A6 wears a non-compression T-shirt under the shirt.

Interpretation: The substitution shall not be granted. Only compression garments may be worn under the uniform.

4-7 Example: A6 wears a compression garment under the shorts extending to

(a) above the knees.

第 4 条　球队

4-1　陈述　球队所有队员所穿戴的所有护臂和护腿的紧身服（包括紧身内衣和紧身内裤）、头饰、护腕、头带及弹力贴必须是相同且单一的颜色。

4-2　举例　在比赛场地上，A1 戴着白色的头带，A2 戴着红色的头带。

解释　不允许 A1 和 A2 戴不同颜色的头带。

4-3　举例　在比赛场地上，A1 戴着白色的头带，A2 戴着红色的护腕。

解释　不允许 A1 戴白色的头带，A2 戴红色的护腕。

4-4　陈述　不允许戴头巾式头带。

图 1　头巾式头带的示例

4-5　举例　A1 戴着一款头巾式头带，其单一的颜色与同队队员所穿戴的任何其他被允许的附加装备的颜色相同。

解释　不允许 A1 戴头巾式头带。头带在其围绕头部处不得有打开或闭合的部分，以及在其表面不得有任何的凸起。

4-6　举例　A6 请求替换。裁判员确认 A6 的球衣里面穿着一件非紧身 T 恤。

解释　不应准予替换。球衣里面只可以穿着紧身服。

4-7　举例　A6 在短裤里面穿着的紧身服长度延伸至：

（a）膝盖上方。

(b) the ankles.

Interpretation: The compression garment (undershorts) is legal and may be worn with any length. All players on the team must have all their compression garments, including undershirts and undershorts, headgear, wristbands, headbands and tapings of the same solid colour.

4-8 **Example:** A6 wears a compression garment (undershirt) under the playing shirt extending to

(a) the shoulders.

(b) the neck.

Interpretation: The compression garment (undershirt) is legal and may be worn

(a) with any length on and below the shoulders.

(b) up to the bottom of the neck.

All players on the team must have all their compression garments, including undershirts and undershorts, headgear, wristbands, headbands and tapings of the same solid colour.

（b）脚踝。

解释 紧身服（内裤）是合法装备，可以穿着任何长度的紧身服。球队所有队员的紧身服(包括紧身内衣和紧身内裤)、头饰、护腕、头带及弹力贴必须是相同且单一的颜色。

4-8 **举例** A6 在球衣里面穿着的紧身服（内衣）长度延伸至:

（a）肩膀。

（b）脖子。

解释 紧身服（内衣）是合法装备，并且可以穿着:

（a）覆盖肩膀上方或下方的任何长度的紧身服。

（b）高度低于脖子底端的紧身服。

球队所有队员的紧身服（包括紧身内衣和紧身内裤）、头饰、护腕、头带及弹力贴必须是相同且单一的颜色。

Article 5 Players: Injury and assistance

5-1 **Statement:** If a player is injured, appears to be injured or in need of assistance and, as a result, any person permitted to sit on the team bench (head coach, first assistant coach, substitutes, excluded players or accompanying delegation members of the same team) enters the court, that player is considered to have received treatment or assistance, whether or not actual treatment or assistance was performed.

5-2 **Example:** A1 appears to have an injured ankle and the game is stopped. The team A

(a) doctor enters the court and treats A1's injured ankle.

(b) doctor enters the court but A1 has already recovered.

(c) head coach enters the court to look after the injured player.

(d) first assistant coach, substitute, excluded player or any other accompanying delegation member enters the court but does not treat A1.

Interpretation: In all cases, A1 received a treatment and shall be substituted.

5-3 **Example:** The team's physiotherapist enters the court and fixes a lose taping on A1.

Interpretation: A1 received an assistance and shall be substituted.

5-4 **Example:** The team's doctor enters the court to find A1's lost contact lens.

Interpretation: A1 received an assistance and shall be substituted.

5-5 **Statement:** Any person permitted to sit on the team's bench, while remaining in the team's bench area, may provide an assistance to a player on the own team. If the assistance does not delay the game from being restarted promptly, that player is not considered to have received an assistance and shall not be required to be substituted.

5-6 **Example:** B1 fouls A1 in the act of shooting, close to the team A bench area. The ball does not enter the basket. While A1 attempts 2 or 3 free throws

第 5 条　队员：受伤和协助

5-1　陈述　如果一名队员受伤或是看似受伤了，或是需要协助，导致被允许坐在球队席上的任何人员（同队的主教练、第一助理教练、替补队员、出局的队员或随队人员）进入比赛场地；无论是否实施了实际的治疗或协助，那名队员应被视为已经接受了治疗或协助。

5-2　举例　A1 看似脚踝受伤了，并且比赛被停止。A 队的：

（a）医生进入比赛场地并治疗 A1 受伤的脚踝。

（b）医生进入比赛场地，但是 A1 已经恢复。

（c）主教练进入比赛场地照看该受伤队员。

（d）第一助理教练、替补队员、出局的队员或任何其他随队人员进入比赛场地，但未治疗 A1。

解释　上述所有情况下，A1 都已经接受了治疗并应被替换。

5-3　举例　A 队的理疗师进入比赛场地，并对 A1 身上脱落的弹力贴进行了固定。

解释　A1 已经接受了协助并应被替换。

5-4　举例　A 队的队医进入比赛场地，并寻找 A1 掉落的隐形眼镜片。

解释　A1 已经接受了协助并应被替换。

5-5　陈述　任何被允许坐在球队席的人员在其球队席区域时，可以向一名本队队员提供协助。如果该协助没有给应及时重新开始的比赛造成延误，那么该队员不被视为已经接受了协助，也不应被要求替换。

5-6　举例　B1 在 A 队球队席区域附近对正在做投篮动作的 A1 犯规。球未进入球篮。在 A1 将要执行 2 次或 3 次罚球时：

(a) the team A manager or A6 from the team's bench area passes a towel, a water bottle or a headband to any other team A player on the court.

(b) the team A physiotherapist from the team's bench area fixes a lose taping of any other team A player on the court or sprays the player's leg or massages the player's neck, etc.

Interpretation: In both cases, the team A player has not received an assistance that delays the game from being restarted promptly. The team A player shall not be required to be substituted. A1 shall continue to attempt 2 or 3 free throws.

5-7 **Example:** B1 fouls A1 in the act of shooting, close to the team A bench area. The ball does not enter the basket. After the foul, A1 falls on the court and into the team's bench area. A6 stands up and helps A1 to the feet. A1 is ready to play immediately, at the latest within approximately 15 seconds.

Interpretation: A1 has not received an assistance that delays the game from being restarted promptly. A1 shall not be required to be substituted. A1 shall attempt 2 or 3 free throws.

5-8 **Example:** A1 is awarded 2 free throws. While the referee communicates the foul at the scorer's table, A1 goes to a place in front of the team's bench area at the far end of the court and asks for a towel or a water bottle. Any person from the team's bench area passes A1 a towel or a water bottle. A1 dries the hands or takes a drink. A1 is ready to play immediately, at the latest within approximately 15 seconds.

Interpretation: A1 has not received an assistance that delays the game from being restarted promptly. A1 shall not be required to be substituted. A1 shall attempt 2 free throws.

5-9 **Example:** A1 scores a goal. Thrower-in B1 indicates to the referee that the ball is wet. The referee stops the game. Any person from the team B bench area comes on to the court and dries the ball or gives a towel to B1 to dry the ball.

Interpretation: In both cases, B1 has not received an assistance that delays the game from being restarted promptly. B1 shall not be required to be substituted. The game shall be resumed with a team B throw-in from any place behind the endline, except from directly behind the backboard. The referee shall hand the ball to a team B player for the throw-in.

（a）A 队的管理人员或 A6 从球队席区域递给比赛场地上 A 队任一其他队员毛巾、水壶或头带。

（b）A 队的理疗师在球队席区域给比赛场地上 A 队任一其他队员固定脱落的弹力贴，用喷剂喷洒腿部或按摩颈部，等等。

解释 在这两种情况下，A 队队员接受的协助没有给应及时重新开始的比赛造成延误。A 队队员不应被要求替换。A1 应继续执行 2 次或 3 次罚球。

5-7 **举例** B1 在 A 队球队席区域附近对正在做投篮动作的 A1 犯规。球未进入球篮。犯规后，A1 在比赛场地上摔倒并跌入其球队席区域。A6 起身并扶起 A1。A1 最晚在大约 15 秒内就做好了比赛准备。

解释 A1 接受的协助没有给应及时重新开始的比赛造成延误。A1 不应被要求替换。A1 应执行 2 次或 3 次罚球。

5-8 **举例** A1 获得 2 次罚球。在裁判员向记录台报告该犯规期间，A1 走到比赛场地远端的球队席区域前并提出要一条毛巾或一个水壶。该球队席区域任一人员将毛巾或水壶递给了 A1。A1 擦了手或喝了水。A1 最晚在大约 15 秒内就做好了比赛准备。

解释 A1 接受的协助没有给应及时重新开始的比赛造成延误。A1 不应被要求替换。A1 应执行 2 次罚球。

5-9 **举例** A1 中篮得分。掷球入界队员 B1 示意裁判员篮球湿了。裁判员停止了比赛。B 队球队席区域任一人员进入比赛场地并擦干篮球或将毛巾递给 B1 去擦干篮球。

解释 在这两种情况下，B1 接受的协助没有给应及时重新开始的比赛造成延误。B1 不应被要求替换。应由 B 队在其后场端线后的任意地点执行掷球入界继续比赛，篮板正后方除外。裁判员应将球递交给 B 队掷球入界队员。

5-10 **Example:** A1 has the ball in the hands for a throw-in from the frontcourt. The team A physiotherapist leaves the team bench area in the backcourt, remains outside the court and fixes the taping of A1.

Interpretation: The team A physiotherapist provided an assistance to A1 outside of the team bench area. A1 shall be required to be substituted.

5-11 **Example:** A1 does not yet have the ball in the hands for a throw-in from the frontcourt. The team A physiotherapist remains in the team bench area in the frontcourt and fixes the taping of A1.

Interpretation: The team A physiotherapist provided an assistance to A1 within the team bench area. If the assistance is completed within 15 seconds, A1 shall not be required to be substituted. If the assistance lasts more than 15 seconds, A1 shall be required to be substituted.

5-12 **Statement:** There is no limit to the time required for the removal of a seriously injured player from the court if, according to a doctor's opinion, the removal is dangerous for the player.

5-13 **Example:** A1 appears to be seriously injured and the game is stopped for about 15 minutes because the doctor believes that removal from the court could be dangerous for the player.

Interpretation: The doctor's opinion shall determine the appropriate time for the removal of the injured player from the court. After the substitution, the game shall be resumed without any penalty.

5-14 **Statement:** If a player is injured or bleeding or has an open wound and cannot continue to play immediately (within approximately 15 seconds), or if assisted by any person permitted to sit on that team's bench, the player must be substituted. If a time-out is granted to either team in the same game clock stopped period, and that player recovers or the assistance is completed during the time-out, the player may continue to play only if the timer's signal for the end of the time-out sounds before a referee beckons a substitute to replace the injured or assisted player.

5-15 **Example:** A1 is injured and the game is stopped. As A1 is not able to continue to play immediately, a referee blows the whistle making the conventional sign for a substitution. Either team requests a time-out

(a) before a substitute for A1 enters the game.

(b) after a substitute for A1 enters the game.

At the end of the time-out, A1 has recovered and requests to remain in the game.

5-10 **举例** A1 双手持球在前场执行掷球入界时，A 队的理疗师离开了其后场的球队席区域并在比赛场地外为 A1 固定弹力贴。

解释 A 队的理疗师在球队席区域外为 A1 提供了协助。A1 应被要求替换。

5-11 **举例** A1 在前场执行掷球入界期间尚未持球时，A 队的理疗师在其前场的球队席区域内为 A1 固定弹力贴。

解释 A 队的理疗师在球队席区域内为 A1 提供了协助。如果该协助在 15 秒内完成，A1 不应被要求替换。如果该协助持续时间超过 15 秒，A1 应被要求替换。

5-12 **陈述** 如果根据医生的意见，从比赛场地上移出一名严重受伤的队员是危险的，那么对将其移出比赛场地的时间没有限制。

5-13 **举例** A1 看似严重受伤，医生认为将其从比赛场地上移出可能是危险的，导致比赛停止了大约 15 分钟。

解释 医生的意见将决定把受伤队员从比赛场地上移出所需的适当时间。在替换后，应继续比赛，不作任何处罚。

5-14 **陈述** 如果一名队员受伤或正在流血，或者有开放性伤口，并且不能立即（大约 15 秒内）继续比赛，或者被允许坐在该队球队席的任何人员给予了该队员协助，该队员就必须被替换。如果在同一停止比赛计时钟期间任一队被准予了暂停，并且在暂停期间该队员恢复了或协助已完成，那么在计时员发出暂停结束信号以后以及裁判员招呼替补队员替换该队员之前，该队员可以继续比赛。

5-15 **举例** A1 受伤了并且比赛停止。因为 A1 不能立即继续比赛，裁判员鸣哨做出了替换的常规手势。任一队请求了一次暂停，在：

（a）替换 A1 的队员进入比赛之前。

（b）替换 A1 的队员进入比赛之后。

在暂停结束时，A1 已经恢复了，并要求留在比赛场地上。

Interpretation:

(a) If A1 recovers during the time-out, A1 may continue to play.

(b) A substitute for A1 has already entered the game, therefore A1 cannot re-enter until the next game clock running period has ended.

5-16 **Statement:** Players designated by their head coach to start the game may be substituted in case of an injury.

Players who receive treatment between free throws must be substituted in case of an injury.

In both cases, the opponents are also entitled to substitute the same number of players, if they wish.

5-17 **Example:** A1 is fouled and is awarded 2 free throws. After the first free throw the referees recognise that

(a) A1 is bleeding and is substituted by A6. Team B requests to substitute 2 players.

(b) B1 is bleeding and is substituted by B6. Team A requests to substitute 1 player.

Interpretation:

In (a) team B is entitled to substitute only 1 player. A6 shall attempt the second free throw.

In (b) team A is entitled to substitute 1 player. A1 shall attempt the second free throw.

解释

（a）如果 A1 在暂停期间已恢复，A1 可以继续比赛。

（b）替换 A1 的队员已经进入比赛。因此，A1 不能重新进入比赛，直到下一个比赛计时钟运行时段结束为止。

5-16 陈述 因为受伤，已经被主教练指定为比赛首发的队员可以被替换。

因为受伤，在罚球之间接受了治疗的队员必须被替换。

在这两种情况下，如果对方也希望替换，他们有权替换相同数量的队员。

5-17 举例 A1 被犯规并获得 2 次罚球。在第 1 次罚球后，裁判员确认：

（a）A1 正在流血，并由 A6 替换 A1。B 队要求替换 2 名队员。

（b）B1 正在流血，并由 B6 替换 B1。A 队要求替换 1 名队员。

解释

在（a）中，B 队只有权替换 1 名队员。A6 应执行第 2 次罚球。

在（b）中，A 队有权替换 1 名队员。A1 应执行第 2 次罚球。

Article 7 Head coach and first assistant coach: Duties and Powers

7-1 **Statement:** At least 40 minutes before the game is scheduled to start, each team's head coach or the team's representative shall give the scorer a team list with the names and corresponding numbers of the team members who are eligible to play in the game, as well as the name of the captain, the head coach and the first assistant coach.

The head coach is personally responsible to ensure that the numbers in the team list correspond to the numbers on the shirts of the players. At least 10 minutes before the game is scheduled to start, each head coach shall sign the scoresheet confirming that the names and corresponding numbers of the team members are entered on the scoresheet correctly, as well as the names of the captain, the head coach, and the first assistant coach.

7-2 **Example:** Team A presents in due time the team list to the scorer. The shirt numbers of 2 players are different than their actual shirt numbers or the name of a player is omitted on the scoresheet. This is recognised

(a) before the start of the game.

(b) after the start of the game.

Interpretation:

(a) The wrong numbers shall be corrected or the name of the player shall be added on the scoresheet without any penalty.

(b) The referee stops the game at a convenient time so as not to disadvantage either team. The wrong numbers shall be corrected without any penalty. However, the name of the omitted player cannot be added on the scoresheet.

7-3 **Example:** Team A head coach wishes to have injured players or players not intended to play to be permitted to sit on the team bench during the game.

Interpretation: The teams are free to decide who of the maximum of 12 team members eligible to play shall be entered on the scoresheet and entitled to sit on the team bench during the game, in addition to a maximum of 8 team accompanying delegation members.

第 7 条　主教练和第一助理教练：职责和权力

7-1　陈述　至少在预定的比赛开始前 40 分钟，每名主教练或其代表应向记录员提交一份球队名单，列有该场比赛中有参赛资格的球队成员的姓名和相应的号码，以及队长、主教练和第一助理教练的姓名。

主教练本人应负责确认球队名单上的号码和队员球衣上的号码相符。至少在预定的比赛开始前 10 分钟，每名主教练应以在记录表上签字来确认其已正确地在记录表上填入了球队成员的姓名和相应的号码，以及队长、主教练、第一助理教练的姓名。

7-2　举例　A 队按时提交球队名单给记录员。有 2 名队员的球衣号码与他们实际的球衣号码不同，或者在记录表上一名队员的姓名被遗漏了。这被确认在：

（a）比赛开始前。

（b）比赛开始后。

解释

（a）错误的号码应被纠正，或者应将遗漏队员的姓名加入记录表，不作任何处罚。

（b）裁判员在不将任一队置于不利的合适时机停止比赛。错误的号码应被纠正，不作任何处罚，但不能再将遗漏队员的姓名加入记录表。

7-3　举例　A 队主教练希望已经受伤的队员或不参加比赛的队员在比赛期间被允许坐在球队席上。

解释　球队可以自由决定哪些有参赛资格的球队成员（最多 12 名）应被登记在记录表上并有权在比赛期间与最多 8 名随队人员坐在球队席。

7-4 **Statement:** At least 10 minutes before the game is scheduled to start, each team's head coach shall confirm the 5 players who are to start the game. Before the game starts the scorer shall check if there is an error regarding these 5 players and if so, the scorer shall notify the nearest referee as soon as possible. If the error is recognised before the start of the game, the starting 5 players shall be corrected. If the error is recognised after the start of the game, the error shall be disregarded.

7-5 **Example:** It is recognised that one of the players on the court is not one of the confirmed starting 5 players. This occurs

(a) before the start of the game.

(b) after the start of the game.

Interpretation:

(a) The player shall be replaced by one of the 5 players who were to start the game without any penalty.

(b) The error shall be disregarded. The game shall continue without any penalty.

7-6 **Example:** The head coach requests the scorer to enter the small 'x' on the scoresheet for the 5 players who are to start the game.

Interpretation: The head coach shall personally confirm the 5 players who are to start the game by marking a small 'x' beside each player's number in the 'Player in' column on the scoresheet.

7-7 **Example:** The team A head coach and the team A first assistant coach are disqualified.

Interpretation: The team A captain shall act as the team A player head coach.

7-4 陈述 至少在预定的比赛开始前 10 分钟，每名主教练应确认比赛首发的 5 名队员。在比赛开始前，记录员应检查是否有与这 5 名队员相关的错误。如果有错误，记录员应尽快通知最靠近的裁判员。如果在比赛开始之前确认错误，应纠正首发的 5 名队员。如果在比赛开始之后确认错误，应忽略该错误。

7-5 举例 确认了一名比赛场地上的队员不是确认的 5 名首发队员之一。这一情况发生在：

（a）比赛开始前。

（b）比赛开始后。

解释

（a）该队员应被正确的比赛首发的 5 名队员之一替换，不作任何处罚。

（b）应忽略该错误，比赛应继续，不作任何处罚。

7-6 举例 主教练要求记录员在记录表上填入小“x”标明比赛首发的 5 名队员。

解释 主教练本人应在记录表上队员号码旁边的“上场队员”栏标上小“x”来确认比赛首发的 5 名队员。

7-7 举例 A 队主教练和 A 队第一助理教练都被取消了比赛资格。

解释 应由 A 队队长担任 A 队的队员兼主教练。

Article 8 Playing time, tied score and overtime

8-1 **Statement:** An interval of play starts

- 20 minutes before the game is scheduled to start.
- when the game clock signal sounds for the end of the quarter or any overtime, except the last one.

When the backboard is equipped with red lighting around its perimeter, the lighting takes precedence over the game clock signal sound.

8-2 **Example:** B1 fouls A1 in the

(a) unsuccessful

(b) successful

act of shooting before the game clock signal sounds for the end of the quarter.

Interpretation: The referees shall consult each other immediately and determine whether B1's foul occurred before the game clock signal sounded for the end of the quarter.

If they decide that B1's foul occurred before the game clock signal sounded, B1 shall be charged with a personal foul. In

(a) A1 shall attempt 2 free throws.

(b) A1's goal shall count. A1 shall attempt 1 free throw.

The game clock shall be reset to the time remaining when the foul occurred. The game shall be resumed as after any last free throw.

If they decide that B1's foul occurred after the game clock signal sounded, the foul shall be disregarded. The goal, if made, shall not count. If B1's foul meets the criteria of an unsportsmanlike foul or a disqualifying foul and there is a quarter or overtime to follow, B1's foul shall not be disregarded and shall be penalised accordingly before the next quarter or overtime starts. The foul shall count towards the team B fouls in the next quarter.

第 8 条　比赛时间、比分相等和决胜期

8-1　陈述　一次比赛休息期间开始于：

- 预定的比赛开始前 20 分钟。
- 结束一节或任一决胜期（除了最后一个）的比赛计时钟信号响时。

如果篮板四周配备了红色灯带，亮起的灯带优先于比赛计时钟发出的信号。

8-2　举例　在结束该节的比赛计时钟信号响之前，B1 对正在做投篮动作的 A1 犯规

（a）球未中篮。

（b）球中篮。

解释　裁判员应立即就 B1 的犯规是否发生在比赛计时钟信号响之前相互商议并作出决定。

如果他们判定 B1 的犯规发生在比赛计时钟信号响之前，B1 应被登记 1 次侵人犯规。

在（a）中，A1 应执行 2 次罚球。

在（b）中，A1 的中篮应计得分，A1 应执行 1 次罚球。

比赛计时钟应复位到犯规发生时的剩余时间。应如同任何最后一次罚球后那样继续比赛。

如果他们判定 B1 的犯规发生在比赛计时钟信号响之后，该犯规应被忽略。如中篮，不应计得分。如果 B1 的犯规达到了一起违反体育运动精神的犯规或是取消比赛资格的犯规的标准，并且随后还有另一节或是决胜期的比赛，则 B1 的犯规不应被忽略，并应在下一节或决胜期开始之前执行相应的罚则。该犯规应被计入 B 队下一节的全队犯规。

8-3 **Example:** A1 attempts a shot for a 3-point goal. The ball is in the air when the game clock signal sounds for the end of the game. After the signal, B1 fouls A1 who is still airborne. The ball enters the basket.

Interpretation: A1 shall be awarded 3 points. B1's foul against A1 shall be disregarded as it occurred after the end of playing time, unless B1's foul meets the criteria of an unsportsmanlike foul or a disqualifying foul and there is a quarter or overtime to follow.

8-3 **举例** A1 尝试 3 分投篮。当球在空中时，结束比赛的计时钟信号响起。在信号之后，B1 对仍在空中的 A1 犯规。球进入球篮。

解释 应判给 A1 得 3 分。B1 对 A1 的犯规应被忽略，因为此犯规是在比赛时间结束之后发生的，除非 B1 的犯规达到了一起违反体育运动精神的犯规或是取消比赛资格的犯规的标准，并且随后还有另一节或是决胜期的比赛。

Article 9 Start and end of a quarter, overtime or the game

9-1 **Statement:** A game shall not start unless each team has a minimum of 5 players on the court ready to play.

9-2 **Example:** At the start of the second half, team A cannot present 5 players on the court because of injuries, disqualifications etc.

Interpretation: The obligation to present a minimum of 5 players is valid only at the start of the game. Team A may continue to play with fewer than 5 players.

9-3 **Example:** Close to the end of the game, A1 is charged with a fifth foul and becomes an excluded player. Team A is reduced to 4 players as they have no more substitutes available. As team B is leading by a large margin, the team B head coach demonstrating fair play wants to remove one of the players to also play with 4 players.

Interpretation: The request by the team B head coach to play with fewer than 5 players shall be denied. If a team has sufficient players available, 5 players shall be on the court.

9-4 **Statement:** Article 9 clarifies which basket a team is to defend and which basket it is to attack. If by confusion any quarter or overtime starts with both teams attacking/defending the wrong baskets, the situation shall be corrected as soon as it is recognised, without placing either team at a disadvantage. Any points scored, time used, fouls charged, etc. before the stopping of the game remain valid.

9-5 **Example:** After the start of the game, the referees recognise that teams are playing in the wrong direction.

Interpretation: The game shall be stopped as soon as possible without placing either team at a disadvantage. Teams shall correct the direction of play. The game shall be resumed from the mirror-opposite place to where the game was stopped.

9-6 **Statement:** The game shall start with a jump ball at the centre circle.

9-7 **Example:** At the start of the game jumper B1 is charged with a personal foul against A1

(a) before

第 9 条 比赛或节、决胜期的开始和结束

9-1 陈述 除非每队有至少 5 名队员在比赛场地上准备比赛，否则比赛不能开始。

9-2 举例 在下半时开始时，A 队由于队员受伤、被取消比赛资格等原因，能上场的队员不足 5 人。

解释 有至少 5 名队员上场比赛的要求仅适用于比赛开始时。A 队可以以少于 5 名队员继续比赛。

9-3 举例 临近比赛结束时，A1 被登记了第 5 次犯规并成为一名出局的队员，A 队因已经没有替补队员而被减少至 4 名队员。因 B 队正在大比分领先，B 队主教练为表示公平比赛，希望撤下 1 名队员并也以 4 名队员进行比赛。

解释 B 队主教练以少于 5 名队员进行比赛的请求应被拒绝。如果某队有足够的队员可以比赛，比赛场地上就应有 5 名队员。

9-4 陈述 规则第 9 条阐明了球队防守的球篮和进攻的球篮。任一节或任一决胜期比赛开始时，如果双方球队因混淆而进攻或防守着错误的球篮，此情况一经确认，只要不将任一队置于不利，应立即纠正。比赛停止之前的任何得分、消耗的时间和登记的犯规等均保留有效。

9-5 举例 在比赛开始之后，裁判员确认双方球队正朝着错误方向的球篮进行着攻防。

解释 在不将任一队置于不利的情况下，应尽快停止比赛。双方球队应纠正进攻方向。应在与比赛被停止的地点镜面对称的对面位置继续比赛。

9-6 陈述 比赛应由中圈跳球开始。

9-7 举例 比赛开始的开场跳球中，在主裁判员的抛球已经离手

（a）之前

(b) after

the ball has left the hands of the crew chief on the toss for the opening jump ball.

Interpretation:

(a) The first quarter has not yet started. Therefore, this is a foul during the interval of play before the start of the game. The game shall start with a jump ball.

(b) The first quarter has started. Therefore, this is a foul during the first quarter. The game shall be resumed with a team A throw-in from behind the sideline in its frontcourt nearest to the centre line, with 14 seconds on the shot clock.

In both cases, the foul shall be entered on the scoresheet and the foul shall count towards the team B fouls in the first quarter.

9-8 **Example:** During the interval of play before the game, A1 is charged with a technical foul. Before the start of the game, the team B head coach designates B6 to attempt 1 free throw, however B6 is not one of the team B starting 5 players.

Interpretation: Only one of the designated team B starting 5 players shall attempt the free throw with no line-up. A substitution cannot be granted before playing time has started.

The game shall start with a jump ball.

9-9 **Example:** During the interval of play before the game, A1 is charged with an unsportsmanlike foul against B1.

Interpretation: Before the start of the game, B1 shall attempt 2 free throws with no line-up.

If B1 is confirmed as one of the 5 players to start the game, B1 shall remain on the court.

If B1 is not confirmed as one of the 5 players to start the game, B1 shall not remain on the court.

The game shall start with a jump ball and with the 5 team B players confirmed to start the game.

（b）之后

跳球队员 B1 对 A1 发生了一起侵人犯规。

解释

（a）第 1 节比赛尚未开始。因此，这是发生在比赛开始前的比赛休息期间的一起犯规。比赛应由跳球开始。

（b）第 1 节比赛已经开始。因此，这是发生在第 1 节中的一起犯规。应判给 A 队在其前场最靠近中线的边线后执行掷球入界继续比赛，A 队应拥有 14 秒进攻时间。

在这两种情况下，犯规应被登记在记录表上，并应计入第 1 节 B 队的全队犯规。

9-8 **举例** 在赛前的比赛休息期间，A1 被判一起技术犯规，比赛开始前，B 队主教练指定 B6 执行 1 次罚球，然而 B6 不是 B 队的 5 名首发队员之一。

解释 应由 B 队被指定的 5 名首发队员之一执行 1 次不占位的罚球。比赛时间开始之前不能准予替换。

比赛应由跳球开始。

9-9 **举例** 在赛前的比赛休息期间，A1 对 B1 发生了一起违反体育运动精神的犯规。

解释 在比赛开始前，B1 应执行 2 次不占位的罚球。

如果确认 B1 是比赛首发的 5 名队员之一，B1 应留在比赛场地上。

如果确认 B1 不是比赛首发的 5 名队员之一，B1 不应留在比赛场地上。

比赛应由跳球开始，并且 B 队应以其确认的比赛首发的 5 名队员开始比赛。

9-10 **Statement:** If during an interval of play before the game a player designated as one of the starting 5 players is no longer able or entitled to start the game, that player shall be replaced by another player. In this case, the opponents are entitled to replace one player of its starting 5 players, if they wish.

9-11 **Example:** A1 is one of the team A starting 5 players. During the interval of play 7 minutes before the game

(a) A1 becomes injured.

(b) A1 is charged with a disqualifying foul.

Interpretation: In both cases, A1 shall be replaced with another team A player. Team B is entitled to replace one of its starting 5 players, if they wish.

9-10 陈述 如果在赛前的比赛休息期间，一名被指定为 5 名首发之一的队员不能或不再有资格开始比赛，该队员应被另一名队员替换。在这种情况下，如果对方也希望替换，他们有权替换一名他们的首发队员。

9-11 举例 A1 是 A 队的 5 名首发队员之一。在距离比赛开始还有 7 分钟时的比赛休息期间：

（a）A1 受伤了。

（b）宣判了 A1 取消比赛资格的犯规。

解释 在这两种情况下，A1 应被另一名 A 队队员替换。如果 B 队也希望替换，他们有权替换一名他们的首发队员。

Article 10 Status of the ball

10-1 **Statement:** The ball does not become dead and the goal, if made, shall count when a player is in the act of shooting for a goal and finishes the shot with a continuous motion while any player of the defensive team is charged with a foul against any opponent after the continuous motion of the shooter has started. This statement is equally valid if any person permitted to sit on the defensive team bench is charged with a technical foul.

10-2 **Example:** A1 is in the act of shooting for a goal when B2 fouls A2. A1 finishes the shot with a continuous motion.

(a) This is the third team B foul in the quarter.

(b) This is the fifth team B foul in the quarter.

Interpretation: In both cases, A1's goal, if made, shall count.

In (a) the game shall be resumed with a team A throw-in from the place nearest to where B2's foul occurred.

In (b) A2 shall attempt 2 free throws. The game shall be resumed as after any last free throw.

10-3 **Example:** A1 is in the act of shooting for a goal when A2 fouls B2. A1 finishes the shot with a continuous motion.

Interpretation: The ball becomes dead when A2 is charged with a team control foul. If A1's shot is successful, the goal shall not count. Regardless of the number of team A fouls in the quarter, the game shall be resumed with a team B throw-in from the free-throw line extended. If A1's shot is unsuccessful, the game shall be resumed with a team B throw-in from the place nearest to where the foul occurred, except from directly behind the backboard.

第 10 条　球的状态

10-1　陈述　当一名正在做投篮动作的队员以连续动作完成该投篮时，任一防守队员在该投篮队员的该连续动作开始之后对任一对方队员犯规，球不成死球，如中篮应计得分。这一陈述对被允许坐在防守队球队席的任何人员被判技术犯规时同样有效。

10-2　举例　A1 正在做投篮动作，此时 B2 对 A2 犯规。A1 以连续动作完成了投篮。

（a）这是该节 B 队的第 3 次全队犯规。

（b）这是该节 B 队的第 5 次全队犯规。

解释　在这两种情况下，如果 A1 中篮，应计得分。

在（a）中，应由 A 队在最靠近 B2 发生犯规的地点执行掷球入界继续比赛。

在（b）中，应由 A2 执行 2 次罚球。应如同任何最后一次罚球后那样继续比赛。

10-3　举例　A1 正在做投篮动作，此时 A2 对 B2 犯规。A1 以连续动作完成了投篮。

解释　当 A2 被判控制球队犯规时，球成为死球。如果 A1 投中，不应计得分。无论 A 队在该节的全队犯规次数是多少，应由 B 队在罚球线延长线处执行掷球入界继续比赛。如果 A1 未投中，应由 B 队在最靠近发生犯规的地点执行掷球入界继续比赛，篮板正后方除外。

Article 12 Jump ball and alternating possession

12-1 **Statement:** The team that does not gain the first team control of a live ball after the opening jump ball at the start of the game shall be awarded the ball for a throw-in from the place nearest to where the next jump ball situation occurs, except from directly behind the backboard.

12-2 **Example:** Two minutes before the start of the game, A1 is charged with a technical foul.

Interpretation: One of the 5 team B starting players shall attempt the free throw with no line-up. As the game has not yet started, the direction of the alternating possession arrow cannot be placed in favour of any team yet. The game shall start with a jump ball.

12-3 **Example:** The crew chief tosses the ball for the opening jump ball. Before the ball reaches its highest point, jumper A1 touches the ball.

Interpretation: This is a jump ball violation by A1. Team B shall be awarded a throw-in from its frontcourt, close to the centre line. Team B shall have 14 seconds on the shot clock. As soon as the ball is placed at the disposal of the team B thrower-in, team A shall be entitled to the first alternating possession throw-in.

12-4 **Example:** The crew chief tosses the ball for the opening jump ball. Before the ball reaches its highest point, non-jumper A2 enters the centre circle from the

(a) backcourt.

(b) frontcourt.

Interpretation: In both cases, this is a jump ball violation by A2. Team B shall be awarded a throw-in close to the centre line, if from its

(a) frontcourt, with 14 seconds on the shot clock.

(b) backcourt, with 24 seconds on the shot clock.

As soon as the ball is placed at the disposal of the team B thrower-in, team A shall be entitled to the first alternating possession throw-in.

第 12 条　跳球和交替拥有

12-1　**陈述**　开场跳球后，未首先获得控制活球的球队应被判给在最靠近下一次跳球情况发生的地点执行掷球入界，篮板正后方除外。

12-2　**举例**　比赛开始前 2 分钟，A1 被判一起技术犯规。

解释　应由 B 队 5 名首发队员的其中一名执行这次不占位的罚球。因为比赛尚未开始，交替拥有箭头还不能指向任一队。比赛应由跳球开始。

12-3　**举例**　主裁判员抛球执行开场跳球。在球到达它的最高点前，跳球队员 A1 触及了球。

解释　这是 A1 的一起跳球违例。应判给 B 队在其前场靠近中线处执行掷球入界。B 队应拥有 14 秒进攻时间。一旦球被置于 B 队掷球入界队员可处理后，A 队应拥有第一次交替拥有掷球入界权。

12-4　**举例**　主裁判员抛球执行开场跳球。在球到达它的最高点前，非跳球队员 A2：

（a）从其后场进入了中圈。

（b）从其前场进入了中圈。

解释　在这两种情况下，A2 发生了一起跳球违例。应判给 B 队在靠近中线处执行掷球入界。如果在：

（a）B 队的前场执行掷球入界，进攻计时钟应显示 14 秒。

（b）B 队的后场执行掷球入界，进攻计时钟应显示 24 秒。

一旦球被置于 B 队掷球入界队员可处理后，A 队应拥有第一次交替拥有掷球入界权。

12-5 **Example:** The crew chief tosses the ball for the opening jump ball. Immediately after the ball is legally tapped by jumper A1

(a) a held ball between A2 and B2 occurs.

(b) a double foul between A2 and B2 occurs.

Interpretation: In both cases, as the control of a live ball was not yet established, the referee cannot use the alternating possession procedure. The crew chief shall administer another jump ball in the centre circle and A2 and B2 shall jump. The time consumed on the game clock, after the ball was legally tapped and before the held ball/double foul occurred, shall remain valid.

12-6 **Example:** The crew chief tosses the ball for the opening jump ball. Immediately after the ball is legally tapped by jumper A1, the ball

(a) goes directly out-of-bounds.

(b) is caught by A1 before it touches one of the non-jumpers or the court.

Interpretation: In both cases, team B shall be awarded a throw-in as the result of A1's violation. If the throw-in is administered from its backcourt, team B shall have 24 seconds on the shot clock. If from its frontcourt, team B shall have 14 seconds on the shot clock. As soon as the ball is placed at the disposal of the team B thrower-in, team A shall be entitled to the first alternating possession throw-in.

12-7 **Example:** The crew chief tosses the ball for the opening jump ball. Immediately after the ball is legally tapped by jumper A1, B1 is charged with a technical foul.

Interpretation: Any team A player shall attempt 1 free throw with no line-up. As soon as a team A player receives the ball for the free throw, the direction of the alternating possession arrow shall be placed in favour of team B. The game shall be resumed with a team B alternating possession throw-in from the place nearest to where the ball was located when a technical foul occurred. If the throw-in is administered from its backcourt, team B shall have 24 seconds on the shot clock. If from its frontcourt, team B shall have 14 seconds on the shot clock.

12-5 **举例** 主裁判员抛球执行开场跳球。在球被跳球队员 A1 合法拍击后，随即发生了：

（a）一起 A2 和 B2 之间的争球。

（b）一起 A2 和 B2 之间的双方犯规。

解释 在这两种情况下，因为对活球的控制尚未建立，裁判员不能运用交替拥有程序。主裁判员应在中圈再执行一次由 A2 和 B2 进行的跳球。在球被合法拍击之后及发生争球或双方犯规之前，比赛计时钟消耗的时间应有效。

12-6 **举例** 主裁判员抛球执行开场跳球。在球被跳球队员 A1 合法拍击后，球随即：

（a）直接出界。

（b）在触及一名非跳球队员或比赛场地之前被 A1 拿住。

解释 在这两种情况下，作为 A1 违例的结果，应判给 B 队执行掷球入界。B 队如果在其后场执行掷球入界，应拥有 24 秒进攻时间；如果在其前场执行掷球入界，应拥有 14 秒进攻时间。一旦球被置于 B 队掷球入界队员可处理后，A 队应拥有第一次交替拥有掷球入界权。

12-7 **举例** 主裁判员抛球执行开场跳球，在球被跳球队员 A1 合法拍击后，随即宣判了 B1 一起技术犯规。

解释 应由 A 队任一队员执行 1 次不占位的罚球。当 A 队的罚球队员获得球时，交替拥有箭头应指向 B 队的进攻方向。应由 B 队在最靠近发生技术犯规时球所在位置的地点执行交替拥有的掷球入界继续比赛。B 队如果在其后场执行掷球入界，应拥有 24 秒进攻时间；如果在其前场执行掷球入界，应拥有 14 秒进攻时间。

12-8 **Example:** The crew chief tosses the ball for the opening jump ball. Immediately after the ball is legally tapped by jumper A1, A2 is charged with an unsportsmanlike foul against B2.

Interpretation: B2 shall attempt 2 free throws with no line-up. As soon as B2 receives the ball for the first free throw, the direction of the alternating possession arrow shall be placed in favour of team A. The game shall be resumed with a team B throw-in from the throw-in line in its frontcourt (as part of the unsportsmanlike foul penalty). Team B shall have 14 seconds on the shot clock.

12-9 **Example:** Team B is entitled to a throw-in under the alternating possession procedure. A referee and/or a scorer makes an error and the throw-in is erroneously awarded to team A.

Interpretation: After the ball touches or is legally touched by a player on the court, the error cannot be corrected. As the result of the error, team B shall not lose its right to the next alternating possession throw-in at the next jump ball situation.

12-10 **Example:** Simultaneously with the game clock signal sounding for the end of the first quarter, B1 is charged with an unsportsmanlike foul against A1. The referees decide that the game clock signal sounded before B1's foul occurred. Team A is entitled to the alternating possession throw-in to start the second quarter.

Interpretation: The unsportsmanlike foul occurred during an interval of play. Before the start of the second quarter, A1 shall attempt 2 free throws with no line-up. The game shall be resumed with a team A throw-in from the throw-in line in its frontcourt. Team A shall have 14 seconds on the shot clock. Team A shall not lose its right to the next alternating possession throw-in at the next jump ball situation.

12-11 **Example:** Shortly after the game clock signal sounds for the end of the third quarter, B1 is charged with a technical foul. Team A is entitled to the alternating possession throw-in to start the fourth quarter.

12-8 **举例** 主裁判员抛球执行开场跳球。在球被跳球队员 A1 合法拍击后，随即宣判了一起 A2 对 B2 的违反体育运动精神的犯规。

解释 B2 应执行 2 次不占位的罚球。当 B2 在第 1 次罚球中获得球时，交替拥有箭头应指向 A 队的进攻方向。应由 B 队在其前场的掷球入界线处执行掷球入界继续比赛（作为违反体育运动精神的犯规罚则一部分）。B 队应拥有 14 秒进攻时间。

12-9 **举例** 根据交替拥有程序，B 队拥有掷球入界权。一名裁判员和 / 或一名记录员出现了一个失误，并错误地给予了 A 队掷球入界。

解释 在球触及一名场上队员或被一名场上队员合法触及后，该失误就不能被纠正了。B 队不应因该失误失去在下一次跳球情况发生时的交替拥有掷球入界权。

12-10 **举例** 结束第 1 节的比赛计时钟信号响的同时，宣判了一起 B1 对 A1 的违反体育运动精神的犯规。裁判员判定 B1 的犯规发生在比赛计时钟信号响之后。A 队拥有第 2 节开始时的交替拥有掷球入界权。

解释 该违反体育运动精神的犯规发生在比赛休息期间。在第 2 节开始前，A1 应执行 2 次不占位的罚球。应由 A 队在其前场的掷球入界线处执行掷球入界继续比赛。A 队应拥有 14 秒进攻时间。A 队不应失去在下一次跳球情况发生时的交替拥有掷球入界权。

12-11 **举例** 在结束第 3 节的比赛计时钟信号响后不久，B1 被判了一起技术犯规。A 队拥有第 4 节开始时的交替拥有掷球入界权。

Interpretation: Any team A player shall attempt 1 free throw with no line-up before the start of the fourth quarter. The fourth quarter shall start with a team A throw-in from the centre line extended. Team A shall have 24 seconds on the shot clock.

12-12 **Example:** A1 jumps with the ball in the hands and is legally blocked by B1. Both players then return to the court with both of them having 1 hand or both hands firmly on the ball.

Interpretation: This is a jump ball situation.

12-13 **Example:** A1 jumps with the ball in the hands and is legally blocked by B1. A1 then returns to the court having 1 hand or both hands still firmly on the ball, while B1 is no longer touching the ball.

Interpretation: This is a travelling violation by A1.

12-14 **Example:** A1 and B1 in the air have their hands firmly on the ball. After returning to the court, A1 lands with 1 foot on the boundary line.

Interpretation: This is a jump ball situation.

12-15 **Example:** A1 jumps with the ball in the hands from the frontcourt and is legally blocked by B1. Both players then return to the court with both of them having 1 hand or both hands firmly on the ball. A1 lands with 1 foot in the backcourt.

Interpretation: This is a jump ball situation.

12-16 **Statement:** It is a jump ball situation resulting in an alternating possession throw-in whenever a live ball lodges between the ring and the backboard, unless between free throws and unless after the last free throw followed by a possession of the ball as part of the foul penalty. Under the alternating possession procedure, the team shall have 14 seconds on the shot clock if the offensive team is entitled to a throw-in or 24 seconds if the defensive team is entitled to a throw-in.

12-17 **Example:** During A1's shot for a goal, the ball lodges between the ring and the backboard.

(a) Team A

解释 在第 4 节开始前，应由 A 队任一队员执行 1 次不占位的罚球。应由 A 队在中线延长线处执行掷球入界开始第 4 节比赛，A 队应拥有 24 秒进攻时间。

12-12 **举例** A1 双手持球跳起，球在手中时被 B1 合法封盖。两名队员随后落回比赛场地且双方都有一手或双手牢牢地置于球上。

解释 这是一次跳球情况。

12-13 **举例** A1 双手持球跳起，球在手中时被 B1 合法封盖。A1 随后落回比赛场地且一手或双手牢牢地置于球上，此时，B1 已不再触球。

解释 这是 A1 的一起带球走违例。

12-14 **举例** A1 和 B1 在空中，他们的手都牢牢地置于球上。落回比赛场地后，A1 的一脚落在界线上。

解释 这是一次跳球情况。

12-15 **举例** A1 双手持球从其前场跳起，球在手中时被 B1 合法封盖。两名队员随后落回比赛场地且双方都有一手或双手牢牢置于球上，A1 有一脚落在其后场。

解释 这是一次跳球情况。

12-16 **陈述** 每当一个活球停留在篮圈和篮板之间时，一次跳球情况发生，应执行交替拥有掷球入界，除非一个活球停留在篮圈和篮板之间的情况是出现在罚球之间，或是出现在最后一次罚球后还要执行属于犯规罚则一部分的球权。按交替拥有的程序，如果进攻队获得掷球入界权，该队应拥有 14 秒进攻时间；如果防守队获得掷球入界权，该队应拥有 24 秒进攻时间。

12-17 **举例** A1 投篮，球停留在篮圈和篮板之间。按交替拥有程序：

（a）A 队拥有掷球入界权。

(b) Team B

is entitled to a throw-in under the alternating possession procedure.

Interpretation: After the throw-in from behind the endline in team B's backcourt

(a) team A shall have 14 seconds

(b) team B shall have 24 seconds

on the shot clock.

12-18 **Example:** A1's shot for a goal is in the air when the shot clock signal sounds, followed by the ball lodging between the ring and the backboard. The alternating possession arrow favours team A.

Interpretation: This is a jump ball situation. After the throw-in from behind the endline in its frontcourt, team A shall have 14 seconds on the shot clock.

12-19 **Example:** B2 is charged with an unsportsmanlike foul against A1 during the act of shooting for a 2-point goal. During the last free throw with no line-up

(a) the ball lodges between the ring and the backboard.

(b) A1 steps on the free-throw line while releasing the ball.

(c) the ball misses the ring.

Interpretation: In all cases, the free throw is unsuccessful. The game shall be resumed with a team A throw-in from the throw-in line in its frontcourt. Team A shall have 14 seconds on the shot clock.

12-20 **Example:** After A1's throw-in from the centre line extended to start a quarter, the ball lodges between the ring and the backboard in team A's frontcourt.

Interpretation: This is a jump ball situation. The direction of the alternating possession arrow shall be reversed immediately in favour of team B. The game shall be resumed with a team B throw-in from behind its endline, except from directly behind the backboard. Team B shall have 24 seconds on the shot clock.

（b）B 队拥有掷球入界权。

解释 从 B 队后场的端线后执行掷球入界后：

（a）A 队应拥有 14 秒进攻时间。

（b）B 队应拥有 24 秒进攻时间。

12-18 **举例** 当 A1 投篮的球在空中时，进攻计时钟信号响，随后球停留在篮圈和篮板之间。交替拥有箭头指向 A 队的进攻方向。

解释 这是一次跳球情况。A 队从其前场的端线后执行掷球入界后应拥有 14 秒进攻时间。

12-19 **举例** B2 被判一起对正在做 2 分试投的 A1 违反体育运动精神的犯规。在最后一次不占位的罚球期间：

（a）球停留在篮圈和篮板之间。

（b）A1 在球离手时踩在罚球线上。

（c）球未触及篮圈。

解释 上述所有情况都应视为罚球未中篮。应判给 A 队在其前场的掷球入界线处执行掷球入界继续比赛。A 队应拥有 14 秒进攻时间。

12-20 **举例** A1 在中线延长线处执行开始一节的掷球入界后，球停留在 A 队前场的篮圈和篮板之间。

解释 这是一次跳球情况。交替拥有箭头的方向应立即反转并指向 B 队的进攻方向。应由 B 队在其端线后（篮板正后方除外）执行掷球入界继续比赛。B 队应拥有 24 秒进攻时间。

12-21 **Example:** The alternating possession arrow favours team A. During the interval of play after the first quarter, B1 is charged with an unsportsmanlike foul against A1. A1 shall attempt 2 free throws with no line-up, followed by a team A throw-in from the throw-in line in its frontcourt to start the second quarter. The alternating possession arrow in favour of team A remains unchanged. After the throw-in, the ball lodges between the ring and the backboard in team A's frontcourt.

Interpretation: This is a jump ball situation. The game shall be resumed with a team A throw-in from behind the endline in its frontcourt, except from directly behind the backboard. Team A shall have 14 seconds on the shot clock. The direction of the alternating possession arrow shall be reversed immediately after the team A throw-in has ended.

12-22 **Statement:** A held ball occurs when one or more players from opposing teams have one or both hands firmly on the ball so that neither player can gain control of the ball without undue roughness.

12-23 **Example:** A1 with the ball in the hands is in the continuous motion to the basket to score. At this time, B1 places the hands firmly on the ball and A1 now takes more steps than allowed by the traveling rule.

Interpretation: This is a jump ball situation.

12-24 **Statement:** A violation by a team during its alternating possession throw-in causes that team to lose the alternating possession throw-in.

12-25 **Example:** With 4:17 on the game clock in a quarter, during an alternating possession throw-in

(a) thrower-in A1 steps on the court while having the ball in the hands.

(b) A2 moves the hands over the boundary line before the ball is thrown-in over the boundary line.

(c) thrower-in A1 takes more than 5 seconds to release the ball.

Interpretation: In all cases, this is a throw-in violation by A1 or A2. The game shall be resumed with a team B throw-in from the place of the original throw-in. The direction of the alternating possession arrow shall be reversed immediately in favour of team B.

12-21 **举例** 交替拥有箭头指向 A 队的进攻方向。在第 1 节结束后的比赛休息期间，宣判了一起 B1 对 A1 的违反体育运动精神的犯规。应由 A1 执行 2 次不占位的罚球，随后由 A 队在其前场的掷球入界线处执行掷球入界开始第 2 节的比赛。交替拥有箭头指向 A 队的进攻方向保持不变。掷球入界后，球停留在 A 队前场的篮圈和篮板之间。

解释 这是一次跳球情况。应由 A 队在其前场端线后（篮板正后方除外）执行掷球入界继续比赛。A 队应拥有 14 秒进攻时间。在 A 队的掷球入界结束之后，交替拥有箭头的方向应立即反转。

12-22 **陈述** 当双方球队各有一名或多名队员有一手或双手牢牢地置于球上，以致不采用粗暴动作任一队员就不能获得控制球时，一次争球发生。

12-23 **举例** A1 双手持球正在做向球篮移动尝试得分的连续动作，此时，B1 将手牢牢地置于球上并致使 A1 移动的步数超出了带球走规则允许的范围。

解释 这是一次跳球情况。

12-24 **陈述** 某队在执行其交替拥有的掷球入界中违例，将使该队失去该次交替拥有掷球入界权。

12-25 **举例** 在某节比赛计时钟显示 4:17 时的一次交替拥有掷球入界中：

（a）掷球入界队员 A1 在球仍在手中时步入场内。

（b）A2 在球被掷过界线前，伸手越过界线。

（c）掷球入界队员 A1 超过 5 秒使球离手。

解释 在上述所有情况下，A1 或 A2 发生了掷球入界违例。应由 B 队在原掷球入界地点执行掷球入界继续比赛，交替拥有箭头的方向应立即反转并指向 B 队的进攻方向。

12-26 **Statement:** Whenever a jump ball situation occurs with no time remaining on the shot clock and the alternating possession arrow favours team A, the alternating possession procedure shall not be applied. This is a shot clock violation. Therefore, the ball shall be awarded to team B for a throw-in.

12-27 **Example:** A1's shot for a goal is in the air when the shot clock signal sounds. The ball then

(a) enters the basket.

(b) rebounds from the ring but does not enter the basket.

(c) misses the ring.

Immediately after (b) and (c), a held ball is called.

Interpretation:

In (a) no shot clock violation has occurred. A1's goal shall count. The game shall be resumed with a team B throw-in from behind its endline.

In (b) if the possession arrow favours team A, team A shall have a throw-in from the place nearest to where the held ball occurred, with 14 seconds on the shot clock. If the possession arrow favours team B, team B shall have a throw-in from the place nearest to where the held ball occurred, with 24 seconds on the shot clock.

In (c) a shot clock violation has occurred. The direction of the possession arrow is not relevant. Team B shall have a throw-in from the place nearest to where the held ball occurred, with 24 seconds on the shot clock.

12-28 **Example:** A1's shot for a goal is in the air when the shot clock signal sounds. The ball

(a) enters the basket.

(b) rebounds from the ring but does not enter the basket.

(c) misses the ring.

Immediately after, A2 or B2 is charged with a technical foul.

12-26 陈述 当一次跳球情况发生在进攻计时钟已没有剩余时间，且交替拥有箭头指向 A 队的进攻方向时，不应使用交替拥有程序。这是一起进攻时间违例。因此，应判给 B 队执行掷球入界。

12-27 举例 A1 投篮的球在空中时进攻计时钟信号响，随后该球：

（a）进入球篮。

（b）从篮圈上弹起，但未进入球篮。

（c）未触及篮圈。

在（b）和（c）后，随即宣判了一起争球。

解释

在（a）中，没有发生进攻时间违例。A1 的中篮应计得分。应由 B 队从其端线后执行掷球入界继续比赛。

在（b）中，如果箭头指向 A 队的进攻方向，应由 A 队在最靠近发生争球的地点执行掷球入界，A 队应拥有 14 秒进攻时间。如果箭头指向 B 队的进攻方向，应由 B 队在最靠近发生争球的地点执行掷球入界，B 队应拥有 24 秒进攻时间。

在（c）中，已发生一起进攻时间违例。与箭头的方向无关。应由 B 队在最靠近发生争球的地点执行掷球入界，B 队应拥有 24 秒进攻时间。

12-28 举例 A1 投篮的球在空中时进攻计时钟信号响，该球：

（a）进入球篮。

（b）从篮圈上弹起，但未进入球篮。

（c）未触及篮圈。

随即宣判了 A2 或 B2 的一起技术犯规。

Interpretation:

In all cases, any player of team A (for the B2 technical foul) or any player of team B (for the A2 technical foul) shall attempt 1 free throw with no line-up. Then

In (a) no shot clock violation has occurred. A1's goal shall count. The game shall be resumed with a team B throw-in from behind its endline.

In (b) if the possession arrow favours team A, team A shall have a throw-in from the place nearest to where the ball was located when the technical foul occurred, with 14 seconds on the shot clock. If the possession arrow favours team B, team B shall have a throw-in from the place nearest to where the ball was located when the technical foul occurred, with 24 seconds on the shot clock.

In (c) a shot clock violation has occurred. The direction of the possession arrow is not relevant. Team B shall have a throw-in from the place nearest to where the ball was located when the technical foul occurred, with 24 seconds on the shot clock.

解释

在上述所有情况下，应由A队（因为B2的技术犯规）或B队（因为A2的技术犯规）的任一队员执行1次不占位的罚球。然后：

在（a）中，没有发生进攻时间违例。A1 的中篮应计得分。应由B队从其端线后执行掷球入界继续比赛。

在（b）中，如果箭头指向A队的进攻方向，应由A队在最靠近发生技术犯规时球所在位置的地点执行掷球入界，A队应拥有14秒进攻时间。如果箭头指向B队的进攻方向，应由B队在最靠近发生技术犯规时球所在位置的地点执行掷球入界，B队应拥有24秒进攻时间。

在（c）中，已发生一起进攻时间违例。与箭头的方向无关。应由B队在最靠近发生技术犯规时球所在位置的地点执行掷球入界，B队应拥有24秒进攻时间。

Article 13 How the ball is played

13-1 **Statement:** During the game, the ball is played with the hands only. It is a violation if a player

- places the ball between the legs to fake a pass or shot.
- deliberately uses the head, fist, legs or feet to play the ball.

13-2 **Example:** A1 ends a dribble. A1 places the ball between the legs and fakes a pass or shot.

Interpretation: This is a violation by A1 for illegally touching the ball with the leg.

13-3 **Example:** A1 passes the ball to A2 who runs on a fast break towards the opponents' basket. Before catching the ball, A2 deliberately touches the ball with the head.

Interpretation: This is a violation by A2 for illegally using the head to play the ball.

13-4 **Statement:** It is not permitted to increase a player's height or reach. It is a violation to lift a team-mate to play the ball.

13-5 **Example:** A1 embraces and lifts team-mate A2 under the opponents' basket. A3 passes the ball to A2 who dunks the ball into the basket.

Interpretation: This is a violation by team A. A2's goal shall not count. The game shall be resumed with a team B throw-in from the free-throw line extended in its backcourt.

第 13 条 如何打球

13-1 陈述 比赛中，只能用手打球。队员出现下列情况是违例。

- 将球置于双腿之间以假装传球或投篮。
- 故意地用头、拳、腿或脚来打球。

13-2 举例 A1 结束了一次运球。A1 将球置于双腿之间以假装传球或投篮。

解释 这是 A1 非法用腿触及球的违例。

13-3 举例 A1 传球给跑向对方球篮快攻的 A2。在接到传球之前，A2 故意用头触及球。

解释 这是 A2 非法用头打球的违例。

13-4 陈述 不允许增加队员的身高或伸展范围。举起同队队员去打球是违例。

13-5 举例 在对方的球篮下，A1 抱着同队队员 A2 并将其举起。A3 将球传给 A2，A2 将球扣进球篮。

解释 这是 A 队违例。A2 的中篮不应计得分。应由 B 队在其后场的罚球线延长线处执行掷球入界继续比赛。

Article 14 Control of the ball

14-1 **Statement:** Team control starts when a player of that team is in control of a live ball by holding or dribbling it or has a live ball at the disposal for a throw-in or a free throw.

14-2 **Example:** Regardless of whether the game clock is stopped or not, a player deliberately delays the process of taking the ball for a throw-in or for a free throw.

Interpretation: The ball becomes live and team control of the ball starts when the referee places the ball on the floor nearest to the throw-in place or on the court at the free-throw line.

14-3 **Example:** Team A is in control of the ball for 15 seconds. A1 passes the ball to A2 and the ball in the air moves over the boundary line. B1 tries to catch the ball and jumps from the court over the boundary line. B1 still airborne

(a) taps the ball with 1 or both hands,

(b) catches the ball with both hands or the ball comes to rest in one hand

and the ball returns to the court where it is caught by A2.

Interpretation:

(a) Team A shall remain in control of the ball. Team A shall have the time remaining on the shot clock.

(b) B1 gained team B control of the ball. A2 re-gained team A control of the ball. Team A shall have a new 24 seconds on the shot clock.

第 14 条　控制球

14-1　陈述　球队控制球开始于该队一名队员正拿着或运着一个活球，或者在掷球入界或罚球中可处理一个活球时。

14-2　举例　无论比赛计时钟是否停止，一名队员在掷球入界或罚球中故意延长拿球过程。

解释　当球被裁判员置于最靠近掷球入界的地点或罚球线的比赛地板上时，球成活球，并且球队控制球开始。

14-3　举例　A 队已经控制球达 15 秒。A1 将球传给 A2 时，球在空中越过了界线。B1 从比赛场地跳起越过界线，试图拿球。B1 仍在空中时：

（a）用单手或双手拍击球。

（b）用双手拿球，或者球在单手上停留。

随即，球回到比赛场地上并被 A2 接住。

解释

（a）A 队仍然保持着控制球。A 队应拥有进攻计时钟显示的剩余时间。

（b）B1 已经获得 B 队控制球。A2 重新获得 A 队控制球。A 队应拥有新的 24 秒进攻时间。

Article 15 Player in the act of shooting

15-1 **Statement:** The act of shooting starts when the player starts to move the ball upwards to the opponents' basket.

15-2 **Example:** A1 on a drive to the basket comes to a legal stop with both feet on the court without moving the ball upwards. At this time, B1 fouls A1.

Interpretation: B1's foul did not occur against a player in the act of shooting as A1 has not yet started to move the ball upwards to the basket.

15-3 **Statement:** The act of shooting on a continuous movement on a drive to the basket starts when the ball has come to rest in the player's hands upon completion of a dribble or a catch in the air and the player starts the shooting motion preceding the release of the ball on a shot for a goal.

15-4 **Example:** A1 on a drive to the basket ends a dribble with the ball in the hands and starts the shooting motion. At this time, B1 fouls A1. The ball does not enter the basket.

Interpretation: B1's foul occurred against a player in the act of shooting. A1 shall attempt 2 free throws. The game shall be resumed as after any last free throw.

15-5 **Example:** A1 jumps in the air and releases the ball on an attempt for a 3-point goal. B1 fouls A1 before A1 returns with both feet to the court. The ball does not enter the basket.

Interpretation: A1 remains in the act of shooting until returning with both feet to the court. A1 shall attempt 3 free throws. The game shall be resumed as after any last free throw.

15-6 **Example:** A1 fouls B1 while holding the ball in the frontcourt. This is a team control foul. In a continuous forward motion, A1 throws the ball into the basket.

Interpretation: A1's goal shall not count. Team B shall be awarded a throw-in from the free-throw line extended in its backcourt.

第 15 条　正在做投篮动作的队员

15-1　陈述　当队员将球朝着对方球篮向上移动时，投篮动作开始。

15-2　举例　A1 在突破上篮期间双脚着地合法停步，但未将球向上移动。此时，B1 对 A1 犯规。

解释　B1 的犯规不是发生在一名正在做投篮动作的队员身上，因为 A1 尚未开始将球朝着对方球篮向上移动。

15-3　陈述　突破上篮期间投篮动作的连续动作开始于：当队员结束运球或腾空接到球后，球已在手中停留时，该队员在投篮球离手前开始做投篮动作。

15-4　举例　A1 在突破上篮期间结束了运球，随即双手持球开始做投篮动作。此时，B1 对 A1 犯规。球未进入球篮。

解释　B1 的犯规发生在一名正在做投篮动作的队员身上。应由 A1 执行 2 次罚球。应如同任何最后一次罚球后那样继续比赛。

15-5　举例　A1 跳起在空中并尝试 3 分投篮，球离手。A1 在其双脚落回地面之前被 B1 犯规了。球未进入球篮。

解释　在 A1 双脚落回地面之前，其投篮动作仍未结束。应由 A1 执行 3 次罚球。应如同任何最后一次罚球后那样继续比赛。

15-6　举例　A1 在其前场持球时对 B1 犯规。这是一起控制球队犯规。在其连续向前的动作中，A1 将球掷进球篮。

解释　A1 的中篮不应计得分。应判给 B 队在其后场的罚球线延长线处执行掷球入界。

15-7 **Example:** B1 fouls A1 on a drive to the basket, with A1's front foot still on the court. A1 continues the act of shooting and because of B1's foul, the ball momentarily leaves A1's hands. A1 catches the ball with both hands and scores a goal.

Interpretation: B1's foul against A1 occurred in the act of shooting. When the ball momentarily leaves A1's hands, A1 still remains in control of the ball and therefore the act of shooting continues. The goal shall count. A1 shall attempt 1 free throw. The game shall continue as after any last free throw.

15-8 **Statement:** When a player is in the act of shooting and, after being fouled passes the ball off, that player is no longer in the act of shooting.

15-9 **Example:** B1 fouls A1 in the act of shooting. This is the third team B foul in the quarter. After the foul A1 passes the ball to A2.

Interpretation: When A1 passed the ball to A2, the act of shooting ended. The game shall be resumed with a team A throw-in from the place nearest to where the foul occurred.

15-10 **Statement:**If a player is fouled in the act of shooting, after which that player scores while committing a travelling violation, the goal shall not count and 2 or 3 free throws shall be awarded.

15-11 **Example:** A1 with the ball in the hands drives to the basket for a 2-point goal attempt. B1 fouls A1, after which A1 commits a travelling violation. The ball enters the basket.

Interpretation: A1's goal shall not count. A1 shall be awarded 2 free throws.

15-7 举例 B1 对突破上篮的 A1 犯规时 A1 的前脚还在地面上。A1 继续其投篮动作，但 B1 的犯规导致球短暂地离开了 A1 的手。A1 再次双手拿球并且中篮得分。

解释 B1 对 A1 的犯规发生在正在做投篮动作时。当球短暂地离开 A1 的手时，A1 仍然保持控制球，因此该投篮动作还在继续，中篮应计得分。应由 A1 执行 1 次罚球。应如同任何最后一次罚球后那样继续比赛。

15-8 陈述 一名正在做投篮动作的队员被犯规后将球传出，该队员就不再是在做投篮动作。

15-9 举例 B1 对正在做投篮动作的 A1 犯规。这是该节 B 队的第 3 次全队犯规。该犯规后，A1 将球传给 A2。

解释 当 A1 将球传给 A2 时，该投篮动作结束。应由 A 队在最靠近发生犯规的地点执行掷球入界继续比赛。

15-10 陈述 如果一名队员在做投篮动作时被犯规，接着该队员在发生带球走违例期间得分了。该中篮不应计得分，应判给 2 次或 3 次罚球。

15-11 举例 A1 双手持球突破上篮尝试 2 分中篮时，B1 对 A1 犯规。随后，A1 发生了带球走违例。球进入球篮。

解释 A1 的中篮不应计得分。应由 A1 执行 2 次罚球。

Article 16 Goal: When made and its value

16-1 **Statement:** The value of a goal is defined by the place on the court where the shot was released from. A goal released from the 2-point goal area shall count 2 points, a goal released from the 3-point goal area shall count 3 points. A goal is credited to the team attacking the opponents' basket into which the ball entered.

16-2 **Example:** A1 releases the ball on a shot from the 3-point goal area. The ball on its upward flight is legally touched by any player who is within the team A 2-point goal area. The ball enters the basket.

Interpretation: A1 shall be awarded 3 points as A1's shot was released from the 3-point goal area.

16-3 **Example:** A1 releases the ball on a shot from the 2-point goal area. The ball on its upward flight is legally touched by B1 who jumped from the team A 3-point goal area. The ball enters the basket.

Interpretation: A1 shall be awarded 2 points as A1's shot was released from the 2-point goal area.

16-4 **Example:** At the start of a quarter, team A is defending its own basket when B1 erroneously dribbles to the own basket and scores a goal.

Interpretation: The team A captain on the court shall be awarded 2 points.

16-5 **Statement:** If the ball enters the opponents' basket, the value of the goal is defined by the place on the court where the ball was released from. The ball may enter the basket directly or indirectly when during a pass the ball touches any player or touches the court before entering the basket.

16-6 **Example:** A1 passes the ball from the 3-point goal area.

(a) The ball enters the basket directly.

(b) The ball touches any player or the court in the team A 2-point or 3-point goal area and then enters the basket.

第 16 条 球中篮及其分值

16-1 陈述 中篮的分值由投篮球离手的比赛场地位置决定。从 2 分中篮区域球离手的中篮应计 2 分，从 3 分中篮区域球离手的中篮应计 3 分。中篮计入使球进入对方球篮的进攻球队名下。

16-2 举例 A1 在 3 分中篮区域投篮球离手。球在向上飞行时，被在 A 队 2 分中篮区域的任一队员合法触及。球进入球篮。

解释 应判给 A1 得 3 分，因为 A1 的投篮是从 3 分中篮区域球离手的。

16-3 举例 A1 从 2 分中篮区域投篮球离手。球在向上飞行时，被从 A 队 3 分中篮区域跳起的 B1 合法触及。球进入球篮。

解释 应判给 A1 得 2 分，因为 A1 的投篮是从 2 分中篮区域球离手的。

16-4 举例 某节比赛开始时，A 队正防守着本方球篮，此时 B1 错误地向本方球篮运球并中篮得分。

解释 应判给 A 队场上队长得 2 分。

16-5 陈述 如果球进入对方的球篮，中篮的分值由投篮球离手的比赛场地位置决定。在一次传球中，球可能在触及了任一队员或触及了比赛场地后直接或间接地进入球篮。

16-6 举例 A1 从 3 分中篮区域传球。

（a）球直接进入球篮。

（b）球触及了位于 A 队的 2 分或 3 分中篮区域中的任一队员或比赛场地后进入球篮。

Interpretation: In both cases, A1 shall be awarded 3 points as the pass was released from the 3-point goal area.

16-7 **Example:** A1 attempts a shot for a 3-point goal. After the ball has left A1's hands, it touches the court in the team A 2-point goal area. The ball enters the basket.

Interpretation: A1's goal shall count for 3 points, as it was released from the 3-point goal area. The game shall be resumed as after any successful goal.

16-8 **Example:** B1 fouls A1 in the act of shooting for a 3-point goal. The ball touches the court and then enters the basket.

Interpretation: A1's goal shall not count. A shot for a goal shall end when the ball touches the court. After a referee blows the whistle and as the ball is no longer a shot, the ball becomes dead immediately. A1 shall attempt 3 free throws.

16-9 **Example:** A1 attempts a shot for a 3-point goal. After the ball has left A1's hands, the game clock signal sounds for the end of the quarter. The ball touches the court and then enters the basket.

Interpretation: A1's goal shall not count. A shot for a goal shall end when the ball touches the court. As the ball is no longer a shot, it becomes dead when the game clock signal sounds for the end of the quarter.

16-10 **Example:** Thrower-in A1 in the frontcourt passes the ball. The ball is then legally touched by any player in team A's frontcourt in the 3-point goal area and then enters the basket.

Interpretation: The goal shall count 2 points as the ball was released from a throw-in. The touch is legal. The value of the goal can only be 3 points when the ball is released from the court on a shot or a pass from behind the 3-point line.

解释 在这两种情况下，应判给 A1 得 3 分，因为 A1 的传球是从 3 分中篮区域球离手的。

16-7 **举例** A1 尝试 3 分投篮。球离开 A1 的手后，触及了 A 队 2 分中篮区域的比赛场地。球进入球篮。

解释 A1 的中篮应计 3 分，因为球是从 3 分中篮区域球离手的。应如同任一中篮后那样继续比赛。

16-8 **举例** B1 对正在做 3 分试投的 A1 犯规。球触及了比赛场地后进入球篮。

解释 A1 的中篮不应计得分。当球触及比赛场地时，投篮应结束。因为已不再是投篮的球，在裁判员鸣哨后，球立即成为死球。应由 A1 执行 3 次罚球。

16-9 **举例** A1 尝试 3 分投篮。球离开 A1 的手后，结束该节的比赛计时钟信号响。球触及了比赛场地后进入球篮。

解释 A1 的中篮不应计得分。当球触及比赛场地时，投篮应结束。因为已不再是投篮的球，当结束该节的比赛计时钟信号响时，球成死球。

16-10 **举例** 位于前场的掷球入界队员 A1 将球传出。随后，球被位于 A 队前场 3 分中篮区域中的任一队员合法触及后进入球篮。

解释 中篮应计 2 分，因为球是从一次掷球入界中离手的。该接触是合法的。只有当球是从比赛场地上 3 分线后的一次投篮或传球中离手时，中篮的分值才是 3 分。

16-11 **Statement:** In a throw-in situation or on a rebound after the last free throw, there is always a time period from the time the inbounds player touches the ball until that player releases the ball on a shot. This is particularly important to take into consideration close to the end of a quarter or overtime. There must be a minimum amount of time available for such a shot before time expires. If 0.3 of a second or more is shown on the game clock or on the shot clock, it is the duty of the referee(s) to determine whether the shooter released the ball before the game clock or shot clock signal sounded for the end of a quarter or overtime. If 0.2 or 0.1 of a second is shown on the game clock or on the shot clock, the only type of a valid goal that can be scored by a player is by tapping or directly dunking the ball, provided that the hands of the player are no longer touching the ball when the game clock or the shot clock shows 0.0.

16-12 **Example:** Team A is awarded a throw-in with

(a) 0.3

(b) 0.2 or 0.1

of a second shown on the game clock or on the shot clock.

Interpretation:

The referees shall ensure that the correct playing time remaining is shown on the clocks.

(a) If during a shot for a goal the game clock or the shot clock signal sounds for the end of the quarter or overtime [①], it is the responsibility of the referees to determine whether the ball was released before the game clock or the shot clock signal sounded for the end of the quarter or overtime.

(b) A goal can only be scored if the ball, while in the air on the throw-in pass, is tapped or directly dunked into the basket.

16-13 **Example:** At the end of a quarter A1 is directly dunking the ball into the basket. The ball is still touching A1's hands when the game clock shows 0.0 seconds.

Interpretation: A1's goal shall not count. The ball was touching A1's hands when the game clock signal sounded for the end of a quarter.

①英文原文表述有误，请参考中文翻译。

16-11 陈述 在掷球入界情况下，或在最后一次罚球后的篮板球情况下，从界内队员触及球的瞬间直到该队员投篮球离手，总会有一个时间段。裁判员应在一节或决胜期临近结束时考虑到这格外重要的一点。要在时间终了之前做出一次投篮，前提是必须有最少量却足够的时间。如果比赛计时钟或进攻计时钟显示 0.3 秒或更多，确定投篮队员是否在该节或该决胜期结束的比赛计时钟或进攻计时钟信号响之前球离手，是裁判员的职责。如果比赛计时钟或进攻计时钟显示 0.2 秒或者 0.1 秒，一名队员唯一有效的中篮得分方式只能是拍击球或直接扣篮，且在比赛计时钟或进攻计时钟显示 0.0 时，该队员的手已不再触及球。

16-12 举例 判给 A 队执行掷球入界，此时，比赛计时钟或进攻计时钟显示：

（a）0.3 秒。

（b）0.2 秒或 0.1 秒。

解释

裁判员应确保两个计时钟显示的是正确的剩余比赛时间。

（a）如果在投篮时，进攻计时钟信号响或结束该节或该决胜期的比赛计时钟信号响，那么，确定球是否在进攻计时钟信号响或结束该节或该决胜期的比赛计时钟信号响之前离开投篮队员的手，是裁判员的职责。

（b）只有掷球入界的球传在空中时被拍入或直接被扣入球篮，中篮得分才有效。

16-13 举例 在某节比赛结束时，A1 直接将球扣入球篮。当比赛计时钟显示 0.0 秒时，球仍触及 A1 的手。

解释 A1 的中篮不应计得分。当结束该节的比赛计时钟信号响时，球仍触及 A1 的手。

16-14 **Statement:** A goal is scored when a live ball enters the basket from above and remains within or passes through the basket entirely. When

(a) a defensive team requests a time-out at any time during the game and a goal is then scored, or

(b) the game clock shows 2:00 or less in the fourth quarter or overtime

the game clock shall be stopped when the ball remains within or has entirely passed through the basket as shown in Diagram 2.

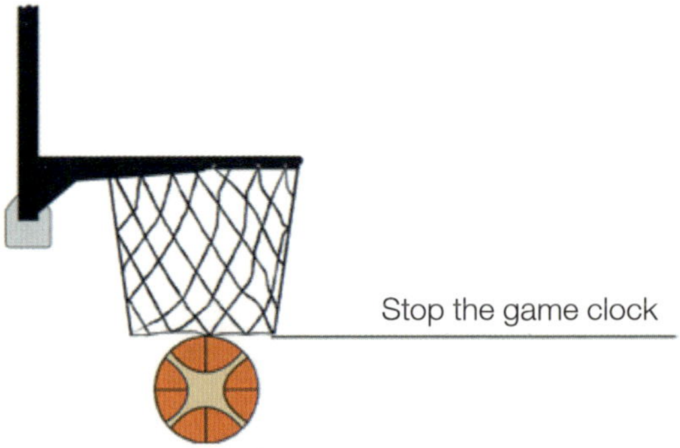

Diagram 2 A goal is scored

16-15 **Example:** With 2:02 on the game clock in the fourth quarter, A1 scores a goal when the ball passes through the basket. With 2:00 on the game clock B1 is ready for the throw-in from the endline.

Interpretation: The goal was scored with more than 2:00 on the game clock. Therefore, the game clock shall not be stopped.

16-14 **陈述** 当一个活球从上方进入球篮并保持停留其中，或完整地穿过球篮时是中篮。在：

（a）比赛的任何时间，防守队请求暂停，随后球中篮得分，或

（b）第 4 节或决胜期比赛计时钟显示 2:00 或更少时，

在球保持停留其中，或完整地穿过球篮时（如图 2 所示），应停止比赛计时钟。

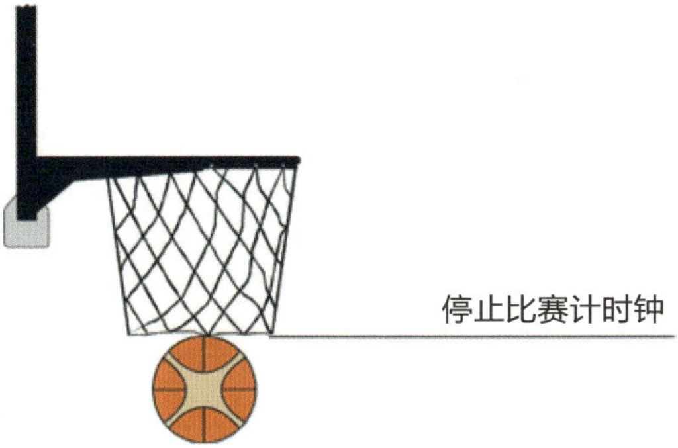

图 2 中篮得分

16-15 **举例** 第 4 节，比赛计时钟显示 2:02 时球穿过球篮，A1 中篮得分。比赛计时钟显示 2:00 时，B1 在端线后准备执行掷球入界。

解释 中篮得分时，比赛计时钟显示的时间多于 2:00。因此，比赛计时钟不应停止。

Article 17 Throw-in

17-1 **Statement:** During the throw-in players, other than the thrower-in, shall not have any part of their bodies over the boundary line.

Before the thrower-in releases the ball, it is possible that the throwing-in motion could cause that player's hands with the ball to move over the boundary line separating the inbounds area from the out-of-bounds area. In such situations, it continues to be the responsibility of the defensive player to avoid interfering with the throw-in by contacting the ball while it is still in the hands of the thrower-in.

17-2 **Example:** In the third quarter, team A is awarded a throw-in from its backcourt. While holding the ball

(a) thrower-in A1 moves the hands over the boundary line so that the ball is above the inbounds area. B1 grabs the ball from A1's hands or taps the ball out of A1's hands without any physical contact against A1.

(b) B1 moves the hands over the boundary line towards thrower-in A1 to stop a pass to A2 on the court.

Interpretation: In both cases, B1 interfered with the throw-in and therefore delayed the game. The referee calls a delay of the game violation. In addition, a verbal warning shall be given to B1 and also communicated to the team B head coach. This warning shall apply to all team B players for the remainder of the game. Any repetition of a similar action by any team B player may result in a technical foul. The team A throw-in shall be repeated. Team A shall have 24 seconds on the shot clock.

17-3 **Example:** In the third quarter, team A is awarded a throw-in from its frontcourt. Thrower-in A1 is holding the ball when B1 moves the hands over the boundary line, with

(a) 7 seconds

(b) 17 seconds

on the shot clock.

第 17 条　掷球入界

17-1　陈述　在执行掷球入界中，除掷球入界队员外，其他队员不得将其身体的任何部分越过界线。

在掷球入界队员的球离手之前，掷入动作有可能造成持球的手越过分隔界内区域与界外区域的界线垂直面。在这种情况下，当球仍然在掷球入界队员的手中时，避免触及球以防干扰掷球入界仍然是防守队员的责任。

17-2　举例　第 3 节，判给 A 队在其后场执行掷球入界。当 A1 持球时：

（a）掷球入界队员 A1 伸手越过界线，使球位于界内区域的上方。B1 在与 A1 无任何身体接触的情况下拿住 A1 手中的球，或将 A1 手中的球拍离。

（b）B1 向掷球入界队员 A1 伸手越过界线，并阻止 A1 将球传给比赛场地上的 A2。

解释　在这两种情况下，B1 都干扰了掷球入界，因而延误了比赛。裁判员宣判一起延误比赛违例，此外，应给予 B1 一次口头警告并通知 B 队主教练。该警告应适用于在剩余比赛中的所有 B 队队员。任一 B 队队员重复出现类似行为都将导致一起技术犯规。A 队应重新执行该掷球入界。A 队应拥有 24 秒进攻时间。

17-3　举例　第 3 节，判给 A 队在其前场执行掷球入界。掷球入界队员 A1 持球时，B1 伸手越过界线，此时，进攻计时钟显示：

（a）7 秒。

（b）17 秒。

Interpretation: This is a throw-in violation by B1. In addition, a verbal warning shall be given to B1 and also communicated to the team B head coach. This warning shall apply to all team B players for the remainder of the game. Any repetition of a similar action by any team B player may result in a technical foul. The team A throw-in shall be repeated. Team A shall have

(a) 14 seconds

(b) 17 seconds

on the shot clock.

17-4 **Statement:** When the game clock shows 2:00 or less in the fourth quarter and in each overtime, the player of the defensive team shall not move any part of the body over the boundary line to interfere with the throw-in.

17-5 **Example:** With 54 seconds on the game clock in the fourth quarter, team A is entitled to a throw-in. Before handing the ball to thrower-in A1, the referee shows to B1 the warning with an 'illegal boundary line crossing' signal. B1 then moves the body towards A1 over the boundary line before the ball was thrown-in over the boundary line.

Interpretation: B1 shall be charged with a technical foul.

17-6 **Example:** With 51 seconds on the game clock in the fourth quarter, team A is entitled to a throw-in. Before handing the ball to thrower-in A1, the referee does not show the warning 'illegal boundary line crossing' signal. B1 then moves the body towards A1 over the boundary line before the ball was thrown-in over the boundary line.

Interpretation: As the referee did not show the warning 'illegal boundary line crossing' signal before handing the ball to A1, the referee shall blow the whistle and B1 shall now be given a warning. This warning shall also be communicated to the team B head coach. The warning shall apply to all team B players for the remainder of the game. Any repetition of similar action by any team B player may result in a technical foul. The throw-in shall be repeated, and the referee shall show the 'illegal boundary line crossing' signal.

解释 这是 B1 的掷球入界违例。此外，应给予 B1 一次口头警告并通知 B 队主教练。该警告应适用于在剩余比赛中的所有 B 队队员。任一 B 队队员重复出现类似行为都将导致一起技术犯规。A 队应重新执行掷球入界。A 队应拥有：

（a）14 秒进攻时间。

（b）17 秒进攻时间。

17-4 **陈述** 在第 4 节和每一决胜期比赛计时钟显示 2:00 或更少时，防守队员不应将其身体的任何部分移动越过界线以干扰掷球入界。

17-5 **举例** 第 4 节，比赛计时钟显示 54 秒时，A 队拥有掷球入界权。在递交球给掷球入界队员 A1 之前，裁判员做出了“非法越过界线”的警告手势。之后，在掷球入界的球越过界线前，B1 的身体朝 A1 移动并越过了界线。

解释 应宣判 B1 一起技术犯规。

17-6 **举例** 第 4 节，比赛计时钟显示 51 秒时，A 队拥有掷球入界权。在递交球给掷球入界队员 A1 之前，裁判员没有做出“非法越过界线”的警告手势。之后，在掷球入界的球越过界线前，B1 的身体朝 A1 移动并越过了界线。

解释 因为裁判员在递交球给掷球入界队员 A1 之前没有做出“非法越过界线”的警告手势，该裁判员应鸣哨并给予 B1 一次警告。应将该警告通知 B 队主教练。该警告应适用于在剩余比赛中的所有 B 队队员。任一 B 队队员重复出现类似行为都将导致一起技术犯规。应重新执行掷球入界，并且裁判员应做出“非法越过界线”的警告手势。

17-7	**Statement:** The thrower-in must pass the ball (not hand the ball) to a team-mate on the court.

17-8 **Example:** Thrower-in A1 hands the ball to A2 on the court.

Interpretation: This is a throw-in violation by A1. The ball must leave A1's hands on the throw-in. Team B shall be awarded a throw-in from the place of the original throw-in.

17-9	**Statement:** During a throw-in, other player(s) shall not have any part of their bodies over the boundary line before the ball is passed on to the court.

17-10 **Example:** After an infraction, thrower-in A1 receives the ball from the referee and A1

(a) places the ball on the floor after which the ball is taken by A2.

(b) hands the ball to A2 in the out-of-bounds area.

Interpretation: In both cases, this is a violation by A2 for moving the body over the boundary line before A1 passes the ball over the boundary line.

17-11 **Example:** After a team A successful goal or a successful last free throw, team B is granted a time-out. After the time-out, thrower-in B1 behind the endline receives the ball from the referee. B1 then

(a) places the ball on the floor after which the ball is taken by B2, who is also behind the endline.

(b) hands the ball to B2, who is also behind the endline.

Interpretation: In both cases, this is a legal play by B2. After a successful goal or a successful last free throw, the only restriction for team B is that its players must pass the ball on to the court within 5 seconds.

17-7 **陈述** 掷球入界队员必须将球传（而不是递交）给比赛场地上的同队队员。

17-8 **举例** 掷球入界队员 A1 将球递交给在比赛场地上的 A2。

解释 这是 A1 的掷球入界违例。在掷球入界中，球必须离开 A1 的手。应判给 B 队在原掷球入界的地点执行掷球入界。

17-9 **陈述** 掷球入界中，在球被传入比赛场地前，其他队员不得将其身体的任何部分越过界线。

17-10 **举例** 在一起规则违犯后，掷球入界队员 A1 从裁判员处获得了球，然后 A1：

（a）将球置于比赛地板上，随后球被 A2 拿到。

（b）将球递交给位于界外区域的 A2。

解释 在这两种情况下，A2 都违例了，因为在 A1 将球传过界线前，A2 移动了其身体并越过了界线。

17-11 **举例** 在 A 队中篮或最后一次罚球成功后，准予了 B 队一次暂停。暂停后，掷球入界队员 B1 在端线后从裁判员处获得了球。然后 B1：

（a）将球置于比赛地板上，随后球被同样位于端线后的 B2 拿到。

（b）将球递交给同样位于端线后的 B2。

解释 这两种 B2 的比赛情况均合法。在一次中篮或最后一次罚球成功后，对于 B 队仅有的限制是其掷球入界队员必须在 5 秒之内将球传入比赛场地。

17-12 **Statement:** If a time-out is granted to a team that is entitled to possession of the ball from its backcourt when the game clock shows 2:00 or less in the fourth quarter and in each overtime, the head coach, after the time-out, has the right to decide whether the throw-in shall be administered from a throw-in line in the team's frontcourt or from the team's backcourt.

After a successful goal or a successful last free throw, the head coach, after the time-out, shall decide whether the throw-in shall take place from the throw-in line on the table side or on the opposite side.

After a foul, violation (including out-of-bounds) or a jump ball situation, the throw-in shall take place from the throw-in line at the same side of the court (table side or opposite side) as the original throw-in.

After a time-out following an unsportsmanlike foul or disqualifying foul or fight the game shall be resumed with a throw-in from the throw-in line in the team's frontcourt, opposite the scorer's table.

After the head coach has decided, the decision is final and irreversible. Further requests of both head coaches to change the throw-in place, after additional time-outs during the same game clock stopped period, shall not lead to a change of the original decision.

17-13 **Example:** With 35 seconds on the game clock in the fourth quarter, A1 dribbles in the backcourt when a team B player taps the ball out-of-bounds at the free-throw line extended. Team A is granted a time-out.

Interpretation: After the time-out at the latest, the crew chief shall request the team A head coach's decision as to where the throw-in shall be administered from. The team A head coach shall say loudly in English 'frontcourt' or 'backcourt' and at the same time show with the arm the place (frontcourt or backcourt), where the throw-in shall be administered from. The team A head coach's decision shall be final and irreversible. The crew chief shall inform the team B head coach of the team A head coach's decision.

If the throw-in is from the frontcourt it shall be from the frontcourt throw-in line on the same side of the court where the ball was tapped out-of-bounds.

17-12 陈述 如果在第 4 节和每一决胜期比赛计时钟显示 2:00 或更少时，在后场拥有球权的队已被准予了暂停，暂停结束后，该队主教练有权决定是在其前场的掷球入界线处还是在其后场执行掷球入界。

在一次中篮或最后一次罚球成功后，该队主教练应在暂停后决定是从记录台侧还是对侧的掷球入界线处执行掷球入界。

在一起犯规、违例（包括球出界）或跳球情况后，应从与最初的掷球入界位置相同的场地一侧（记录台侧或对侧）的掷球入界线处执行掷球入界。

如果在一起违反体育运动精神的犯规，或取消比赛资格的犯规，或打架出现后准予了暂停，那么暂停结束后，应在该队前场记录台对侧的掷球入界线处执行掷球入界继续比赛。

在该主教练作出决定后，该决定就是最终且不能更改的。在同一个比赛计时钟停止的时段中，即使两位主教练想通过请求额外的暂停去改变该掷球入界的地点，在这些额外的暂停后，仍然应按照该主教练最初决定的地点继续比赛。

17-13 举例 第 4 节，比赛计时钟显示 35 秒，A1 在其后场运球时，球被一名 B 队队员拍击后从罚球线延长线处出界。准予了 A 队一次暂停。

解释 最迟在该暂停结束后，主裁判员应询问 A 队主教练决定在哪里执行掷球入界。A 队主教练应大声用英语说出“frontcourt”（前场）或“backcourt”（后场），并同时用其手臂指向执行掷球入界的地点（前场或后场）。A 队主教练的决定是最终且不能更改的。主裁判员应将 A 队主教练的决定通知 B 队主教练。

如果在其前场执行掷球入界，应从其前场位于与球被拍出界相同的场地一侧的掷球入界线处执行。

The game shall be resumed with a team A throw-in only when the positions of the players of both teams on the court show their understanding of where the game shall be resumed from.

17-14 **Example:** With 44 seconds on the game clock in the fourth quarter and with 17 seconds on the shot clock, A1 dribbles in the backcourt when a team B player taps the ball out-of-bounds in team A's backcourt at the throw-in line on the table side or the opposite side. A time-out is then granted

(a) to team B.

(b) to team A.

(c) first to team B and immediately after to team A (or vice-versa).

Interpretation:

(a) The game shall be resumed with a team A throw-in from the throw-in line in its backcourt, where the ball went out-of-bounds. Team A shall have 17 seconds on the shot clock.

(b) and (c) If the team A head coach decides on a throw-in from the frontcourt, the game shall be resumed with a team A throw-in from the throw-in line in its frontcourt on the table side or on the opposite side to match the side the ball went out-of-bounds. Team A shall have 14 seconds on the shot clock. If from the backcourt, team A shall have 17 seconds on the shot clock.

17-15 **Example:** With 57 seconds on the game clock in the fourth quarter, A1 attempts 2 free throws. During the second free throw A1 steps on the free-throw line and a violation is called. Team B is granted a time-out.

Interpretation: After the time-out, if the team B head coach decides on a throw-in from

(a) the frontcourt, the throw-in shall be held from the throw-in line on the opposite side. Team B shall have 14 seconds on the shot clock.

只有当双方队员在比赛场地上的位置显示他们都明白将从何处继续比赛时，才由A队执行掷球入界继续比赛。

17-14 **举例** 第4节，比赛计时钟显示44秒，进攻计时钟显示17秒，当A1在其后场运球时，球被一名B队队员拍击后从A队后场记录台侧或对侧的掷球入界线处出界。随后：

（a）准予了B队一次暂停。

（b）准予了A队一次暂停。

（c）先准予了B队一次暂停，紧接着准予了A队一次暂停（或顺序相反）。

解释

（a） 应由A队在其后场球出界一侧的掷球入界线处执行掷球入界继续比赛。A队应拥有17秒进攻时间。

（b）和（c）如果A队主教练决定在其前场执行掷球入界，那么应由A队在其前场记录台侧或对侧（与球出界位置相同的一侧）的掷球入界线处执行掷球入界继续比赛，A队应拥有14秒进攻时间。如果在其后场执行掷球入界，那么A队应拥有17秒进攻时间。

17-15 **举例** 第4节，比赛计时钟显示57秒时，A1执行2次罚球。在第2次罚球时，A1踩在罚球线上被判违例。此时，准予了B队一次暂停。

解释 暂停后，如果B队主教练决定继续比赛的掷球入界地点在：

（a）其前场，应在对侧的掷球入界线处执行掷球入界，B队应拥有14秒进攻时间。

(b) the backcourt, the throw-in shall be held from the free-throw line extended on the opposite side. Team B shall have 24 seconds on the shot clock.

17-16 **Example:** With 26 seconds on the game clock in the fourth quarter, A1 dribbles for 6 seconds in the backcourt, when

(a) B1 taps the ball out-of-bounds.

(b) B1 is charged with the third team B foul in the quarter.

Team A is granted a time-out.

Interpretation: After the time-out:

In both cases, if the team A head coach decides on a throw-in from the throw-in line in the frontcourt, team A shall have 14 seconds on the shot clock.

If the throw-in is from the frontcourt it shall be from the frontcourt throw-in line on the same side of the court where the ball was when the game was stopped.

If the throw-in is from the backcourt, team A shall have

(a) 18 seconds

(b) 24 seconds

on the shot clock.

17-17 **Example:** With 1:24 on the game clock in the fourth quarter, A1 dribbles in the frontcourt when B1 taps the ball to the team A backcourt where any team A player starts to dribble again. B2 now taps the ball out-of-bounds on the table side in the team A backcourt with

(a) 6 seconds

(b) 17 seconds

on the shot clock. Team A is granted a time-out.

（b）其后场，应在对侧的罚球线延长线处执行掷球入界，B 队应拥有 24 秒进攻时间。

17-16 **举例** 第 4 节，比赛计时钟显示 26 秒，A1 在其后场运球已达 6 秒时：

（a）B1 将球拍出界。

（b）判了 B1 犯规，这是该节 B 队的第 3 次全队犯规。

准予了 A 队一次暂停。

解释 暂停后，

在这两种情况下，如果 A 队主教练决定在其前场的掷球入界线处执行掷球入界，那么 A 队应拥有 14 秒进攻时间。

如果在其前场执行掷球入界，应从其前场位于停止比赛时与球所在位置相同的场地一侧的掷球入界线处执行。

如果在其后场执行掷球入界，A 队应拥有：

（a）18 秒进攻时间。

（b）24 秒进攻时间。

17-17 **举例** 第 4 节，比赛计时钟显示 1:24，A1 在其前场运球时，球被 B1 拍击到 A 队的后场，接着，A 队任一队员在其后场再次开始运球。此时，B2 将球拍击到 A 队后场记录台侧的界外，进攻计时钟显示：

（a）6 秒。

（b）17 秒。

准予了 A 队一次暂停。

Interpretation: After the time-out:

If the team A head coach decides on a throw-in from the throw-in line in the frontcourt, it shall be held at the table side. Team A shall have

(a) 6 seconds

(b) 14 seconds

on the shot clock.

If from the backcourt, it shall be held at the original place where the ball went out-of-bounds. Team A shall have

(a) 6 seconds

(b) 17 seconds

on the shot clock.

17-18 **Example:** With 48 seconds on the game clock in the fourth quarter, A1 dribbles in the frontcourt when B1 taps the ball to the team A backcourt where A2 starts to dribble again. B2 now fouls A2 close to the table side. This is the third team B foul in the quarter with

(a) 6 seconds

(b) 17 seconds

on the shot clock. Team A is granted a time-out.

Interpretation: In both cases, if after the time-out the team A head coach decides on a throw-in from the throw-in line in the frontcourt, it shall be held on the table side. Team A shall have 14 seconds on the shot clock. If from the backcourt, team A shall have 24 seconds on the shot clock.

17-19 **Example:** With 1:32 on the game clock in the fourth quarter, team A is in control of the ball for 5 seconds when A1 and B1 are disqualified for punching each other in the team A backcourt. Team A is granted a time-out.

解释 暂停后，

如果A队主教练决定在其前场的掷球入界线处执行掷球入界，该掷球入界应在记录台侧执行。A 队应拥有：

（a）6 秒进攻时间。

（b）14 秒进攻时间。

如果在其后场执行掷球入界，应从球出界的原地点执行。A 队应拥有：

（a）6 秒进攻时间。

（b）17 秒进攻时间。

17-18 **举例** 第 4 节，比赛计时钟显示 48 秒，A1 在其前场运球时，球被 B1 拍击到 A 队的后场，接着，A2 在其后场再次开始运球。这时，B2 对靠近记录台侧的 A2 犯规，这是该节 B 队的第 3 次全队犯规，进攻计时钟显示：

（a）6 秒。

（b）17 秒。

准予了 A 队一次暂停。

解释 在这两种情况下，如果暂停后 A 队主教练决定在其前场的掷球入界线处执行掷球入界，该掷球入界应在记录台侧执行。A 队应拥有 14 秒进攻时间；如果 A 队主教练决定在其后场执行掷球入界，那么 A 队应拥有 24 秒进攻时间。

17-19 **举例** 第 4 节，比赛计时钟显示 1:32，A 队控球已达 5 秒时，A1 和 B1 在 A 队的后场因相互拳击而被取消比赛资格。准予了 A 队一次暂停。

Interpretation: The disqualifying foul penalties shall cancel each other. The game shall be resumed with a team A throw-in from its backcourt. However, if after the time-out the team A head coach decides on a throw-in from the throw-in line in the frontcourt, team A shall have 14 seconds on the shot clock. If from the backcourt, team A shall have 19 seconds on the shot clock.

17-20 **Example:** With 1:29 on the game clock in the fourth quarter and with 19 seconds on the shot clock, team A is in control of the ball in its frontcourt when A6 and B6 are disqualified for entering the court during a fight. Team A is granted a time-out.

Interpretation: The disqualifying foul penalties shall cancel each other. After the time-out, the game shall be resumed with a team A throw-in in its frontcourt, from the place nearest to where the ball was located when the fight has started. Team A shall have 19 seconds on the shot clock.

17-21 **Example:** With 1:18 on the game clock in the fourth quarter, team A is awarded a throw-in from its backcourt. Team A is granted a time-out. After the time-out, the team A head coach decides on a throw-in from the throw-in line in the frontcourt. Before the throw-in is administered, the team B head coach requests a time-out.

Interpretation: The original decision of the team A head coach to administer a throw-in from the frontcourt is final and irreversible and cannot be changed within the same game clock stopped period. This shall be valid also if the team A head coach takes a second time-out, following the first one.

17-22 **Statement:** At the start of all quarters other than the first quarter and at the start of each overtime, a throw-in shall be administered at the centre line extended, opposite the scorer's table. The thrower-in shall have one foot on either side of the centre line extended. If the thrower-in commits a throw-in violation, the ball shall be awarded to the opponents for a throw-in from the centre line extended.

However, if an infraction occurred on the court directly on the centre line, the throw-in shall be administered from the frontcourt at the place nearest to the centre line.

解释 这两起取消比赛资格的犯规的罚则应相互抵消。应由A队在其后场执行掷球入界继续比赛。然而，暂停后，如果A队主教练决定在其前场的掷球入界线处执行掷球入界，A队应拥有14秒进攻时间；如果A队主教练决定在其后场执行掷球入界，A队应拥有19秒进攻时间。

17-20 举例 第4节，比赛计时钟显示1:29，进攻计时钟显示19秒，A队在其前场控制球时，A6和B6在一起打架中因进入比赛场地而被取消比赛资格。准予了A队一次暂停。

解释 这两起取消比赛资格的犯规的罚则应相互抵消。暂停后，应由A队在其前场最靠近打架开始时球所在位置的地点执行掷球入界继续比赛。A队应拥有19秒进攻时间。

17-21 举例 第4节，比赛计时钟显示1:18时，判给A队在其后场执行掷球入界。准予了A队一次暂停。暂停后，A队主教练决定在其前场的掷球入界线处执行掷球入界。在执行掷球入界前，B队主教练请求一次暂停。

解释 A队主教练选择在其前场执行掷球入界的最初决定，在同一比赛计时钟停止的时段内，是最终且不能更改的。即使A队主教练在第1次暂停后又请求了第2次暂停，这个决定也是有效的。

17-22 陈述 除了第1节之外，所有其他节和所有决胜期的开始，应从记录台对侧的中线延长线处执行掷球入界。该掷球入界队员应双脚骑跨中线。如果掷球入界队员发生了掷球入界违例，应判给对方队员在中线延长线处执行掷球入界。

然而，如果比赛场地内直接在中线上发生了一起规则违犯，应从前场最靠近中线的地点执行掷球入界。

17-23 **Example:** At the start of a quarter thrower-in A1 commits a violation at the centre line extended.

Interpretation: The game shall be resumed with a team B throw-in from the place of the original throw-in at the centre line extended, with 10:00 on the game clock and 24 seconds on the shot clock. The thrower-in shall be entitled to pass the ball to any place on the court. The direction of the alternating possession arrow shall be reversed in favour of team B.

17-24 **Example:** At the start of a quarter thrower-in A1 at the centre line extended passes the ball to A2 who touches it before it goes out-of-bounds in the team A

(a) frontcourt.

(b) backcourt.

Interpretation: The game shall be resumed with a team B throw-in from the place nearest to where the ball went out-of-bounds in its

(a) backcourt with 24 seconds

(b) frontcourt with 14 seconds

on the shot clock.

The team A throw-in ends when A2 touched the ball. The direction of the alternating possession arrow shall be reversed in favour of team B.

17-25 **Example:** The following infractions may occur at the centre line on the court:

(a) A1 causes the ball to go out-of-bounds.

(b) A1 is charged with a team control foul.

(c) A1 commits a travelling violation.

Interpretation: In all cases, the game shall be resumed with a team B throw-in from its frontcourt at the place nearest to the centre line. Team B shall have 14 seconds on the shot clock.

17-23 **举例** 在一节开始时，掷球入界队员 A1 在中线延长线处发生了一起违例。

解释 应将球判给 B 队从原掷球入界地点（中线延长线处）执行掷球入界，比赛计时钟显示 10:00，进攻计时钟显示 24 秒。该掷球入界队员应有权将球传到比赛场地上的任何地点。交替拥有箭头的方向应反转并指向 B 队的进攻方向。

17-24 **举例** 在一节比赛开始时，掷球入界队员 A1 在中线延长线处将球传给 A2，A2 触及球后，球从 A 队的：

（a）前场出界。

（b）后场出界。

解释 应由 B 队在最靠近球出界的地点执行掷球入界继续比赛，进攻计时钟应显示：

（a）24 秒（在 B 队的后场执行掷球入界）。

（b）14 秒（在 B 队的前场执行掷球入界）。

当 A2 触及球时，A 队的掷球入界结束。交替拥有箭头的方向应反转并指向 B 队的进攻方向。

17-25 **举例** 在比赛场地上的中线处可能发生下列规则违犯：

（a）A1 使球出界。

（b）A1 发生一起控制球队犯规。

（c）A1 发生一起带球走违例。

解释 在上述所有情况下，应判给 B 队在其前场最靠近中线的地点执行掷球入界。B 队应拥有 14 秒进攻时间。

17-26 **Statement:** A throw-in resulting from an unsportsmanlike foul or disqualifying foul shall always be administered from the throw-in line in the team's frontcourt.

17-27 **Example:** A1 is charged with an unsportsmanlike foul against B1 during the interval of play between the first and second quarter.

Interpretation: Before the start of the second quarter, B1 shall attempt 2 free throws with no line-up. The game shall be resumed with a team B throw-in from the throw-in line in its frontcourt. Team B shall have 14 seconds on the shot clock. The direction of the alternating possession arrow shall remain unchanged.

17-28 **Statement:** During a throw-in, the following situations may occur:

(a) The ball is passed over the basket and a player of either team touches it by reaching through the basket from below. This is an interference violation.

(b) The ball lodges between the ring and the backboard. This is a jump ball situation.

17-29 **Example:** Thrower-in A1 passes the ball over the basket when a player of either team touches it by reaching through the basket from below.

Interpretation: This is an interference violation. The game shall be resumed with a throw-in by the opponents from the free-throw line extended. If a defensive team commits the violation, no points shall be credited to the offensive team as the ball was released from out-of-bounds.

17-30 **Example:** Thrower-in A1 passes the ball towards the team B basket and it lodges between the ring and the backboard.

Interpretation: This is a jump ball situation. The game shall be resumed according to the alternating possession procedure:

- If team A is entitled to the throw-in, the game shall be resumed with the team A throw-in from behind the endline in its frontcourt, nearest to but not directly behind the backboard. Team A shall have 14 seconds on the shot clock.

17-26	**陈述** 源于一起违反体育运动精神的犯规或取消比赛资格的犯规的掷球入界，应总是在球队前场的掷球入界线处执行。

17-27 **举例** 在第 1 节和第 2 节之间的比赛休息期间，宣判了 A1 对 B1 的一起违反体育运动精神的犯规。

解释 在第 2 节比赛开始前，应由 B1 执行 2 次不占位的罚球。应由 B 队在其前场的掷球入界线处执行掷球入界继续比赛。B 队应拥有 14 秒进攻时间。交替拥有箭头的方向保持不变。

17-28	**陈述** 在掷球入界中，可能出现下列情况。 （a）掷入的球越过球篮时，被任一队的队员从下方伸手穿过球篮并触及。这是一起干扰得分违例。 （b）球停留在篮圈和篮板之间。这是一次跳球情况。

17-29 **举例** 掷球入界队员 A1 传出的球越过球篮时，被任一队的队员从下方伸手穿过球篮并触及。

解释 这是一起干扰得分违例。应由对方队在罚球线延长线处执行掷球入界继续比赛。如果防守队发生该违例，不应判给进攻队得分，因为球是从界外区域离手的。

17-30 **举例** 掷球入界队员 A1 将球传向 B 队的球篮，球停留在篮圈和篮板之间。

解释 这是一次跳球情况。应使用交替拥有程序继续比赛。

- 如果 A 队拥有掷球入界权，应由 A 队在其前场端线后最靠近篮板（但不是在篮板正后方）的位置执行掷球入界继续比赛。A 队应拥有 14 秒进攻时间。

- If team B is entitled to the throw-in, the game shall be resumed with the team B throw-in from behind the endline in its backcourt, nearest to but not directly behind the backboard. Team B shall have 24 seconds on the shot clock.

17-31 **Statement:** After the ball is placed at the disposal of the thrower-in, that player may not bounce the ball so as the ball touches the inbounds area and the thrower-in then touches the ball again before it has touched or been touched by another player on the court.

17-32 **Example:** Thrower-in A1 bounces the ball which touches

(a) the inbounds area

(b) the out-of-bounds area

and A1 then catches it again.

Interpretation:

(a) This is a throw-in violation by A1. After the ball leaves A1's hands and the ball touches the inbounds area, A1 shall not touch the ball before it touches or was touched by another player on the court.

(b) If A1 did not move more than a total of 1 meter between bouncing the ball and catching it again, A1's action is legal. The 5-second restriction to release the ball shall continue.

17-33 **Statement:** The thrower-in shall not cause the ball to touch the out-of-bounds area, after it was released on the throw-in.

17-34 **Example:** Thrower-in A1 passes the ball from the

(a) frontcourt

(b) backcourt

to A2 on the court. The ball goes out-of-bounds without touching any player on the court.

Interpretation: This is a throw-in violation by A1. The game shall be resumed with a team B throw-in from the place of the original throw-in, if from the

- 如果 B 队拥有掷球入界权，应由 B 队在其后场端线后最靠近篮板（但不是在篮板正后方）的位置执行掷球入界继续比赛。B 队应拥有 24 秒进攻时间。

17-31 陈述 在球被置于掷球入界队员可处理后，该队员将球反弹使球触及界内区域后，不得在球触及了场上另一名队员或被场上另一名队员触及之前再次触及球。

17-32 举例 掷球入界队员 A1 将球反弹，使球触及了：

（a）界内区域。

（b）界外区域。

随后，A1 再次接住球。

解释

（a）这是 A1 的掷球入界违例。在球离开了 A1 的手触及了界内区域后，并且在球触及了场上另一名队员或被场上另一名队员触及之前，A1 不得触及球。

（b）如果 A1 将球反弹和再次拿球之间移动的总距离不超过 1 米，A1 的行为是合法的。5 秒球离手的限制应继续。

17-33 陈述 在掷球入界中，掷球入界队员不得在球离手后，使球触及界外区域。

17-34 举例 掷球入界队员 A1 在其：

（a）前场

（b）后场

将球传向场上的 A2，但球出界且未触及场上的任一队员。

解释 这是 A1 的掷球入界违例。应由 B 队在原掷球入界的地点执行掷球入界继续比赛。如果该掷球入界的地点是在 B 队的：

(a) backcourt with 24 seconds

(b) frontcourt with 14 seconds

on the shot clock.

17-35 **Example:** Thrower-in A1 passes the ball to A2. A2 catches the ball with one foot touching the boundary line.

Interpretation: This is an out-of-bounds violation by A2. The game shall be resumed with a team B throw-in from the place nearest to where A2 touched the boundary line.

17-36 **Example:** Thrower-in A1 from behind the sideline,

(a) in the backcourt close to the centre line is entitled to pass the ball to any place on the court.

(b) in the frontcourt close to the centre line is entitled to pass the ball only to a team-mate in the frontcourt.

(c) at the centre line extended at the start of a quarter or each overtime is entitled to pass the ball to any place on the court.

With the ball in the hands A1 takes one normal lateral step, therefore changing the position regarding the frontcourt or backcourt.

Interpretation: In all cases, this is a legal play by A1. A1 shall keep the initial throw-in position with the right to pass the ball either to the frontcourt or to the backcourt according to the initial status.

17-37 **Statement:** After a successful goal or successful last free throw, the thrower-in behind the endline may move laterally and/or backwards and the ball may be passed between team-mates behind the endline, but the throw-in period shall not exceed 5 seconds. This is also valid after a time-out is taken by either team or when an illegal interference with the throw-in violation by the defensive team during the throw-in is called and therefore the throw-in shall be repeated.

17-38 **Example:** After an opponents' successful goal or last free throw in the second quarter, A1 has the ball in the hands for a throw-in from behind the endline.

（a）后场，则拥有 24 秒进攻时间。

（b）前场，则拥有 14 秒进攻时间。

17-35 举例 掷球入界队员 A1 将球传给 A2，A2 接球时一只脚正触及界线。

解释 这是 A2 的出界违例。应由 B 队在最靠近 A2 触及界线的地点执行掷球入界继续比赛。

17-36 举例 掷球入界队员 A1 在边线后执行掷球入界的地点在：

（a）其后场靠近中线处，A1 有权将球传到比赛场地上的任何地点。

（b）其前场靠近中线处，A1 只有权将球传给其前场的同队队员。

（c）在中线延长线处开始一节或每一决胜期的比赛时，A1 有权将球传到比赛场地上的任何地点。

A1 双手持球，并侧向移动了正常的 1 步；因此，A1 改变了其原来所在的前场或后场的位置。

解释 上述所有 A1 的比赛情况均合法。A1 应保持其最初的掷球入界位置，并有权根据其最初所处的位置将球传到其前场或后场。

17-37 陈述 在一次中篮或最后一次罚球成功后，掷球入界队员可以在端线后向侧面和/或向后移动，并且可以将球在位于端线后的同队队员之间传递，但是该掷球入界的过程不应超过 5 秒。在掷球入界中，当任一队被准予的暂停结束后或防守队被判非法干扰掷球入界违例并因此重新执行掷球入界时，这个规定也仍然有效。

17-38 举例 第 2 节，在对方队员中篮或最后一次罚球成功后，A1 双手持球在其端线后执行掷球入界。

(a) B2 moves the hands over the boundary line before the ball is thrown-in on the court.

(b) A1 passes the ball to A2 who is also behind the endline. B2 moves the hands over the boundary line and touches the ball on this pass.

Interpretation: B2 shall be given a warning for delaying the game. B2's warning shall also be communicated to the team B head coach and shall apply to all team B members for the remainder of the game. Any repetition of a similar action may result in a technical foul. Any team A player shall keep the right to move along the endline before releasing the ball or passing it to a team-mate.

17-39 **Example:** After an opponents' successful goal, A1 has the ball in the hands for the throw-in from behind the endline. After the ball is thrown-in on to the court, B2 kicks the ball close to the endline.

Interpretation: This is a kick ball violation by B2. The game shall be resumed with a team A throw-in from behind its endline, except from directly behind the backboard. As B2's kick ball violation occurred after the throw-in, team A thrower-in shall not have the right to move along the endline from the designated throw-in place before releasing the ball on to the court.

17-40 **Example:** After an opponents' successful goal, A1 has the ball in the hands for a throw-in from behind the endline. A2 jumps from out-of-bounds behind the endline and while airborne catches the ball from A1's throw-in. After that

(a) A2 passes the ball back to A1 who is still out-of-bounds behind the endline.

(b) A2 passes the ball to A3 who is on the court.

(c) A2 returns to out-of-bounds behind the endline.

(d) A2 lands on the court.

(e) A2 lands on the court and passes the ball back to A1 who is still out-of-bounds behind the endline.

（a）在球被掷入比赛场地前，B2 伸手越过了界线。

（b）A1 将球传给同样位于端线后的 A2。B2 伸手越过界线并触及了这次传球。

解释 应给予 B2 一次延误比赛的警告。也应将给予 B2 的警告通知 B 队主教练，并且该警告应适用于在剩余比赛中的所有 B 队队员。重复出现任一类似行为都将导致一起技术犯规。任一 A 队队员应保持其在球离手前可沿着端线移动或传球给同队队员的权利。

17-39 **举例** 在对方队员中篮后，A1 双手持球在其端线后执行掷球入界。A1 将球掷入比赛场地后，B2 在靠近端线处脚踢球。

解释 这是 B2 的脚踢球违例。应由 A 队在其端线后（篮板正后方除外）执行掷球入界继续比赛。因为 B2 的脚踢球违例发生在掷球入界后，A 队掷球入界队员在将球掷入比赛场地之前已无权从指定的掷球入界地点沿着端线移动。

17-40 **举例** 在对方队员中篮后，A1 双手持球在其端线后执行掷球入界。A2 从该端线后的界外跳起，并在空中时接到了 A1 掷球入界的球。之后：

（a）A2 将球回传给仍在其端线后界外的 A1。

（b）A2 将球传给在比赛场地上的 A3。

（c）A2 落回其端线后的界外。

（d）A2 落在比赛场地上。

（e）A2 落在比赛场地上，并将球回传给仍在其端线后界外的 A1。

Interpretation:

(a), (b) and (c) This is a legal play by team A.

(d) and (e) This is a throw-in violation by A2.

17-41 **Statement:** After the free throw resulting from a technical foul, the game shall be resumed with a throw-in from the place nearest to where the ball was located when the technical foul occurred, unless there is a jump ball situation or before the start of the first quarter.

If a technical foul is called against the defensive team, and the throw-in shall be administered from its backcourt, the offensive team shall have 24 seconds on the shot clock. If from its frontcourt, the shot clock shall be reset as follows:

- If 14 seconds or more are shown on the shot clock, it shall continue with the time remaining on the shot clock.
- If 13 seconds or less are shown on the shot clock, it shall show 14 seconds.

If a technical foul is called against the offensive team, that team shall have the time remaining on the shot clock, regardless of whether the throw-in shall be administered from its backcourt or from its frontcourt.

If a time-out and a technical foul are called during the same game clock stopped period the time-out shall be administered first, followed by the administration of the technical foul penalty.

After a free throw(s) resulting from an unsportsmanlike foul or a disqualifying foul, the game shall be resumed with a throw-in from the throw-in line in the team's frontcourt. The team shall have 14 seconds on the shot clock.

17-42 **Example:** A2 dribbles in the

(a) backcourt

(b) frontcourt

when A1 is charged with a technical foul.

解释

（a）（b）和（c）A 队的比赛情况合法。

（d）和（e）　　这是 A2 的掷球入界违例。

17-41 **陈述** 在一起源于技术犯规的罚球后，应在最靠近发生技术犯规时球所在位置的地点执行掷球入界继续比赛，除非有一次跳球情况或是在第 1 节比赛开始之前。

如果宣判了一起防守队的技术犯规，则进攻队应在其后场执行掷球入界并应拥有 24 秒进攻时间；如果在其前场执行掷球入界，则进攻计时钟应按下述原则复位：

- 如果进攻计时钟显示 14 秒或更多，应从进攻计时钟显示的剩余时间处连续计算。
- 如果进攻计时钟显示 13 秒或更少，则应复位到 14 秒。

如果宣判了一起进攻队的技术犯规，那么随后进攻队的掷球入界无论在其前场还是在其后场执行，该队应拥有进攻计时钟显示的剩余时间。

如果在同一个比赛计时钟停止的时段中，准予了一次暂停，又宣判了一起技术犯规，那么，应先执行暂停，之后再执行技术犯规的罚则。

在执行完一起违反体育运动精神的犯规或取消比赛资格的犯规的罚球后，应在球队前场的掷球入界线处执行掷球入界继续比赛。该队应拥有 14 秒进攻时间。

17-42 **举例** A2 在其：

（a）后场

（b）前场

运球时，宣判了 A1 一起技术犯规。

Interpretation: Any team B player shall attempt 1 free throw with no line-up. In both cases, the game shall be resumed with a team A throw-in from the place nearest to where the ball was located when the technical foul occurred. Team A shall have the time remaining on the shot clock.

17-43 **Example:** A2 dribbles in the

(a) backcourt

(b) frontcourt

when B1 is charged with a technical foul.

Interpretation: Any team A player shall attempt 1 free throw with no line-up. The game shall be resumed with a team A throw-in from the place nearest to where the ball was located when the technical foul occurred. If in its

(a) backcourt, with 24 seconds on the shot clock.

(b) frontcourt, with the time remaining on the shot clock, if 14 seconds or more are shown on the shot clock and with 14 seconds on the shot clock, if 13 seconds or less are shown on the shot clock.

17-44 **Example:** With 1:47 on the game clock in the fourth quarter, A1 dribbles in the frontcourt and is charged with a technical foul. Team A is granted a time-out.

Interpretation: After the time-out, any team B player shall attempt 1 free throw with no line-up. The game shall be resumed with a team A throw-in from the place nearest to where the ball was located when the technical foul occurred. Team A shall have the time remaining on the shot clock.

17-45 **Statement:** When the game clock shows 2:00 or less in the fourth quarter and in each overtime, if a technical foul is called against the offensive team and that team is granted a time-out, the offensive team shall have the time remaining on the shot clock, if the throw-in shall be administered from its backcourt. If from the throw-in line in its frontcourt, the shot clock shall be reset as follows:

解释 应由B队任一队员执行1次不占位的罚球。在这两种情况下，应由A队在最靠近发生技术犯规时球所在位置的地点执行掷球入界继续比赛。A队应拥有进攻计时钟显示的剩余时间。

17-43 **举例** A2在其:

（a）后场

（b）前场

运球时，宣判了B1一起技术犯规。

解释 应由A队任一队员执行1次不占位的罚球。应由A队在最靠近发生技术犯规时球所在位置的地点执行掷球入界继续比赛。如果该掷球入界地点在其:

（a）后场，则拥有24秒进攻时间。

（b）前场，如果进攻计时钟显示14秒或更多，则拥有进攻计时钟显示的剩余时间；如果进攻计时钟显示13秒或更少，则拥有14秒进攻时间。

17-44 **举例** 第4节，比赛计时钟显示1:47，A1在其前场运球时被判一起技术犯规。此时，准予了A队一次暂停。

解释 暂停后，应由B队任一队员执行1次不占位的罚球。应由A队在最靠近发生技术犯规时球所在位置的地点执行掷球入界继续比赛。A队应拥有进攻计时钟显示的剩余时间。

17-45 **陈述** 在第4节和每一决胜期比赛计时钟显示2:00或更少时，如果宣判了进攻队一起技术犯规，并且准予了该队一次暂停；然后，进攻队在其后场执行掷球入界，则该队拥有进攻计时钟显示的剩余时间。如果在该队前场的掷球入界线处执行掷球入界，进攻计时钟应按下述原则复位。

- If 14 seconds or more are shown on the shot clock, it shall show 14 seconds.
- If 13 seconds or less are shown on the shot clock, it shall continue with the time remaining on the shot clock.

17-46 **Example:** With 1:45 on the game clock in the fourth quarter, A1 dribbles in the backcourt and is charged with a technical foul. Team A is granted a time-out.

Interpretation: After the time-out at the latest, the team A head coach shall inform the crew chief of the throw-in place (frontcourt or backcourt). After the time-out, any team B player shall attempt 1 free throw with no line-up. The game shall be resumed with a team A throw-in according to the team A head coach's decision.

If the team A head coach decides on a throw-in from the throw-in line in the frontcourt, team A shall have 14 seconds, if 14 seconds or more are shown on the shot clock or the time remaining on the shot clock, if 13 seconds or less are shown on the shot clock.

If from the backcourt, team A shall have the time remaining on the shot clock.

17-47 **Example:** With 1:43 on the game clock in the fourth quarter, A1 dribbles in the backcourt and is charged with a technical foul. Any team B player shall attempt 1 free throw with no line-up. Team A is granted a time-out.

Interpretation: After the time-out at the latest, the team A head coach shall inform the crew chief of the throw-in place (frontcourt or backcourt). The game shall be resumed with a team A throw-in according to the team A head coach's decision.

If the team A head coach decides on a throw-in from the throw-in line in the frontcourt, team A shall have 14 seconds, if 14 seconds or more are shown on the shot clock or the time remaining on the shot clock, if 13 seconds or less are on the shot clock.

If from the backcourt, team A shall have the time remaining on the shot clock.

- 如果进攻计时钟显示 14 秒或更多，进攻计时钟应显示 14 秒。
- 如果进攻计时钟显示 13 秒或更少，应从进攻计时钟显示的剩余时间处连续计算。

17-46 **举例** 第 4 节，比赛计时钟显示 1:45，A1 在其后场运球时被判一起技术犯规。此时，准予了 A 队一次暂停。

解释 最迟在该暂停结束后，A 队主教练应将掷球入界的地点（前场或后场）告知主裁判员。暂停后，应由 B 队任一队员执行 1 次不占位的罚球。应由 A 队在其主教练决定的地点执行掷球入界继续比赛。

如果A队主教练决定在其前场的掷球入界线处执行掷球入界，且进攻计时钟显示 14 秒或更多，A 队应拥有 14 秒进攻时间；如果进攻计时钟显示 13 秒或更少，则 A 队应拥有进攻计时钟显示的剩余时间。

如果在其后场执行掷球入界，A 队应拥有进攻计时钟显示的剩余时间。

17-47 **举例** 第 4 节，比赛计时钟显示 1:43，A1 在其后场运球时被判一起技术犯规。B 队任一队员执行 1 次不占位的罚球。此时，准予了 A 队一次暂停。

解释 最迟在该暂停结束后，A 队主教练应将掷球入界的地点（前场或后场）告知主裁判员。应由 A 队在其主教练决定的地点执行掷球入界继续比赛。

如果A队主教练决定在其前场的掷球入界线处执行掷球入界，且进攻计时钟显示 14 秒或更多，A 队应拥有 14 秒进攻时间；如果进攻计时钟显示 13 秒或更少，则 A 队应拥有进攻计时钟显示的剩余时间。

如果在其后场执行掷球入界，A 队应拥有进攻计时钟显示的剩余时间。

17-48 **Example:** With 1:41 on the game clock in the fourth quarter, A1 dribbles in the backcourt when B1 taps the ball out-of-bounds. Team A is granted a time-out. Immediately after, A1 is charged with a technical foul.

Interpretation: After the time-out at the latest, the team A head coach shall inform the crew chief of the throw-in place (frontcourt or backcourt). Any team B player shall attempt 1 free throw with no line-up. The game shall be resumed with a team A throw-in according to the team A head coach's decision.

If the team A head coach decides on a throw-in from the throw-in line in the frontcourt, team A shall have 14 seconds, if 14 seconds or more are shown on the shot clock or the time remaining on the shot clock, if 13 seconds or less are shown on the shot clock.

If from the backcourt, team A shall have the time remaining on the shot clock.

17-49 **Example:** With 58 seconds on the game clock in the fourth quarter, in A1's backcourt

(a) B1 deliberately kicks the ball.

(b) B1 fouls A1. This is the third team B foul in the quarter.

(c) B1 taps the ball out-of-bounds.

With 19 seconds on the shot clock, team A is granted a time-out.

Interpretation: The team A head coach shall decide whether the game shall be resumed with a throw-in from the throw-in line in the frontcourt or from the backcourt.

In all cases, if from the throw-in line in its frontcourt, team A shall have 14 seconds on the shot clock.

(a) and (b) If from its backcourt, team A shall have 24 seconds on the shot clock.

(c) If from its backcourt, team A shall have 19 seconds on the shot clock.

17-48 **举例** 第 4 节，比赛计时钟显示 1:41，A1 在其后场运球时，B1 将球拍出界。此时，准予了 A 队一次暂停。随即，A1 被判一起技术犯规。

解释 最迟在该暂停结束后，A 队主教练应将掷球入界的地点（前场或后场）告知主裁判员。应由 B 队任一队员执行 1 次不占位的罚球。应由 A 队在其主教练决定的地点执行掷球入界继续比赛。

如果A队主教练决定在其前场的掷球入界线处执行掷球入界，且进攻计时钟显示 14 秒或更多，A 队应拥有 14 秒进攻时间；如果进攻计时钟显示 13 秒或更少，则 A 队应拥有进攻计时钟显示的剩余时间。

如果在其后场执行掷球入界，A 队应拥有进攻计时钟显示的剩余时间。

17-49 **举例** 第 4 节，比赛计时钟显示 58 秒时，在 A1 的后场：

（a）B1 故意脚踢球。

（b）B1 对 A1 犯规，这是该节 B 队的第 3 次全队犯规。

（c）B1 将球拍出界。

进攻计时钟显示 19 秒，准予了 A 队一次暂停。

解释 A 队主教练应决定，是在其前场的掷球入界线处还是在其后场执行掷球入界继续比赛。

在上述所有情况下，如果 A 队在其前场的掷球入界线处执行掷球入界，A 队应拥有 14 秒进攻时间。

（a）和（b） 如果在其后场执行掷球入界，A 队应拥有 24 秒进攻时间。

（c） 如果在其后场执行掷球入界，A 队应拥有 19 秒进攻时间。

17-50 Statement: Whenever the ball enters the basket, but the goal or the last free throw is not valid, the game shall be resumed with a throw-in from the free-throw line extended.

If after a last free throw that is not valid due to a violation by the free-throw shooter, the throw-in shall be from the free-throw line extended opposite the table side.

If after a goal that is not valid the throw-in shall be from the free-throw line extended on the same side of the floor, where the action to cancel the goal occurred.

17-51 Example: A1 in the act of shooting commits a travelling violation and then the ball enters the basket.

Interpretation: A1's goal shall not count. Team B shall be awarded a throw-in from the free-throw line extended in its backcourt, on the same side of the court where the travelling violation occurred. Team B shall have 24 seconds on the shot clock.

17-52 Example: A1 attempts a shot for a goal. While the ball is on its downward flight, A2 touches the ball which then enters the basket.

Interpretation: A1's goal shall not count. Team B shall be awarded a throw-in from the free-throw line extended in its backcourt, on the same side of the court where A2 illegally touched the ball. Team B shall have 24 seconds on the shot clock.

17-50 **陈述** 每当球进入球篮，但该中篮或最后一次罚球无效，应在罚球线延长线处执行掷球入界继续比赛。

如果罚球队员违例致使最后一次罚球无效，该掷球入界应在记录台对侧的罚球线延长线处执行。

如果中篮无效，该掷球入界应在位于发生取消得分的行为相同的场地一侧的罚球线延长线处执行。

17-51 **举例** 正在做投篮动作的 A1 发生了带球走违例，随后球进入球篮。

解释 A1 的中篮不应计得分。应判给 B 队在其后场位于发生带球走违例相同的场地一侧的罚球线延长线处执行掷球入界。B 队应拥有 24 秒进攻时间。

17-52 **举例** A1 尝试投篮。球在下落飞行中，被 A2 触及，随后球中篮。

解释 A1 的中篮不应计得分。应判给 B 队在其后场位于 A2 非法触及球相同的场地一侧的罚球线延长线处执行掷球入界。B 队应拥有 24 秒进攻时间。

Article 18/19 Time-out / Substitution

18/19-1 **Statement:** A time-out cannot be granted before the playing time for a quarter or overtime has started or after the playing time for a quarter or overtime has ended.

A substitution cannot be granted before the playing time for the first quarter has started or after the playing time for the game has ended. A substitution can be granted during intervals of play between quarters and overtimes.

18/19-2 **Example:** After the ball has left the hands of the crew chief on the opening jump ball but before the ball is legally tapped, jumper A2 commits a violation. Team B is awarded a throw-in. At this time, either team requests a time-out or a substitution.

Interpretation: Despite the fact that the game has started, the time-out or substitution shall not be granted because the game clock has not yet started.

18/19-3 **Statement:** If the shot clock signal sounds while the ball is in the air during a shot for a goal, it is not a violation and the game clock shall not stop. If the shot is successful then it is, under certain conditions, a time-out and substitution opportunity for both teams.

18/19-4 **Example:** The ball is in the air on a shot for a goal when the shot clock signal sounds. The ball enters the basket. Either or both teams request

(a) a time-out.

(b) a substitution.

Interpretation:

(a) This is a time-out opportunity only for the non-scoring team.

If the non-scoring team is granted a time-out, the opponents may also be granted a time-out and both teams are also granted a substitution, if they request it.

第 18/19 条　暂停 / 替换

18/19-1　**陈述**　在一节或决胜期的比赛时间开始前，或一节或决胜期的比赛时间已结束后不能准予暂停。

在第 1 节比赛时间开始前，或整场比赛的比赛时间结束后不能准予替换。在每两节之间和每两个决胜期之间的比赛休息期间可以准予替换。

18/19-2　**举例**　开场跳球时，在球离开主裁判员的手后但在球被合法拍击之前，跳球队员 A2 发生了一起违例，判给 B 队执行掷球入界。此时，任一队请求暂停或替换。

解释　尽管比赛已经开始，但该暂停或替换不应被准予，因为比赛计时钟尚未开动。

18/19-3　**陈述**　如果投篮的球在空中时进攻计时钟信号响，这不是一起违例，比赛计时钟不应停止。如果该投篮成功，那么在某些条件下，这对于双方球队都是一次暂停和替换的机会。

18/19-4　**举例**　投篮的球在空中时，进攻计时钟信号响。球进入球篮。此时，任一队或双方球队请求：

（a）一次暂停。

（b）一次替换。

解释

（a）这只是非得分队的一次暂停机会。

如果非得分队被准予了暂停，那么，也可以准予对方暂停，并且双方球队都可以在他们提出请求的情况下被准予替换。

(b) This is a substitution opportunity only for the non-scoring team and only when the game clock shows 2:00 or less in the fourth quarter and in each overtime. If the non-scoring team is granted a substitution, the opponents may also be granted a substitution and both teams may also be granted a time-out, if they request it.

18/19-5 **Statement:** Articles 18 and 19 clarify when a time-out or substitution opportunity starts and ends. If the request for a time-out or substitution (for any player, including the free-throw shooter) is made after the ball is at the disposal of the free-throw shooter for the first free throw, the time-out or substitution shall be only granted for both teams if

(a) the last free throw is successful, or

(b) the last free throw is followed by a throw-in, or

(c) for any valid reason, the ball remains dead after the last free throw.

After the ball is at the disposal of the free-throw shooter for the first of 2 or 3 consecutive free throws for the same foul penalty, no time-out or substitution shall be granted before the ball becomes dead following the last free throw.

When a technical foul occurs between such free throws, the free throw with no line-up shall be administered immediately. A time-out or substitution for either team shall not be granted before and/or after the free throw, unless the substitute shall become the player to attempt the free throw for the technical foul penalty. In this case, the opponents are also entitled to substitute 1 player, if they wish.

18/19-6 **Example:** A1 is awarded 2 free throws. Either team requests a time-out or substitution

(a) before the ball is at the disposal of the free-throw shooter A1.

(b) after the first free-throw attempt.

（b）这只是非得分队仅在第 4 节和每一决胜期比赛计时钟显示 2:00 或更少时的一次替换机会。如果非得分队被准予了替换，那么，也可以准予对方替换，并且双方球队都可以在他们提出请求的情况下被准予暂停。

18/19-5 **陈述** 规则第 18 条和第 19 条阐明了暂停或替换机会的开始和结束。如果在罚球队员第 1 次罚球可处理球之后提出了暂停或替换（任一队员，包括罚球队员）的请求；那么，应仅在下列情况中准予双方球队的暂停或替换：

（a）最后一次罚球成功，或

（b）最后一次罚球后还要执行掷球入界，或

（c）因为任何正当原因，在最后一次罚球之后球仍是死球。

罚球队员在执行同一个罚则中连续 2 次或 3 次罚球的第 1 次罚球可处理球后，只有在最后一次罚球后球成死球之后可以准予暂停或替换。

当在这样的罚球之间发生了一起技术犯规时，应立即执行该次不占位的罚球。在该罚球之前和 / 或之后，不应准予任一队的暂停或替换，除非由一名替补队员成为队员去执行技术犯规罚则的罚球。在这种情况下，如果对方队希望，他们也有权替换 1 名队员。

18/19-6 **举例** 判给 A1 执行 2 次罚球。在下列情况中，任一队请求暂停或替换：

（a）在罚球队员 A1 可处理球之前。

（b）在第 1 次罚球之后。

(c) after the successful second free throw but before the ball is at the disposal of any team B thrower-in.

(d) after the successful second free throw and after the ball is at the disposal of any team B thrower-in.

Interpretation:

(a) The time-out or substitution shall be granted immediately, before the first free-throw attempt.

(b) The time-out or substitution shall not be granted after the first free throw, even if successful.

(c) The time-out or substitution shall be granted immediately, before the throw-in.

(d) The time-out or substitution shall not be granted.

18/19-7 **Example:** A1 is awarded 2 free throws. After the first free-throw attempt, either team requests a time-out or substitution. During the last free-throw attempt

(a) the ball rebounds from the ring and the game continues.

(b) the free throw is successful.

(c) the ball misses the ring.

(d) A1 steps on the free-throw line while shooting and the violation is called.

(e) B1 steps on the restricted area before the ball has left A1's hands. B1's violation is called and A1's free throw is not successful.

Interpretation:

(a) The time-out or substitution shall not be granted.

(b), (c) and (d) The time-out or substitution shall be granted immediately.

（c）在第 2 次罚球成功之后，但在 B 队任一掷球入界队员可处理球之前。

（d）在第 2 次罚球成功之后，并在 B 队任一掷球入界队员可处理球之后。

解释

（a）在第 1 次罚球之前应立即准予暂停或替换。

（b）即使第 1 次罚球成功，在第 1 次罚球之后也不应准予暂停或替换。

（c）在执行掷球入界之前应立即准予暂停或替换。

（d）不应准予暂停或替换。

18/19-7 **举例** 判给 A1 执行 2 次罚球。第 1 次罚球后，任一队请求了暂停或替换。在最后一次罚球中：

（a）球从篮圈上弹起，比赛继续。

（b）罚球成功。

（c）球未触及篮圈。

（d）A1 投球时脚踩罚球线，被判违例。

（e）B1 在球离开 A1 的手之前步入限制区。宣判了 B1 的违例，且 A1 的罚球未成功。

解释

（a） 不应准予暂停或替换。

（b）（c）和（d）应立即准予暂停或替换。

(e) A1 shall attempt a substitute free throw and, if made, the time-out or substitution shall be granted immediately.

18/19-8 **Example:** A substitution opportunity has just ended when substitute A6 runs to the scorer's table, loudly requesting a substitution. The timer reacts and erroneously sounds the signal. The referee blows the whistle.

Interpretation: The ball is dead and the game clock is stopped which normally shall be a substitution opportunity. However, because A6's request was made too late, the substitution shall not be granted. The game shall be resumed immediately.

18/19-9 **Example:** A goaltending or an interference violation occurs during the game. A time-out has been requested by either coach or a substitution has been requested by a substitute of either team.

Interpretation: The violation causes the game clock to be stopped and the ball to become dead. Time-outs or substitutions shall be granted.

18/19-10 **Example:** B1 fouls A1 on an unsuccessful attempt for a 2-point goal. After A1's first of 2 free throws, A2 is charged with a technical foul. Either team now requests a time-out or substitution.

Interpretation: Any team B player may attempt 1 free throw with no line-up. If a team B substitute has become a player to attempt the free throw, team A shall also be entitled to substitute 1 player, if they wish. If the free throw is attempted by a team B substitute, who has become a player or if team A also substituted 1 player, they cannot be substituted until the next game clock running period has ended. After the team B player's free throw for A2's technical foul, A1 shall attempt the second free throw. The game shall be resumed as after any last free throw. If successful and if requested, the time-out or further substitution shall be granted for both teams.

(e) 应由A1重新执行1次罚球；如中篮，应立即准予暂停或替换。

18/19-8 **举例** 一次替换机会刚刚结束，替补队员A6跑到记录台大声请求替换。计时员做出了反应并错误地发出了信号。裁判员鸣了哨。

解释 通常，球成死球并且比赛计时钟停止时应是一次替换机会。然而，由于A6的请求提出得太晚了，不应准予替换。应立即继续比赛。

18/19-9 **举例** 比赛期间发生了一起干涉得分或干扰得分违例。任一队的主教练已请求了暂停，或任一队的替补队员已请求了替换。

解释 违例致使比赛计时钟停止，且球成死球。应准予暂停或替换。

18/19-10 **举例** A1在做2分试投时被B1犯规，球未中篮。在A1执行2次罚球中的第1次罚球后，A2被判一起技术犯规。此时，任一队请求暂停或替换。

解释 B队任一队员可以执行1次不占位的罚球。如果B队由一名替补队员成为队员去执行这次罚球，那么，如果A队希望的话，也有权替换一名队员。如果B队的确是由一名替补队员成为队员去执行这次罚球的，或如果A队也的确替换了一名队员，那么他们在接下来的比赛计时钟运行时段结束前，不得被替换。在B队队员执行A2技术犯规罚则的罚球后，A1应执行其第2次罚球。应如同任何最后一次罚球后那样继续比赛。如该罚球中篮，两队提出暂停或进一步替换的请求应被准予。

18/19-11 **Example:** B1 fouls A1 on an unsuccessful attempt for a 2-point goal. After A1's first of 2 free throws, A2 is charged with a technical foul. Any team B player shall attempt 1 free throw with no line-up. Either team now requests a time-out or substitution.

Interpretation: At this time, no time-out or substitution shall be granted. A1 shall attempt the second free throw. The game shall be resumed as after any last free throw. If successful and if requested, the time-out or further substitution shall be granted for both teams.

18/19-12 **Example:** B1 fouls A1 on an unsuccessful attempt for a 2-point goal. After A1's first of 2 free throws, A2 is charged with a technical foul. This is A2's fifth foul. Either team now requests a time-out or substitution.

Interpretation: A2 shall be substituted immediately. Any team B player may attempt 1 free throw with no line-up. If a team B substitute has become a player to attempt the free throw, team A is also entitled to substitute 1 player, if they wish. If the free throw is attempted by a team B substitute, who has become a player or if team A also substituted 1 player, they cannot be substituted until the next game clock running period has ended. After the team B player's free throw for A2's technical foul, A1 shall attempt the second free throw. The game shall be resumed as after any last free throw. If successful and if requested, the time-out or further substitution shall be granted for both teams.

18/19-13 **Example:** Dribbler A1 is charged with a technical foul. B6 requests to become a player to attempt the free throw.

Interpretation: This is a substitution opportunity for both teams. After becoming a player, B6 may attempt 1 free throw with no line-up but B6 may not become a substitute until the next game clock running period has ended.

18/19-11 **举例** A1 在做 2 分试投时被 B1 犯规，球未中篮。在 A1 执行 2 次罚球中的第 1 次罚球后，A2 被判一起技术犯规。应由 B 队任一队员执行 1 次不占位的罚球。此时，任一队请求暂停或替换。

解释 此时，不应准予暂停或替换。A1 应执行其第 2 次罚球。应如同任何最后一次罚球后那样继续比赛。如该罚球中篮，两队提出暂停或进一步替换的请求应被准予。

18/19-12 **举例** A1 在做 2 分试投时被 B1 犯规，球未中篮。在 A1 执行 2 次罚球中的第 1 次罚球后，A2 被判一起技术犯规。这是 A2 的第 5 次犯规。此时，任一队请求暂停或替换。

解释 A2 应立即被替换。由 B 队任一队员执行 1 次不占位的罚球。如果 B 队由一名替补队员成为队员去执行这次罚球，那么，如果 A 队希望的话，也有权替换 1 名队员。如果 B 队的确是由一名替补队员成为队员去执行这次罚球的，或 A 队也的确替换了 1 名队员，那么他们在接下来的比赛计时钟运行时段结束前，不得被替换。在 B 队队员执行 A2 技术犯规罚则的罚球后，A1 应执行其第 2 次罚球；应如同任何最后一次罚球后那样继续比赛。如该罚球中篮，双方球队提出暂停或进一步替换的请求应被准予。

18/19-13 **举例** 运球队员 A1 被判一起技术犯规。B6 请求成为队员去执行罚球。

解释 这对双方球队都是一次替换的机会。B6 在成为一名队员后，可以去执行 1 次不占位的罚球；但是 B6 在接下来的比赛计时钟运行时段结束前，不能成为替补队员。

18/19-14 Statement: A substitute who has become a player can leave the game only after the end of the next game clock running period of the game.

18/19-15 Example: B1 is substituted by B6. Before the game clock has started, B6 is charged with a personal foul. This is B6's

(a) third

(b) fifth

foul.

Interpretation: In

(a) B6 cannot be substituted until the end of the game clock running period of the game.

(b) B6 shall be substituted.

18/19-16 Statement: If, following a request for a time-out a foul is called against either team, the time-out shall not start until the referee has completed all communication related to that foul with the scorer's table. In the case of a player's fifth foul, this communication includes the necessary substitution procedure. After all communication is completed, the time-out period shall start when a referee blows the whistle and shows the time-out signal.

18/19-17 Example: During the game, the team A head coach requests a time-out after which

(a) B1 is charged with a fifth foul.

(b) a player of either team is charged with a foul.

Interpretation:

In (a) the time-out period shall not start until all communication with the scorer's table is completed and a substitute for B1 becomes a player.

18/19-14 陈述 一名替补队员在成为队员后，只有在接下来的比赛计时钟运行时段结束后，才能被替换下场。

18/19-15 举例 B6 替换 B1。在比赛计时钟开动之前，B6 被判一起侵人犯规。这是 B6 的：

（a）第 3 次犯规。

（b）第 5 次犯规。

解释

在（a）中，B6 在接下来的比赛计时钟运行时段结束前不能被替换。

在（b）中，B6 应被替换。

18/19-16 陈述 如果暂停请求提出后，宣判了任一队的犯规，暂停应该等到裁判员就该起犯规已完成了与记录台的所有联系后才开始。如果出现了队员的第 5 次犯规，那么这个联系还包括了必要的替换程序。在所有的联系完成后，裁判员鸣哨并做出暂停手势时，该暂停时段才开始。

18/19-17 举例 比赛中，A 队主教练请求暂停，随后：

（a）宣判了 B1 的第 5 次犯规。

（b）宣判了任一队员的犯规。

解释

在（a）中，应等到裁判员与记录台完成所有联系，并且替换 B1 的队员已成为队员后，该暂停时段才开始。

In both cases, the players shall be permitted to go to their benches even though the time-out period has not formally started.

18/19-18 **Statement:** Each time-out shall last 1 minute. Teams must return promptly to the court after the referee blows the whistle and beckons the teams on to the court. If a team extends the time-out beyond 1 minute, it is gaining an advantage by extending the time-out and causing a delay of the game. A warning to the head coach of that team shall be given by a referee. If that head coach does not respond to the warning, an additional time-out shall be charged against that team. If the team has no time-outs remaining, a technical foul for delaying the game may be charged against the head coach, entered on the scoresheet as a 'B_1'. If a team does not return to the court promptly after the half-time interval of play, a time-out shall be charged against that team. Such a charged time-out shall not last 1 minute. The game shall be resumed immediately.

18/19-19 **Example:** The time-out ends and the referee beckons team A on to the court. The team A head coach continues to instruct the team which remains in the team bench area. The referee re-beckons team A on to the court and

(a) team A finally returns to the court.

(b) team A continues to remain in the team bench area.

Interpretation:

(a) After team A starts to return to the court, the referee shall give a warning to the team A head coach that if the same behaviour is repeated, an additional time-out shall be charged against team A.

(b) A time-out, without warning shall be charged against team A. This time-out shall last 1 minute. If team A has no time-outs remaining, a technical foul for delaying the game shall be charged against the team A head coach, entered as a 'B_1' .

在这两种情况下，即使暂停时段没有正式开始，也应允许双方队员回到他们的球队席。

18/19-18 **陈述** 每次暂停应持续 1 分钟。在裁判员鸣哨并招呼球队上场后，球队必须及时回到比赛场地上。如果某队延误暂停并使其超过了 1 分钟，该队是在通过延误暂停获得利益，并造成了比赛的延误。裁判员应给予该队主教练一次警告。如果那名主教练对该警告不予理会，则应再登记该队 1 次暂停。如果该队没有剩余的暂停，可宣判主教练 1 次延误比赛的技术犯规，在记录表上登记为"B_1"。如果有球队在半时比赛休息期间后没有尽快返回比赛场地，应登记该队 1 次暂停。该情况下登记的暂停不应是持续 1 分钟的，应立即继续比赛。

18/19-19 **举例** 暂停结束了，裁判员招呼 A 队回到比赛场地上。A 队主教练继续指导其球队，并且该队仍然滞留在其球队席区域。裁判员再次招呼 A 队回到比赛场地上，并且：

（a）A 队最终回到了比赛场地上。

（b）A 队继续滞留在其球队席区域。

解释

（a）在 A 队开始回到比赛场地上后，裁判员应给予 A 队主教练一次警告。如果相同的行为再次出现，就应再登记 A 队 1 次暂停。

（b）应登记 A 队 1 次暂停，无须警告。该暂停应持续 1 分钟。如果 A 队没有剩余的暂停，应登记 A 队主教练 1 次延误比赛的技术犯规，登记为"B_1"。

18/19-20 **Example:** After the end of the half-time interval of play, team A is still in its dressing room and therefore the start of the third quarter is delayed.

Interpretation: After team A finally enters the court a time-out, without warning shall be charged against team A. This time-out shall not last 1 minute. The game shall be resumed immediately.

18/19-21 **Statement:** If a team was not granted a time-out in the second half before the game clock shows 2:00 in the fourth quarter, the scorer shall mark 2 horizontal lines on the scoresheet in the first box for the team's second half time-outs. The scoreboard shall show the first time-out as taken.

18/19-22 **Example:** With 2:00 on the game clock in the fourth quarter, both teams have not taken a time-out in the second half.

Interpretation: The scorer shall mark 2 horizontal lines in the first box of both teams' time-outs for the second half. The scoreboard shall show the first time-out as taken.

18/19-23 **Example:** With 2:09 on the game clock in the fourth quarter, the team A head coach requests the first time-out in the second half while the game clock is running. With 1:58 on the game clock, the ball goes out-of-bounds and the game clock is stopped. Team A is granted a time-out.

Interpretation: The scorer shall mark 2 horizontal lines in the first box of team A's time-outs as a time-out was not granted before the game clock showed 2:00 in the fourth quarter. The time-out granted at 1:58 shall be entered in the second box and team A shall have only 1 more time-out left. After the time-out, the scoreboard shall show 2 time-outs as taken.

18/19-24 **Statement:** Whenever a time-out is requested, regardless of whether before or after a technical foul, an unsportsmanlike foul or a disqualifying foul is called, the time-out shall be granted before the start of the administration of the free throw(s). If during a time-out a technical foul, an unsportsmanlike foul or a disqualifying foul is called, the free throw(s) shall be administered after the time-out has ended.

18/19-20 **举例** 在半时比赛休息期间结束后，A 队仍滞留在其球队更衣室里，并就此延误了第 3 节比赛的开始时间。

解释 在 A 队最终进入比赛场地后，应登记 A 队 1 次暂停，无须警告。这个暂停不应是持续 1 分钟的，应立即继续比赛。

18/19-21 **陈述** 如果某队在下半时的第 4 节比赛计时钟显示 2:00 之前都没有被准予过暂停，记录员应在记录表上该队下半时登记暂停的第 1 个空格内画 2 条水平线。记录屏应显示第 1 次暂停已被使用。

18/19-22 **举例** 第 4 节，比赛计时钟显示 2:00 时，双方球队在下半时都没有使用过暂停。

解释 记录员应在记录表上双方球队下半时登记暂停的第 1 个空格内画 2 条水平线。记录屏应显示他们的第 1 次暂停均已被使用。

18/19-23 **举例** 第 4 节，比赛计时钟显示 2:09 时，A 队主教练提出了其下半时的第 1 次暂停请求。此时，比赛计时钟还在运行。在比赛计时钟显示 1:58 时，球出界且比赛计时钟停止。准予了 A 队暂停。

解释 因为在第 4 节比赛计时钟显示 2:00 之前，A 队未被准予暂停，记录员应在记录表上 A 队登记暂停的第 1 个空格内画 2 条水平线。A 队在比赛计时钟显示 1:58 时被准予的暂停，应被记录在第 2 个空格内，并且 A 队仅剩 1 次暂停。暂停后，记录屏应显示已使用过 2 次暂停。

18/19-24 **陈述** 当有球队请求了一次暂停时，该请求无论是在宣判了一起技术犯规、违反体育运动精神的犯规或取消比赛资格的犯规之前或之后，在执行罚球开始前应准予该暂停。如果在暂停期间宣判了一起技术犯规、违反体育运动精神的犯规或取消比赛资格的犯规，那么应在暂停结束之后执行罚球。

18/19-25 **Example:** The team B head coach requests a time-out. A1 is charged with an unsportsmanlike foul against B1, followed by a technical foul against A2.

Interpretation: The team B time-out shall be granted. After the time-out, any team B player shall attempt 1 free throw with no line-up. B1 shall then attempt 2 free throws with no line-up. The game shall be resumed with a team B throw-in from the throw-in line in its frontcourt. Team B shall have 14 seconds on the shot clock.

18/19-26 **Example:** The team B head coach requests a time-out. A1 is charged with an unsportsmanlike foul against B1. Team B is granted a time-out. During the time-out, A2 is charged with a technical foul.

Interpretation: After the time-out, any team B player shall attempt 1 free throw with no line-up. B1 shall then attempt 2 free throws with no line-up. The game shall be resumed with a team B throw-in from the throw-in line in its frontcourt. Team B shall have 14 seconds on the shot clock.

18/19-25 **举例** B 队主教练请求暂停。宣判了 A1 对 B1 的一起违反体育运动精神的犯规，接着又宣判了 A2 的一起技术犯规。

解释 应准予 B 队暂停。暂停后，应由 B 队任一队员执行 1 次不占位的罚球。然后，应由 B1 执行 2 次不占位的罚球。应由 B 队在其前场的掷球入界线处执行掷球入界继续比赛。B 队应拥有 14 秒进攻时间。

18/19-26 **举例** B 队主教练请求暂停。宣判了 A1 对 B1 的一起违反体育运动精神的犯规。随后准予了 B 队暂停。在暂停期间，宣判了 A2 的一起技术犯规。

解释 暂停后，应由 B 队任一队员执行 1 次不占位的罚球。然后，应由 B1 执行 2 次不占位的罚球。应由 B 队在其前场的掷球入界线处执行掷球入界继续比赛。B 队应拥有 14 秒进攻时间。

Article 23 Player out-of-bounds and ball out-of-bounds

23-1 **Statement:** If the ball is out-of-bounds because of touching or being touched by a player who is on or outside the boundary line, this player causes the ball to go out-of-bounds.

23-2 **Example:** Close to the sideline, A1 with the ball in the hands is closely guarded by B1. A1 touches B1 with the body. B1 has 1 foot out-of-bounds.

Interpretation: This is a legal play by A1. A player is out-of-bounds when any part of the body is in contact with something other than a player. The game shall continue.

23-3 **Example:** Close to the sideline, A1 with the ball in the hands is closely guarded by B1 and B2. A1 touches with the ball B1 who has 1 foot out-of-bounds.

Interpretation: This is an out-of-bounds violation by B1. The ball is out-of-bounds when it touches a player who is out-of-bounds. The game shall be resumed with a team A throw-in from the place nearest to where the ball went out-of-bounds. Team A shall have the time remaining on the shot clock.

23-4 **Example:** A1 dribbles close to the sideline in front of the scorer's table. The ball rebounds high from the court and touches B6's knee sitting on the substitution chair. The ball returns to A1 on the court.

Interpretation: The ball is out-of-bounds when it touches B6 who is out-of-bounds. The ball is caused to go out-of-bounds by A1 who touched the ball before it goes out-of-bounds. The game shall be resumed with a team B throw-in from the place nearest to where the ball went out-of-bounds.

第 23 条　队员出界和球出界

23-1　陈述　如果球出界是由于触及了界线上或界线外的队员或是被其触及了，是该队员使球出界。

23-2　举例　在靠近边线处，A1 双手持球被 B1 严密防守着。A1 用身体触及了一只脚踩在界外的 B1。

解释　A1 的比赛情况合法。只有当一名队员身体的任何部分触及了在界外除队员外的其他物体时，该队员才出界。比赛应继续。

23-3　举例　在靠近边线处，A1 双手持球被 B1 和 B2 严密防守着。A1 用球触及了一只脚踩在界外的 B1。

解释　这是 B1 的出界违例。当球触及了在界外的队员时，球出界。应由 A 队在最靠近球出界的地点执行掷球入界继续比赛。A 队应拥有进攻计时钟显示的剩余时间。

23-4　举例　A1 在靠近记录台前方的边线处运球。球从比赛场地上高高弹起并触及了正坐在替换座椅上的 B6 的膝盖。之后，球又回到了比赛场地上并触及了 A1。

解释　当球触及在界外的 B6 时，球便出界了。A1 在球出界前触及了球，所以是 A1 使球出界。应由 B 队在最靠近球出界的地点执行掷球入界继续比赛。

Article 24 Dribbling

24-1 **Statement:** It is not a dribble if a player deliberately throws the ball against either the opponents' or the team's own backboard.

24-2 **Example:** A1 has not yet dribbled and is standing still when A1 deliberately throws the ball against a backboard and catches or touches the ball again before it touches another player.

Interpretation: This is a legal play by A1. After catching the ball, A1 may shoot, pass the ball or start a dribble.

24-3 **Example:** After ending a dribble either in a continuous motion or standing still, A1 deliberately throws the ball against the backboard. A1 catches or touches the ball again

(a) after it bounced on the court and starts a dribble.

(b) before it touches any other player.

Interpretation:

In (a) this is a double dribble violation by A1. A1 shall not dribble for a second time after the first dribble has ended.

In (b) this is a legal play by A1. After catching or touching the ball, A1 may shoot or pass but shall not start a new dribble.

24-4 **Example:** A1's shot for a goal misses the ring. A1 catches the ball and deliberately throws it against the backboard, after which A1 catches or touches the ball again before it touches any other player.

Interpretation: This is a legal play by A1. After catching the ball, A1 may shoot, pass or start a dribble.

24-5 **Example:** A1 dribbles and comes to a legal stop.

(a) A1 then loses the balance and without moving the pivot foot, A1 touches the court with the ball once or twice while holding the ball in the hands.

(b) A1 then tosses the ball from 1 hand to another without moving the pivot foot.

第 24 条　运球

24-1　**陈述**　如果一名队员故意地将球抛中对方或该队本方的篮板，这不是一次运球。

24-2　**举例**　A1 尚未运球并在站定时故意将球抛中篮板，随后 A1 在球触及另一队员之前再次拿到或触及球。

解释　A1 的比赛情况合法。拿到球后，A1 可以投篮、传球或开始运球。

24-3　**举例**　结束运球后，A1 以连续动作或在站定后故意将球抛中篮板。A1 在：

（a）球在比赛场地上弹起后再次拿到或触及球，并开始了一次运球。

（b）球触及任一其他队员之前再次拿到或触及球。

解释

在（a）中，这是 A1 的两次运球违例，因为 A1 不应在第一次运球已结束后又开始第二次运球。

在（b）中，A1 的比赛情况合法。拿到或触及球后，A1 可以投篮或传球，但不得开始一次新的运球。

24-4　**举例**　A1 的投篮未触及篮圈。A1 拿到球并故意将球抛中篮板，随后在球触及任一其他队员之前，A1 再次拿到或触及球。

解释　A1 的比赛情况合法。拿到球后，A1 可以投篮、传球或开始运球。

24-5　**举例**　A1 结束运球后合法停步，然后：

（a）A1 失去平衡，在未移动中枢脚的情况下，A1 双手持球并使球触及了比赛场地一次或两次。

（b）在未移动中枢脚的情况下，A1 将球在两手之间抛接。

Interpretation: In both cases, this is a legal play by A1. A1 did not move the pivot foot.

24-6 **Example:** A1 starts a dribble by throwing the ball

(a) over the opponent.

(b) a few meters away from an opponent.

The ball touches the court after which A1 continues to dribble.

Interpretation: In both cases, this is a legal play by A1. The ball touched the court before A1 touched the ball again on a dribble.

24-7 **Example:** A1 ends a dribble and deliberately throws the ball on to B1's leg. A1 catches the ball and starts to dribble again.

Interpretation: This is a double dribble violation by A1. A1's dribble ended as the ball was not touched by B1. It was the ball which touched B1. A1 may not dribble again.

24-8 **Example:** A1 ends a dribble and passes the ball to A2. The ball accidentally touches the body of B2. After that, the ball touches the floor, A1 catches it and starts to dribble again.

Interpretation: This is a legal play. A1 may dribble again as after the first dribble the ball has touched another player.

解释 这两种 A1 的比赛情况均合法。A1 没有移动其中枢脚。

24-6 **举例** A1 通过将球：

（a）抛过对方队员开始运球。

（b）抛到对方队员几米外的地点开始运球。

在球触及比赛场地后，A1 继续运球。

解释 这两种 A1 的比赛情况均合法。在 A1 再次触及球并运球之前，球已经触及了比赛场地。

24-7 **举例** A1 结束运球后故意将球掷在 B1 的腿上，A1 随后拿到球并再次开始运球。

解释 这是 A1 的两次运球违例。A1 的运球已经结束，因为并不是 B1 触及了球，而是球触及了 B1。A1 不得再次运球。

24-8 **举例** A1 结束运球后向 A2 传球，球意外地触及了 B2 的身体。随后球触及了比赛场地，A1 拿到球并再次开始运球。

解释 该比赛情况合法。A1 可以再次运球，因为在第一次运球后，球已触及另一名队员。

Article 25 Travelling

25-1 **Statement:** It is legal if a player who is lying on the court gains control of the ball. It is legal if a player who is holding the ball falls on the court. It is also legal if a player, after falling on the court with the ball, slides because of momentum. However, if the player then rolls or attempts to stand up while holding the ball, it is a violation.

25-2 **Example:** A1 holds the ball, then

(a) loses balance and falls on the court.

(b) after falling on the court A1's momentum causes that player to slide.

Interpretation: In both cases, this is a legal play by A1. Falling on the court is not a travelling violation. However, if A1 now rolls to avoid the defence or attempts to stand up while holding the ball, a travelling violation occurs.

25-3 **Example:** A1, while lying on the court, gains control of the ball. A1 then

(a) passes the ball to A2.

(b) starts a dribble while still lying on the court.

(c) attempts to stand up while dribbling the ball.

(d) attempts to stand up while still holding the ball.

Interpretation:

(a), (b) and (c) This is a legal play by A1.

(d) This is a travelling violation by A1.

25-4 **Statement:** A player may not touch the court consecutively with the same foot or both feet after ending a dribble or gaining control of the ball.

25-5 **Example:** A1 ends a dribble with the ball in the hands. In a continuous motion, A1 jumps off the left foot, lands on the left foot, then on the right foot and attempts a shot for a goal.

Interpretation: This is a travelling violation by A1. After ending a dribble, a player may not touch the court consecutively with the same foot.

第 25 条　带球走

25-1 陈述　如果一名躺在比赛场地上的队员获得了控制球，这是合法的。如果正持着球的队员摔倒在比赛场地上，这是合法的。如果一名队员持球摔倒在比赛地板上，由于动量使其滑行，这也是合法的。然而，如果该队员随后在持球时滚动或试图站起来，这是一起违例。

25-2 举例　A1 持球，然后，

（a）失去了平衡并且摔倒在比赛场地上。

（b）摔倒在比赛场地上后，A1 的动量使其滑行。

解释　这两种 A1 的比赛情况均合法。摔倒在比赛场地上不是一起带球走违例。然而，如果此时正持球的 A1 为躲避防守而滚动或试图站起来，则发生了一起带球走违例。

25-3 举例　躺在比赛场地上的 A1 获得了控制球，A1 随后:

（a）传球给 A2。

（b）仍躺在比赛场地上时开始运球。

（c）在运球时试图站起来。

（d）在持球时试图站起来。

解释

（a）（b）和（c）　A1 的比赛情况合法。

（d）　这是 A1 的带球走违例。

25-4 陈述　队员在结束运球或获得控制球后不得用同一只脚或双脚连续地触及地面。

25-5 举例　A1 结束运球时双手持球。在连续动作中，A1 跳起左脚，接着左脚落地，随后右脚落地并尝试投篮。

解释　这是 A1 的带球走违例。队员在结束运球后不得用同一只脚连续地触及地面。

Article 26 3 seconds

26-1 Statement: It is a violation when a player leaves the court at the endline to avoid a 3-second violation and then re-enters the restricted area.

26-2 Example: A1 in the restricted area for less than 3 seconds moves out-of-bounds at the endline to avoid a 3-second violation. A1 then re-enters the restricted area.

Interpretation: This is a 3-second violation by A1.

26-3 Statement: A player shall not remain in the opponents' restricted area for more than 3 consecutive seconds while the player's team is in control of a live ball in the frontcourt and the game clock is running.

26-4 Example: A1 in the restricted area for 2.5 seconds releases the ball on a shot for a goal. The ball misses the backboard and the ring and A1 rebounds it.

Interpretation: This is a legal play by A1. Team A has ended its control of a ball when A1 released it on a shot. With A1's rebound, team A gained a new control of the ball.

26-5 Example: While the thrower-in A1 has the ball in the hands in the frontcourt, A2 remains in the opponents' restricted area for more than 3 seconds.

Interpretation: This is a legal play by A2. Team A has the control of the ball, however, the game clock has not yet started.

第 26 条 3 秒

26-1 陈述 当一名队员为了避免一起 3 秒违例，从端线处离开比赛场地后又重新进入限制区，这是一起违例。

26-2 举例 A1 在限制区内停留少于 3 秒时从端线处移动至界外以避免一起 3 秒违例。随后 A1 又重新进入限制区。

解释 这是 A1 的一起 3 秒违例。

26-3 陈述 某队在其前场控制活球并且比赛计时钟正在运行时，该队的队员不得在对方队的限制区内停留超过持续的 3 秒。

26-4 举例 A1 在限制区内停留 2.5 秒时投篮球离手。球未触及篮板和篮圈，随后 A1 获得篮板球。

解释 A1 的比赛情况合法。当 A1 投篮球离手时，A 队控制球结束。当 A1 获得篮板球时，A 队获得了新的控制球。

26-5 举例 掷球入界队员 A1 在其前场双手持球时，A2 在对方队的限制区内持续停留超过了 3 秒。

解释 A2 的比赛情况合法。虽然 A 队控制球，但比赛计时钟尚未开动。

Article 27 Closely guarded player

27-1 **Statement:** A closely guarded player must pass, shoot or dribble the ball within 5 seconds.

27-2 **Example:** A1 is closely guarded for 4 seconds by B1. Then A1 fumbles the ball and catches it again.

Interpretation: This is a 5-second violation by A1, as A1 within 5 seconds did not pass, shoot or dribble the ball. The fumbling the ball at the start or at the end of the dribble is not a dribble.

第 27 条　被严密防守的队员

27-1　陈述　一名被严密防守的队员必须在 5 秒内传球、投篮或运球。

27-2　举例　A1 被 B1 严密防守 4 秒时，A1 漏接球并再次拿到球。

解释　这是 A1 的一起 5 秒违例，因为 A1 没有在 5 秒内传球、投篮或运球。在开始或结束运球时漏接球不是一次运球。

Article 28 8 seconds

28-1 **Statement:** The shot clock is stopped because of a jump ball situation. If the resulting alternating possession throw-in is awarded to the team that was in control of the ball in its backcourt, the 8-second period shall continue.

28-2 **Example:** A1 dribbles in the backcourt for 5 seconds when a held ball occurs. Team A is entitled to the next alternating possession throw-in.

Interpretation: Team A shall have only 3 seconds to move the ball into its frontcourt.

28-3 **Statement:** During a dribble from the backcourt to the frontcourt, the ball goes into a team's frontcourt when both feet of the dribbler and the ball are completely in contact with the frontcourt.

28-4 **Example:** A1 is straddling the centre line and receives the ball from A2 who is in the backcourt. A1 passes the ball back to A2 who is

(a) still in the backcourt.

(b) straddling the centre line.

(c) straddling the centre line. A2 starts to dribble in the backcourt.

Interpretation: In all cases, this is a legal play by team A. A1 does not have both feet completely in contact with the frontcourt and therefore A1 is entitled to pass the ball into the backcourt. The 8-second period shall continue.

28-5 **Example:** A1 dribbles from the backcourt and stops the forward motion while still dribbling

(a) straddling the centre line.

(b) with both feet in the frontcourt, while the ball is dribbled in the backcourt.

(c) with both feet in the frontcourt while the ball is dribbled in the backcourt, after which A1 returns with both feet to the backcourt.

第 28 条　8 秒

28-1　陈述　进攻计时钟因为一次跳球情况而停止。如果交替拥有的结果是原控制球队在其后场执行掷球入界，8 秒周期应连续计算。

28-2　举例　A1 在其后场运球达 5 秒时发生了一次争球。A 队拥有下一次的交替拥有掷球入界权。

解释　A 队应只有 3 秒使球进入其前场。

28-3　陈述　从后场向前场运球的过程中，当运球队员的双脚和球都完全触及前场时，球才进入了该队的前场。

28-4　举例　A1 骑跨中线时接到了位于其后场的 A2 的传球。A1 随后将球回传给:

（a）仍然位于其后场的 A2。

（b）正骑跨中线的 A2。

（c）正骑跨中线的 A2。A2 在其后场开始运球。

解释　上述所有 A 队的比赛情况均合法。A1 的双脚没有完全触及其前场，因此 A1 有权将球传回其后场。8 秒周期应连续计算。

28-5　举例　A1 在其后场运球，然后 A1 停止向前移动但仍运着球时:

（a）骑跨中线。

（b）双脚位于其前场，但球被运在其后场。

（c）双脚位于其前场，但球被运在其后场，随后 A1 双脚回到其后场。

(d) both feet are in the backcourt, while the ball is dribbled in the frontcourt.

Interpretation: In all cases, this is a legal play by A1. Dribbler A1 continues to be in the backcourt until both the feet, as well as the ball, are completely in contact with the frontcourt. The 8-second period shall continue.

28-6 **Statement:** Each time when the 8-second period continues with the time remaining and the same team that previously had control of the ball is awarded a throw-in from its backcourt, the referee handing the ball to the thrower-in shall inform the thrower-in on the time remaining in the 8-second period.

28-7 **Example:** A1 dribbles in the backcourt for 6 seconds when a double foul occurs in the

(a) backcourt.

(b) frontcourt.

Interpretation:

(a) The game shall be resumed with a team A throw-in in its backcourt from the place nearest to where the double foul occurred. The referee shall inform the team A thrower-in that the team has 2 seconds to move the ball into its frontcourt.

(b) The game shall be resumed with a team A throw-in in its frontcourt from the place nearest to where the double foul occurred.

28-8 **Example:** A1 dribbles in the backcourt for 4 seconds when B1 taps the ball out-of-bounds in the team A backcourt.

Interpretation: The game shall be resumed with a team A throw-in in its backcourt from the place nearest to where the ball went out-of-bounds. The referee shall inform the team A thrower-in that the team has 4 seconds to move the ball into its frontcourt.

28-9 **Statement:** If the game is stopped by a referee for any valid reason not connected with either team and the opponents would be placed at a disadvantage, the 8-second period shall continue.

（d）双脚位于其后场，但球被运在其前场。

解释 上述所有 A1 的比赛情况均合法。在运球队员 A1 的双脚和球完全触及其前场之前，A1 仍然是位于其后场的。8 秒周期应连续计算。

28-6 **陈述** 每当判给原控制球队在其后场执行掷球入界，并且 8 秒周期应以剩余的时间连续计算时，将球递交给掷球入界队员的裁判员应告知该掷球入界队员 8 秒周期剩余的时间。

28-7 **举例** A1 在其后场运球达 6 秒时，一起双方犯规发生在其：

（a）后场。

（b）前场。

解释

（a）应由 A 队在其后场最靠近发生双方犯规的地点执行掷球入界继续比赛，裁判员应告知 A 队的掷球入界队员该队还有 2 秒使球进入其前场。

（b）应由 A 队在其前场最靠近发生双方犯规的地点执行掷球入界继续比赛。

28-8 **举例** A1 在其后场运球达 4 秒时，B1 将球从 A 队的后场拍出界。

解释 应由 A 队在其后场最靠近球出界的地点执行掷球入界继续比赛。裁判员应告知 A 队的掷球入界队员该队还有 4 秒使球进入其前场。

28-9 **陈述** 如果比赛因与任一队都无关的正当原因而被裁判员停止，且对方队将被置于不利，8 秒周期应连续计算。

28-10 **Example:** With 25 seconds on the game clock in the fourth quarter and with the score A 72 – B 72, team A gains control of the ball. A1 dribbles in the backcourt for 5 seconds when the game is stopped by the referees because of

(a) the game clock or the shot clock failing to run or to start.

(b) a bottle being thrown on to the court.

(c) the shot clock being erroneously reset.

Interpretation: In all cases, the game shall be resumed with a team A throw-in from its backcourt, with 3 seconds remaining in the 8-second period. Team B would be placed at a disadvantage if the game were resumed with a new 8-second period.

28-11 **Statement:** Following an 8-second violation, the throw-in place is determined by the location of the ball when the violation occurred.

28-12 **Example:** The 8-second period for team A ends and the violation occurs when

(a) team A controls the ball in its backcourt.

(b) the ball is in the air on A1's pass from the backcourt towards the frontcourt.

Interpretation: The team B throw-in shall be administered in its frontcourt, from the place nearest to the

(a) location of the ball when the 8-second violation occurred, except from directly behind the backboard.

(b) centre line.

Team B shall have 14 seconds on the shot clock.

28-13 **Statement:** Team control ends when the ball has left the player's hands on a shot for a goal.

28-14 **Example:** Just before the end of the 8-second period the ball has left A1's hands from the backcourt on a shot for a goal. The ball enters the basket.

28-10 举例 第 4 节，比赛计时钟显示 25 秒时，比分 A72 – B72，A 队获得控制球。A1 在其后场运球达 5 秒时，裁判员因下列情况而停止比赛:

（a）比赛计时钟或进攻计时钟未能运行或开动。

（b）一个瓶子被扔进比赛场地。

（c）进攻计时钟被错误地复位。

解释 上述所有情况下，应由 A 队在其后场执行掷球入界继续比赛，8 秒周期剩余 3 秒。如果给予一个新的 8 秒周期，将置 B 队于不利。

28-11 陈述 在一起 8 秒违例后，执行掷球入界的地点由发生违例时球的位置所决定。

28-12 举例 A 队 8 秒周期结束，发生违例时:

（a）A 队在其后场控制着球。

（b）A1 从其后场向前场的传球在空中。

解释 B 队执行掷球入界的地点应位于其前场，并且最靠近:

（a）发生 8 秒违例时球的位置，篮板正后方除外。

（b）中线。

B 队应拥有 14 秒进攻时间。

28-13 陈述 在投篮中，球已经离开队员的手时，球队控制球结束。

28-14 举例 A1 在临近 8 秒周期结束时从其后场投篮球离手。球进入球篮。

Interpretation: This is a legal play by team A. The control of the ball has ended when A1 has released the ball on a shot. A1's 3 points goal shall count.

解释 A 队的比赛情况合法。当 A1 投篮球离手时，控制球结束。A1 的 3 分中篮应计得分。

Article 29/50 Shot clock

29/50-1 **Statement:** A shot for a goal is attempted close to the end of the shot clock period and the shot clock signal sounds while the ball is in the air.

- If the ball enters the basket, the goal shall count.
- If the ball touches the ring and rebounds from it, the game shall continue with 24 seconds on the shot clock, if the opponents' team gains control and with 14 seconds on the shot clock, if the same team that was in control of the ball before the ball touched the ring regains control of the ball.
- If the ball misses the ring, the referees shall wait to see whether the opponents gain an immediate and clear control of the ball.
  - If yes, the shot clock signal shall be disregarded.
  - If not, this is a shot clock violation. The ball shall be awarded to the opponents for the throw-in from the place nearest to where the game was stopped, except from directly behind the backboard.

29/50-2 **Example:** A1's shot for a goal is in the air when the shot clock signal sounds. The ball touches the backboard and then rolls on the court, where it is first touched by B1, then by A2 and is finally controlled by B2.

Interpretation: This is a shot clock violation by team A. A1's shot missed the ring and team B did not gain an immediate and clear control of the ball.

29/50-3 **Example:** During A1's shot for a goal the ball touches the backboard but misses the ring. The ball is then touched but not controlled by B1, after which A2 gains control of the ball. The shot clock signal sounds.

Interpretation: This is a shot clock violation by team A.

第 29/50 条　进攻计时钟

29/50-1　**陈述**　当一次投篮尝试临近进攻时间周期结束，并且球在空中时进攻计时钟信号响。

- 如果球进入球篮，中篮应计得分。
- 如果球触及篮圈并弹起：接着如果对方队获得控制球，进攻计时钟应复位到 24 秒并继续比赛；接着如果重新控制球的队和球触及篮圈前控制球的队是同一队，进攻计时钟应复位到 14 秒并继续比赛。
- 如果球未触及篮圈，裁判员应等待并观察对方队员是否立即和清晰地获得控制球。

——如果是，应忽略进攻计时钟的信号。

——如果否，则发生了一起进攻时间违例。应判给对方队员在最靠近比赛被停止的地点执行掷球入界，篮板正后方除外。

29/50-2　**举例**　A1 投篮的球在空中时进攻计时钟信号响。球触及篮板后在比赛场地上滚动，B1 先触及了球，随后 A2 也触及了球，球最后被 B2 控制。

解释　这是 A 队的进攻时间违例。A1 投篮的球未触及篮圈，并且 B 队没有立即和清晰地获得控制球。

29/50-3　**举例**　A1 投篮的球触及篮板，但未触及篮圈。随后球被 B1 触及但未被控制。之后 A2 获得控制球。此时进攻计时钟信号响。

解释　这是 A 队的进攻时间违例。

29/50-4 **Example:** A1's shot for a goal at the end of a shot clock period is legally blocked by B1. The shot clock signal sounds. B1 fouls A1.

Interpretation: This is a shot clock violation by team A. B1's foul against A1 shall be disregarded unless it is an unsportsmanlike foul or a disqualifying foul.

29/50-5 **Example:** A1's shot for a goal is in the air when the shot clock signal sounds. The ball misses the ring, after which

a) a held ball between A2 and B2 occurs.

b) B1 taps it out-of-bounds.

Interpretation: In both cases, this is a shot clock violation by team A. Team B did not gain an immediate and clear control of the ball.

29/50-6 **Example:** B1 fouls A1 in the act of shooting for a goal when at approximately the same time the shot clock expired. The ball enters the basket.

Interpretation: If the ball was

a) still in A1's hands and B1's foul occurred before the shot clock expired, or

b) already in the air on A1's shot for a goal and B1's foul occurred before the shot clock expired, or

c) already in the air on A1's shot for a goal and B1's foul occurred after the shot clock expired,

it is not a shot clock violation. A1's goal shall count. A1 shall attempt 1 additional free throw. The game shall be resumed as after any last free throw.

d) still in A1's hands and B1's foul occurred after the shot clock expired,

it is a shot clock violation. A1's goal shall not count. B1's foul shall be disregarded unless it is an unsportsmanlike foul or a disqualifying foul. The game shall be resumed with a team B throw-in from the free-throw line extended.

29/50-4 **举例** 在进攻时间周期即将结束时，A1 的投篮被 B1 合法封盖，此时进攻计时钟信号响，之后 B1 对 A1 犯规。

解释 这是 A 队的进攻时间违例。应忽略 B1 对 A1 的犯规，除非该犯规是一起违反体育运动精神的犯规或是取消比赛资格的犯规。

29/50-5 **举例** A1 投篮的球在空中时进攻计时钟信号响。球未触及篮圈，随即：

（a）发生了 A2 和 B2 之间的一次争球。

（b）B1 将球拍出界。

解释 在这两种情况下，A 队都发生了进攻时间违例。B 队没有立即和清晰地获得控制球。

29/50-6 **举例** B1 对正在做投篮动作的 A1 犯规，几乎同时，进攻时间终了。球进入球篮。

解释 如果当时：

（a）球仍然在 A1 的手中，并且 B1 的犯规发生在进攻时间终了之前，或

（b）A1 投篮离手的球已在空中，并且 B1 的犯规发生在进攻时间终了之前，或

（c）A1 投篮离手的球已在空中，并且 B1 的犯规发生在进攻时间终了之后，

这不是一起进攻时间违例。A1 的中篮应计得分。A1 应获得 1 次额外的罚球。应如同任何最后一次罚球后那样继续比赛。

（d）球仍然在 A1 的手中，并且 B1 的犯规发生在进攻时间终了之后，

这是一起进攻时间违例。A1 的中篮不应计得分。应忽略 B1 的犯规，除非该犯规是一起违反体育运动精神的犯规或是取消比赛资格的犯规。应由 B 队在罚球线延长线处执行掷球入界继续比赛。

29/50-7 **Example:** With 25.2 seconds on the game clock, team A gains control of the ball. With 1 second on the shot clock, A1 attempts a shot for a goal. While the ball is in the air, the shot clock signal sounds. The ball misses the ring and

a) after another 1.2 seconds, the game clock signal sounds for the end of the quarter.

b) A2 catches the ball on a rebound. The referee calls the violation with the game clock showing 0.8 of a second.

Interpretation:

In (a) this is not a shot clock violation by team A. The referee was waiting to see if team B gained immediate and clear control of the ball and therefore did not call a violation. The quarter has ended.

In (b) this is a shot clock violation by team A. The game shall be resumed with a team B throw-in from the place nearest to where the game was stopped, with the game clock showing 0.8 of a second.

29/50-8 **Example:** With 25.2 seconds on the game clock, team A gains control of the ball. With 1.2 seconds on the game clock and with A1 having the ball in the hands, the shot clock signal sounds. The referee calls a violation with the game clock showing 0.8 of a second.

Interpretation: This is a shot clock violation by team A. As the violation occurred with 1.2 seconds on the game clock, the referees shall correct the game clock. The game shall be resumed with a team B throw-in from the place nearest to where the game was stopped, with the game clock showing 1.2 seconds.

29/50-9 **Statement:** If the shot clock signal sounds and the opponents gain an immediate and clear control of the ball, the shot clock signal shall be disregarded. The game shall continue.

29/50-10 **Example:** Close to the end of the shot clock period, A1's pass is missed by A2 (both players are in their frontcourt) and the ball rolls into team A's backcourt. Before B1 gains control of the ball with a free path to the basket, the shot clock signal sounds.

29/50-7 **举例** 比赛计时钟显示 25.2 秒时，A 队获得控制球。进攻计时钟显示 1 秒时，A1 尝试投篮。当球在空中时，进攻计时钟信号响。球未触及篮圈，随后：

（a）又过了 1.2 秒，结束该节的比赛计时钟信号响。

（b）A2 在抢篮板球中拿到了球。裁判员宣判了该违例，此时比赛计时钟显示 0.8 秒。

解释

在（a）中，这不是 A 队的进攻时间违例。裁判员是在等待并观察 B 队队员是否将立即和清晰地获得控制球，因此没有宣判违例。该节结束。

在（b）中，这是 A 队的进攻时间违例。应由 B 队在最靠近比赛被停止的地点执行掷球入界继续比赛，比赛计时钟显示 0.8 秒。

29/50-8 **举例** 比赛计时钟显示 25.2 秒时，A 队获得控制球。当比赛计时钟显示 1.2 秒且 A1 正双手持球时，进攻计时钟信号响。裁判员宣判了该违例，比赛计时钟显示 0.8 秒。

解释 这是 A 队的进攻时间违例。该违例发生时比赛计时钟显示的是 1.2 秒，因此裁判员应纠正比赛计时钟。应由 B 队在最靠近比赛被停止的地点执行掷球入界继续比赛，比赛计时钟显示 1.2 秒。

29/50-9 **陈述** 如果进攻计时钟信号响，且对方队员立即和清晰地获得控制球，信号应被忽略。比赛应继续。

29/50-10 **举例** 临近进攻时间周期结束，A2 未能接到 A1 的传球（两名队员都在他们的前场），然后，球滚入 A 队的后场。在 B1 即将获得控制球并有一个面向球篮的开放路径之前，进攻计时钟信号响。

Interpretation: If B1 gains an immediate and clear control of the ball, the signal shall be disregarded. The game shall continue.

29/50-11 **Example:** After a goal scored by the opponents and with 25.3 seconds on the game clock, team A has the ball for a throw-in from behind its endline. Close to the end of the shot-clock period, A1's pass to A2 is deflected by B1 and the shot clock signal sounds. The referee calls a shot clock violation with the game clock showing 0.8 of a second.

Interpretation: This is a shot clock violation by team A which occurred with the game clock showing 0.8 of a second. The game shall be resumed with a team B throw-in from the place nearest to where the game was stopped, with the game clock showing 0.8 of a second.

29/50-12 **Statement:** If a team that was in control of the ball is awarded an alternating possession throw-in, that team shall have only the time remaining on the shot clock when the jump ball situation occurred.

29/50-13 **Example:** Team A is in control of the ball in its frontcourt with 10 seconds on the shot clock when a jump ball situation occurs. An alternating possession throw-in is awarded to

(a) team A.

(b) team B.

Interpretation:

(a) Team A shall have 10 seconds on the shot clock.

(b) Team B shall have 24 seconds on the shot clock.

29/50-14 **Statement:** If the game is stopped by a referee for a foul or violation (excluding for the ball having gone out-of-bounds) called against the team not in control of the ball and the possession of the ball is awarded to the same team that previously had control of the ball in its frontcourt, the shot clock shall be reset as follows:

- If 14 seconds or more are shown on the shot clock when the game was stopped, the shot clock shall continue with the time remaining the shot clock.

解释 如果 B1 立即和清晰地获得控制球，信号应被忽略。比赛应继续。

29/50-11 **举例** 在对方队员中篮得分后，比赛计时钟显示 25.3 秒，A 队在其端线后执行掷球入界。在临近进攻时间周期结束时，A1 传向 A2 的球被 B1 碰触，随后进攻计时钟信号响。裁判员宣判进攻时间违例，比赛计时钟显示 0.8 秒。

解释 这是 A 队的进攻时间违例，该违例发生在比赛计时钟显示 0.8 秒时。应由 B 队在最靠近比赛被停止的地点执行掷球入界继续比赛，比赛计时钟显示 0.8 秒。

29/50-12 **陈述** 如果原控制球队被判给交替拥有的掷球入界，该队应拥有在跳球情况发生时进攻计时钟显示的时间。

29/50-13 **举例** 进攻计时钟显示 10 秒时，A 队在其前场控制球，此时发生一次跳球情况。该交替拥有掷球入界权判给：

（a）A 队。

（b）B 队。

解释

（a）A 队应拥有 10 秒进攻时间。

（b）B 队应拥有 24 秒进攻时间。

29/50-14 **陈述** 如果比赛因裁判员宣判非控制球队的一起犯规或违例（使球出界除外）而停止，并且随后的球权判给原控制球队在其前场继续比赛，进攻计时钟应按下述原则复位。

- 如果在比赛停止时进攻计时钟显示 14 秒或更多，进攻计时钟应从剩余时间处连续计算；

- If 13 seconds or less are shown on the shot clock when the game was stopped, the team shall have 14 seconds on the shot clock.

29/50-15 **Example:** With 8 seconds on the shot clock, A1 dribbles in the frontcourt when

(a) B1 taps the ball out-of-bounds in the team A frontcourt.

(b) B1 fouls A1. This is the second team B foul in the quarter.

Interpretation: The game shall be resumed with a team A throw-in in the frontcourt with

(a) 8 seconds

(b) 14 seconds

on the shot clock.

29/50-16 **Example:** With 4 seconds on the shot clock, team A is in control of the ball in its frontcourt when

(a) A1

(b) B1

is injured. The referee stops the game.

Interpretation: Team A shall have

(a) 4 seconds

(b) 14 seconds

on the shot clock.

29/50-17 **Example:** With 6 seconds on the shot clock, A1's shot for a goal is in the air when a double foul between A2 and B2 occurs. The alternating possession arrow favours team A.

(a) The ball misses the ring.

(b) The ball touches the ring.

Interpretation: Team A shall have

- 如果在比赛停止时进攻计时钟显示 13 秒或更少，该队应拥有 14 秒进攻时间。

29/50-15 举例 进攻计时钟显示 8 秒时，A1 在其前场运球，此时：

（a）B1 在 A 队的前场将球拍出界。

（b）B1 对 A1 犯规。这是该节 B 队的第 2 次全队犯规。

解释 应由 A 队在其前场执行掷球入界继续比赛，A 队应拥有：

（a）8 秒进攻时间。

（b）14 秒进攻时间。

29/50-16 举例 进攻计时钟显示 4 秒时，A 队在其前场控制球，此时：

（a）A1 受伤。

（b）B1 受伤。

裁判员停止比赛。

解释 A 队应拥有：

（a）4 秒进攻时间。

（b）14 秒进攻时间。

29/50-17 举例 进攻计时钟显示 6 秒，A1 投篮离手的球在空中时，发生了 A2 和 B2 之间的双方犯规。交替拥有箭头指向 A 队的进攻方向。

（a）球未触及篮圈。

（b）球触及了篮圈。

解释 A 队应拥有：

(a) 6 seconds

(b) 14 seconds

on the shot clock.

29/50-18 **Example:** With 5 seconds on the shot clock, A1 dribbles when B1 is charged with a technical foul, after which the team A head coach is charged with a technical foul.

Interpretation: After the cancellation of equal penalties, the game shall be resumed with a team A throw-in. Team A shall have 5 seconds on the shot clock.

29/50-19 **Example:** With

(a) 16 seconds

(b) 12 seconds

on the shot clock, A1 passes the ball to A2, both in the frontcourt, when B1 in the backcourt deliberately kicks or strikes the ball with the fist.

Interpretation: In both cases, this is a violation by B1 for kicking the ball or striking it with the fist. The game shall be resumed with a team A throw-in from its frontcourt with

(a) 16 seconds

(b) 14 seconds

on the shot clock.

29/50-20 **Example:** With 6 seconds on the shot clock, A1 dribbles in the frontcourt when B2 is charged with an unsportsmanlike foul against A2.

Interpretation: After A2's 2 free throws with no line-up, regardless of whether made or missed, the game shall be resumed with a team A throw-in from the throw-in line in its frontcourt. Team A shall have 14 seconds on the shot clock.

The same interpretation is valid for a disqualifying foul.

（a）6 秒进攻时间。

（b）14 秒进攻时间。

29/50-18 举例 进攻计时钟显示 5 秒时，A1 正在运球，此时宣判了 B1 一起技术犯规，接着宣判了 A 队主教练一起技术犯规。

解释 在这两起相同罚则相互抵消之后，应由 A 队执行掷球入界继续比赛。A 队应拥有 5 秒进攻时间。

29/50-19 举例 进攻计时钟显示：

（a）16 秒，

（b）12 秒，

A1 在其前场将球传向同样位于其前场的 A2，此时 B1 在其后场故意脚踢球或者拳击球。

解释 在这两种情况下，B1 因脚踢球或者拳击球而违例。应由 A 队在其前场执行掷球入界继续比赛，进攻计时钟应显示：

（a）16 秒。

（b）14 秒。

29/50-20 举例 进攻计时钟显示 6 秒时，A1 在其前场运球，此时 B2 对 A2 发生了一起违反体育运动精神的犯规。

解释 在 A2 的 2 次不占位的罚球后，无论罚球是否成功，应由 A 队在其前场的掷球入界线处执行掷球入界继续比赛。A 队应拥有 14 秒进攻时间。

该解释对取消比赛资格的犯规同样适用。

29/50-21 **Statement:** If the game is stopped by a referee for any valid reason not connected with either team and if the opponents would be placed at a disadvantage, the shot clock shall continue with the time remaining.

29/50-22 **Example:** With 25 seconds on the game clock in the fourth quarter and with the score A 72 – B 72, team A gains control of the ball in its frontcourt. A1 dribbles for 20 seconds when the game is stopped by the referees because of

(a) the game clock or the shot clock failing to run or to start.

(b) a bottle being thrown on to the court.

(c) the shot clock being erroneously reset.

Interpretation: In all cases, the game shall be resumed with a team A throw-in from the place nearest to where the game was stopped. Team A shall have 4 seconds on the shot clock. Team B would be placed at a disadvantage if the game were resumed with no time remaining on the shot clock.

29/50-23 **Example:** A1's shot for a goal touches the ring. A2 rebounds the ball and 9 seconds later the shot clock signal sounds in error. The referees stop the game.

Interpretation: This is an error in the shot clock operation of not resetting the shot clock. After consulting the commissioner, if present, and the shot clock operator, the game shall be resumed with a team A throw-in. Team A shall have 5 seconds on the shot clock.

29/50-24 **Example:** With 4 seconds on the shot clock, A1 attempts a shot for a goal. The ball misses the ring but the shot clock operator erroneously resets the clock. A2 rebounds the ball and after a certain time, A3 scores a goal. At this time, the referees recognise the error.

29/50-21 陈述 如果比赛因与任一队都无关的正当原因而被裁判员停止，且对方队将被置于不利，进攻计时钟应从剩余时间处连续计算。

29/50-22 举例 第 4 节，比赛计时钟显示 25 秒，比分 A72 – B72，A 队在其前场获得控制球并且在 A1 运球达 20 秒时，裁判员因下列情况而停止比赛。

（a）比赛计时钟或进攻计时钟未能运行或开动。

（b）一个瓶子被扔进比赛场地。

（c）进攻计时钟被错误地复位。

解释 上述所有情况下，应由 A 队在最靠近比赛被停止的地点执行掷球入界继续比赛。A 队应拥有 4 秒进攻时间。如果没有剩余的进攻时间并继续比赛，将置 B 队于不利。

29/50-23 举例 A1 投篮离手的球触及了篮圈。A2 获得篮板球，9 秒之后进攻计时钟误响。裁判员停止比赛。

解释 这是一起未复位进攻时间钟的操作失误。裁判员在与到场的临场代表和进攻计时员商议之后，应判给 A 队执行掷球入界继续比赛。A 队应拥有 5 秒进攻时间。

29/50-24 举例 进攻计时钟显示 4 秒时，A1 尝试投篮。球未触及篮圈，但是进攻计时员错误地复位了进攻计时钟。A2 获得了篮板球，在一定的时间后 A3 中篮。此时，裁判员确认了这一失误。

Interpretation: The referees, after consulting the commissioner, if present, shall confirm that the ball missed the ring during A1's shot. If so, they shall then decide if the ball had left A3's hands before the shot clock would have sounded if the reset had not taken place. If so, A3's goal shall count. If not, a shot clock violation occurred and A3's goal shall not count.

29/50-25 **Statement:** A shot for a goal is released and a foul is then called against a defensive player in the defensive team's backcourt. If the game is resumed with a throw-in, the shot clock shall be reset as follows:

- If 14 seconds or more are displayed on the shot clock at the time when the game was stopped, the shot clock shall not be reset but shall continue from the time it was stopped.
- If 13 seconds or less are displayed on the shot clock at the time when the game was stopped, the shot clock shall be reset to 14 seconds.

29/50-26 **Example:** A1 attempts a shot for a goal. The ball enters the basket. B2 in the backcourt fouls A2. This is the third team B foul in the quarter.

Interpretation: A1's goal shall count. The game shall be resumed with a team A throw-in from the place nearest to where B2's foul occurred. Team A shall have 14 seconds on the shot clock.

29/50-27 **Example:** With 17 seconds on the shot clock, A1's shot for a goal is in the air when B2 in the backcourt fouls A2. This is the second team B foul in the quarter. The ball

(a) rebounds from the ring but does not enter the basket.

(b) misses the ring.

Interpretation:

In both cases, the game shall be resumed with a team A throw-in in its frontcourt from the place nearest to where B2's foul occurred. Team A shall have 17 seconds on the shot clock.

解释 裁判员在与到场的临场代表商议之后，应确认 A1 投篮的球未触及篮圈。如果确认该球未触及篮圈，他们接着应决定，如果进攻计时钟没有复位，在进攻计时钟响起前 A3 投篮的球是否已离手。如果是，A3 的中篮应计得分；如果否，则发生了一起进攻时间违例，A3 的中篮不应计得分。

29/50-25 **陈述** 在一次投篮球离手之后，随即宣判了在防守队后场的一名防守队员犯规，如果随后以掷球入界继续比赛，进攻时间应按下述原则复位。

- 如果比赛停止时进攻计时钟显示 14 秒或更多，进攻计时钟不应复位，而是应从时间被停止处连续计算。
- 如果比赛停止时进攻计时钟显示 13 秒或更少，进攻计时钟应复位到 14 秒。

29/50-26 **举例** A1 尝试投篮，球进入球篮，B2 在其后场对 A2 犯规。这是该节 B 队的第 3 次全队犯规。

解释 A1 的中篮应计得分。应由 A 队在最靠近 B2 发生犯规的地点执行掷球入界继续比赛。A 队应拥有 14 秒进攻时间。

29/50-27 **举例** 进攻计时钟显示 17 秒，A1 投篮离手的球在空中时，B2 在其后场对 A2 犯规。这是该节 B 队的第 2 次全队犯规。该球：

（a）从篮圈上弹起，但未进入球篮。

（b）未触及篮圈。

解释

在这两种情况下，应由 A 队在其前场最靠近 B2 发生犯规的地点执行掷球入界继续比赛。A 队应拥有 17 秒进攻时间。

29/50-28 **Example:** With 10 seconds on the shot clock, A1's shot for a goal is in the air when B2 in the backcourt fouls A2. This is the second team B foul in the quarter. The ball

(a) enters the basket.

(b) rebounds from the ring but does not enter the basket.

(c) misses the ring.

Interpretation:

In (a) A1's goal shall count.

In all cases, the game shall be resumed with a team A throw-in in its frontcourt from the place nearest to where B2's foul occurred. Team A shall have 14 seconds on the shot clock.

29/50-29 **Example:** A1's shot for a goal is in the air when the shot clock signal sounds. B2 in the backcourt fouls A2. This is the second team B foul in the quarter. The ball

(a) enters the basket.

(b) rebounds from the ring but does not enter the basket.

(c) misses the ring.

Interpretation:

In (a) A1's goal shall count.

In all cases, this is not a shot clock violation by team A. The game shall be resumed with a team A throw-in in its frontcourt from the place nearest to where B2's foul occurred. Team A shall have 14 seconds on the shot clock.

29/50-30 **Example:** With 10 seconds on the shot clock, A1's shot for a goal is in the air when B2 in the backcourt fouls A2. This is the fifth team B foul in the quarter. The ball

(a) enters the basket.

(b) rebounds from the ring but does not enter the basket.

(c) misses the ring.

29/50-28 举例 进攻计时钟显示 10 秒，A1 投篮离手的球在空中时，B2 在其后场对 A2 犯规。这是该节 B 队的第 2 次全队犯规。该球：

（a）进入球篮。

（b）从篮圈上弹起，但未进入球篮。

（c）未触及篮圈。

解释

在（a）中，A1 的中篮应计得分。

上述所有情况下，应由 A 队在其前场最靠近 B2 发生犯规的地点执行掷球入界继续比赛。A 队应拥有 14 秒进攻时间。

29/50-29 举例 A1 投篮离手的球在空中时，进攻计时钟信号响。B2 在其后场对 A2 犯规。这是该节 B 队的第 2 次全队犯规。该球：

（a）进入球篮。

（b）从篮圈上弹起，但未进入球篮。

（c）未触及篮圈。

解释

在（a）中，A1 的中篮应计得分。

上述所有情况下，A 队都没有发生进攻时间违例。应由 A 队在其前场最靠近 B2 发生犯规的地点执行掷球入界继续比赛。A 队应拥有 14 秒进攻时间。

29/50-30 举例 进攻计时钟显示 10 秒，A1 投篮离手的球在空中时，B2 在其后场对 A2 犯规。这是该节 B 队的第 5 次全队犯规。该球：

（a）进入球篮。

（b）从篮圈上弹起，但未进入球篮。

（c）未触及篮圈。

Interpretation:

In (a) A1's goal shall count.

In all cases, A2 shall attempt 2 free throws. The game shall be resumed as after any last free throw.

29/50-31 **Example:** A1's shot for a goal is in the air when the shot clock signal sounds and B2 fouls A2 before the ball

(a) enters the basket.

(b) rebounds from the ring but does not enter the basket.

(c) misses the ring.

B2's foul is the fifth team B in the quarter.

Interpretation:

In (a) A1's goal shall count.

In all cases, this is not a shot clock violation by team A. A2 shall attempt 2 free throws. The game shall be resumed as after any last free throw.

29/50-32 **Statement:** A throw-in resulting from an unsportsmanlike foul or a disqualifying foul penalty shall always be administered from the throw-in line in the team's frontcourt. The team shall have 14 seconds on the shot clock.

29/50-33 **Example:** With 1:12 on the game clock and with 6 seconds on the shot clock in the fourth quarter, A1 dribbles in the frontcourt when B1 is charged with an unsportsmanlike foul against A1. After A1's first free throw, the team A head coach or the team B head coach requests a time-out.

Interpretation: A1 shall attempt the second free throw with no line-up. The time-out shall then be granted. After the time-out, the game shall be resumed with a team A throw-in from the throw-in line in its frontcourt. Team A shall have 14 seconds on the shot clock.

29/50-34 **Example:** With 19 seconds on the shot clock, A1 dribbles in the frontcourt when B2 is charged with an unsportsmanlike foul against A2.

解释

在（a）中，A1 的中篮应计得分。

上述所有情况下，A2 应执行 2 次罚球。应如同任何最后一次罚球后那样继续比赛。

29/50-31 **举例** A1 投篮离手的球在空中时，进攻计时钟信号响并且 B2 对 A2 犯规，随后该球：

（a）进入球篮。

（b）从篮圈上弹起，但未进入球篮。

（c）未触及篮圈。

B2 的犯规是该节 B 队的第 5 次全队犯规。

解释

在（a）中，A1 的中篮应计得分。

上述所有情况下，A 队都没有发生进攻时间违例，A2 应执行 2 次罚球。应如同任何最后一次罚球后那样继续比赛。

29/50-32 **陈述** 源于一起违反体育运动精神的犯规或取消比赛资格的犯规的掷球入界，应总是在球队前场的掷球入界线处执行。该队应拥有 14 秒进攻时间。

29/50-33 **举例** 第 4 节，比赛计时钟显示 1:12，进攻计时钟显示 6 秒，A1 在其前场运球时，B1 被判对 A1 发生了一起违反体育运动精神的犯规。在 A1 的第 1 次罚球后，A 队主教练或 B 队主教练请求了一次暂停。

解释 应由 A1 执行第 2 次不占位的罚球，然后才准予暂停。暂停后，应由 A 队在其前场的掷球入界线处执行掷球入界继续比赛。A 队应拥有 14 秒进攻时间。

29/50-34 **举例** 进攻计时钟显示 19 秒，A1 在其前场运球时，B2 被判对 A2 发生了一起违反体育运动精神的犯规。

Interpretation: After A2's 2 free throws with no line-up, regardless of whether made or missed, the game shall be resumed with a team A throw-in from the throw-in line in its frontcourt. Team A shall have 14 seconds on the shot clock.

The same interpretation is valid for a disqualifying foul.

29/50-35 **Statement:** After the ball touches the ring of the opponents' basket for any reason, the team shall have 14 seconds on the shot clock, if the team which gains control of the ball is the same team that was in control of the ball before the ball touched the ring.

29/50-36 **Example:** During A1's pass to A2, the ball touches B2 after which the ball touches the ring. A3 gains control of the ball.

Interpretation: Team A shall have 14 seconds on the shot clock when A3 gains control of the ball anywhere on the court.

29/50-37 **Example:** A1 attempts a shot for a goal with

(a) 4 seconds

(b) 20 seconds

on the shot clock. The ball touches the ring, rebounds from it and A2 gains control of the ball.

Interpretation: In both cases, team A shall have 14 seconds on the shot clock when A2 gains control of the ball anywhere on the court.

29/50-38 **Example:** A1 attempts a shot for a goal. The ball touches the ring.

(a) B1 touches the ball.

(b) A2 taps the ball.

and A3 then gains control of the ball.

Interpretation: In both cases, team A shall have 14 seconds on the shot clock when A3 gains control of the ball anywhere on the court.

29/50-39 **Example:** A1 attempts a shot for a goal. The ball touches the ring. B1 then touches the ball before it goes out-of-bounds.

解释 在A2的2次不占位的罚球后，无论罚球是否成功，应由A队在其前场的掷球入界线处执行掷球入界继续比赛。A队应拥有14秒进攻时间。

该解释对取消比赛资格的犯规同样适用。

29/50-35 陈述 当球因任何原因触及对方球篮的篮圈后，如果获得控制球的球队和球触及篮圈前控制球的队是同一队，则该队应拥有14秒进攻时间。

29/50-36 举例 在A1向A2传球期间，球被B2触及后又触及了篮圈。之后，A3获得控制球。

解释 无论A3在比赛场地上的哪个地点获得控制球，A队都应拥有14秒进攻时间。

29/50-37 举例 A1尝试投篮，此时进攻计时钟显示：

（a）4秒。

（b）20秒。

球触及了篮圈后弹起，然后A2获得控制球。

解释 在这两种情况下，无论A2在比赛场地上的哪个地点获得控制球，A队都应拥有14秒进攻时间。

29/50-38 举例 A1尝试投篮。球触及篮圈后：

（a）被B1触及。

（b）被A2拍击。

最后A3获得控制球。

解释 在这两种情况下，无论A3在比赛场地上的哪个地点获得控制球，A队都应拥有14秒进攻时间。

29/50-39 举例 A1尝试投篮。球触及篮圈后被B1触及，随后球出界。

Interpretation: The game shall be resumed with a team A throw-in from the place nearest to where the ball went out-of-bounds. Team A shall have 14 seconds on the shot clock regardless of where on the floor the throw-in shall be administered.

29/50-40 **Example:** With 4 seconds on the shot clock, A1 throws the ball towards the ring to reset the shot clock. The ball touches the ring. B1 then touches the ball before it goes out-of-bounds in the team A backcourt.

Interpretation: The game shall be resumed with a team A throw-in in its backcourt from the place nearest to where the ball went out-of-bounds. Team A shall have 14 seconds on the shot clock.

29/50-41 **Example:** With 6 seconds on the shot clock, A1 attempts a shot for a goal. The ball touches the ring and A2 gains control of the ball. B2 then fouls A2 during the rebound. This is the third team B foul in the quarter.

Interpretation: The game shall be resumed with a team A throw-in from the place nearest to where B2's foul occurred. Team A shall have 14 seconds on the shot clock.

29/50-42 **Example:** A1 attempts a shot for a goal. The ball touches the ring and on the rebound a held ball between A2 and B2 occurs. The alternating possession arrow favours team A.

Interpretation: The game shall be resumed with a team A throw-in from the place nearest to where the held ball occurred. Team A shall have 14 seconds on the shot clock.

29/50-43 **Example:** A1 attempts a shot for a goal with

(a) 8 seconds

(b) 17 seconds

on the shot clock. The ball lodges between the ring and the backboard. The alternating possession arrow favours team A.

Interpretation: In both cases, the game shall be resumed with a team A throw-in from behind the endline in its frontcourt nearest to the backboard. Team A shall have 14 seconds on the shot clock.

解释 应由A队在最靠近球出界的地点执行掷球入界继续比赛。无论该掷球入界在比赛场地上的哪个地点执行，A队都应拥有14秒进攻时间。

29/50-40 **举例** 进攻计时钟显示4秒时，A1为了使进攻计时钟复位而将球掷向篮圈。球触及了篮圈。然后，球被B1触及后在A队的后场出界。

解释 应由A队在其后场最靠近球出界的地点执行掷球入界继续比赛。A队应拥有14秒进攻时间。

29/50-41 **举例** 进攻计时钟显示6秒时，A1尝试投篮。在球触及篮圈后，A2获得控制球。然后，B2在抢篮板球中对A2犯规。这是该节B队的第3次全队犯规。

解释 应由A队在最靠近B2发生犯规的位置执行掷球入界继续比赛。A队应拥有14秒进攻时间。

29/50-42 **举例** A1尝试投篮，球触及篮圈后，在抢篮板球中，发生了一次A2和B2的争球。交替拥有箭头指向A队的进攻方向。

解释 应由A队在最靠近发生争球的位置执行掷球入界继续比赛。A队应拥有14秒进攻时间。

29/50-43 **举例** A1尝试投篮，进攻计时钟显示：

（a）8秒

（b）17秒

球停留在篮圈和篮板之间。交替拥有箭头指向A队的进攻方向。

解释 在这两种情况下，应由A队从其前场端线后最靠近篮板的位置执行掷球入界继续比赛。A队应拥有14秒进攻时间。

29/50-44 **Example:** A1 in the frontcourt passes the ball for an alley-oop to A2 who does not catch the ball. The ball touches the ring, after which A3 gains control of the ball in team A's

(a) frontcourt.

(b) backcourt.

Interpretation:

(a) Team A shall have 14 seconds on the shot clock.

(b) This is a team A backcourt violation as team A did not lose the control of the ball.

29/50-45 **Example:** A1's shot for a goal touches the ring. B1 rebounds the ball and B1 lands on the court. A2 taps the ball out of B1's hands. A3 now catches the ball.

Interpretation: Team B (B1) has gained clear control of the ball during the rebound, after which team A (A3) gained a new control. Team A shall have 24 seconds on the shot clock.

29/50-46 **Example:** With 5 seconds on the shot clock, thrower-in A1 passes the ball towards the team B basket. The ball touches the ring and is then touched but not controlled by A2 or B2.

Interpretation: The game clock and the shot clock shall be started simultaneously when the ball touches or is touched by either player on the court.

If team A then gains control of the ball on the court, it shall have 14 seconds on the shot clock.

If team B then gains control of the ball on the court, it shall have 24 seconds on the shot clock.

29/50-47 **Statement:** During the game with the game clock running, whenever a team gains a new possession of a live ball either in its frontcourt or in its backcourt, that team shall have 24 seconds on the shot clock.

29/50-48 **Example:** While the game clock is running, A1 gains new possession of the ball on the court in its

29/50-44 **举例** A1 在其前场向 A2 做出了一次空中接力传球，A2 没能接到该传球。球触及了篮圈，随后 A3 在：

（a）其前场获得控制球。

（b）其后场获得控制球。

解释

（a）A 队应拥有 14 秒进攻时间。

（b）这是 A 队的球回后场违例，因为 A 队没有失去控制球。

29/50-45 **举例** A1 投篮离手的球触及了篮圈。B1 获得篮板球后，B1 落回比赛场地。A2 将 B1 手中的球拍离。球随后被 A3 拿到。

解释 B 队（B1）在抢篮板球中已经获得了明确的控制球，在此之后，A 队（A3）获得新的控制球。A 队应拥有 24 秒进攻时间。

29/50-46 **举例** 进攻计时钟显示 5 秒时，掷球入界队员 A1 将球传向 B 队的球篮。球触及篮圈后被 A2 或 B2 触及，但他们均未控制球。

解释 当球触及任一场上队员或被任一场上队员触及时，比赛计时钟与进攻计时钟应同时开动。然后，

如果 A 队在比赛场地上获得控制球，他们应拥有 14 秒进攻时间。

如果 B 队在比赛场地上获得控制球，他们应拥有 24 秒进攻时间。

29/50-47 **陈述** 比赛期间，当比赛计时钟正在运行时，每当某队在其前场或后场获得了一个新的活球球权，该队都应拥有 24 秒进攻时间。

29/50-48 **举例** 当比赛计时钟正在运行时，A1 在比赛场地上该队的：

(a) backcourt.

(b) frontcourt.

Interpretation: In both cases, team A shall have 24 seconds on the shot clock.

29/50-49 **Example:** After a team B throw-in, A1 gains an immediate and clear new possession of the ball on the court in its

(a) backcourt.

(b) frontcourt.

Interpretation: In both cases, team A shall have 24 seconds on the shot clock.

29/50-50 **Statement:** The game is stopped by a referee for a foul or violation (including for the ball having gone out-of-bounds) called against the team in control of the ball. If the ball is awarded to the opponents with a throw-in from its frontcourt, that team shall have 14 seconds on the shot clock.

29/50-51 **Example:** Within the backcourt A1 passes the ball to A2. A2 touches but does not catch the ball before it goes out-of-bounds in team A's backcourt.

Interpretation: The game shall be resumed with a team B throw-in in its frontcourt from the place nearest to where the ball went out-of-bounds. Team B shall have 14 seconds on the shot clock.

29/50-52 **Statement:** Whenever a team gains or regains control of a live ball anywhere on the court with less than 24 seconds on the game clock, the shot clock shall have no display visible.

After the ball has touched the ring of the opponents' basket and the offensive team regains the control of a live ball anywhere on the court with less than 24 seconds and more than 14 seconds on the game clock, the team shall have 14 seconds on the shot clock. If there are 14 seconds or less on the game clock, the shot clock shall have no display visible.

（a）后场

（b）前场

获得了一个新的球权。

解释 在这两种情况下，A 队应拥有 24 秒进攻时间。

29/50-49 举例 B 队执行掷球入界后，A1 在比赛场地上该队的：

（a）后场

（b）前场

立即和清晰地获得一个新的球权。

解释 在这两种情况下，A 队应拥有 24 秒进攻时间。

29/50-50 陈述 比赛因裁判员宣判控制球队的一起犯规或违例（包括使球出界）而停止。如果随后将球判给对方队在其前场执行掷球入界，那么该队应拥有 14 秒进攻时间。

29/50-51 举例 A1 在其后场将球传给同样位于其后场的 A2，A2 触及了球但没拿到球，随后球从 A 队的后场出界。

解释 应由 B 队在其前场最靠近球出界的地点执行掷球入界继续比赛。B 队应拥有 14 秒进攻时间。

29/50-52 陈述 每当某队在比赛场地上的任何地点获得控制活球，或重新获得控制活球，且此时比赛计时钟显示的时间少于 24 秒，应不显示进攻时间。

在球已触及对方球篮的篮圈后被进攻队在比赛场地上的任何地点重新获得控制活球时，如果比赛计时钟显示多于 14 秒、少于 24 秒，则该队应拥有 14 秒进攻时间；如果比赛计时钟显示 14 秒或更少，则应不显示进攻时间。

29/50-53 **Example:** With 12 seconds on the game clock, thrower-in A1 gains a new control of the ball.

Interpretation: The shot clock shall have no display visible.

29/50-54 **Example:** With 23 seconds on the game clock, A1 gains a new control of the ball on the court. With 18 seconds on the game clock, B1 in the backcourt deliberately kicks the ball.

Interpretation: The game shall be resumed with a team A throw-in in its frontcourt from the place nearest to where B1 kicked the ball. The game clock shows 18 seconds. The shot clock shall have no display visible.

29/50-55 **Example:** With 23 seconds on the game clock, A1 gains a new control of the ball on the court. The shot clock has no display visible. With 19 seconds on the game clock, A1 attempts a shot for a goal. The ball touches the ring. Team A regains the control of the ball by A2 rebounding it, with 16 seconds on the game clock.

Interpretation: The game shall continue with 16 seconds on the game clock. The shot clock shall be switched on. Team A shall have 14 seconds on the shot clock as there were more than 14 seconds on the game clock when team A regained the control of the ball.

29/50-56 **Example:** With 23 seconds on the game clock, A1 gains a new control of the ball on the court. The shot clock has no display visible. With 15 seconds on the game clock, A1 attempts a shot for a goal. The ball touches the ring and B1 taps it out-of-bounds in team B's backcourt, with 12 seconds on the game clock.

Interpretation: The game shall be resumed with a team A throw-in in its frontcourt from the place nearest to where the ball went out-of-bounds, with 12 seconds on the game clock. The shot clock shall continue to have no display visible as there were less than 14 seconds on the game clock when team A regained the control of the ball.

29/50-53 **举例** 比赛计时钟显示 12 秒时，掷球入界队员 A1 获得了一个新的控制球。

解释 应不显示进攻时间。

29/50-54 **举例** 比赛计时钟显示 23 秒时，A1 在比赛场地上获得了一个新的控制球。比赛计时钟显示 18 秒时，B1 在其后场故意脚踢球。

解释 应由 A 队在其前场最靠近 B1 脚踢球的地点执行掷球入界继续比赛。比赛计时钟显示 18 秒。应不显示进攻时间。

29/50-55 **举例** 比赛计时钟显示 23 秒时，A1 在比赛场地上获得了一个新的控制球。进攻时间已不显示。比赛计时钟显示 19 秒时，A1 尝试投篮。球触及了篮圈。A2 通过获得篮板球使 A 队重新获得控制球，此时比赛计时钟显示 16 秒。

解释 应从比赛计时钟显示的 16 秒处继续比赛。进攻计时钟应被打开。因为 A 队重新获得控制球时比赛计时钟的显示多于 14 秒，A 队应拥有 14 秒进攻时间。

29/50-56 **举例** 比赛计时钟显示 23 秒时，A1 在比赛场地上获得了一个新的控制球。进攻时间已不显示。比赛计时钟显示 15 秒时，A1 尝试投篮。球触及了篮圈后被 B1 拍击并从 B 队的后场出界，此时比赛计时钟显示 12 秒。

解释 应由 A 队在其前场最靠近球出界的地点执行掷球入界继续比赛，比赛计时钟显示 12 秒。由于 A 队重新获得控制球时比赛计时钟的显示少于 14 秒，仍应不显示进攻时间。

29/50-57 **Example:** With 22 seconds on the game clock, A1 gains a new control of the ball on the court. The shot clock has no display visible. With 18 seconds on the game clock, A1 attempts a shot for a goal. The ball misses the ring and B1 taps it out-of-bounds in team B's backcourt, with

(a) 15.5 seconds

(b) 12 seconds

on the game clock.

Interpretation: The game shall be resumed with a team A throw-in in its frontcourt from the place nearest to where the ball went out-of-bounds, with the time remaining on the game clock. The shot clock shall continue to have no display visible, as team A had gained a new control of the ball with less than 24 seconds on the game clock.

29/50-57 **举例** 比赛计时钟显示 22 秒时，A1 在比赛场地上获得了一个新的控制球。进攻时间已不显示。比赛计时钟显示 18 秒时，A1 尝试投篮。球未触及篮圈，随即球被 B1 拍击并从 B 队的后场出界，此时比赛计时钟显示

（a）15.5 秒。

（b）12 秒。

解释 应由 A 队在其前场最靠近球出界的地点执行掷球入界继续比赛，比赛计时钟显示剩余的时间。由于 A 队获得一个新的控制球时比赛计时钟的显示少于 24 秒，仍应不显示进攻时间。

Article 30 Ball returned to the backcourt

30-1 **Statement:** An airborne player retains the same status relative to the court as where the player has last touched the court before being airborne.

When a player jumps from the frontcourt and gains a new team control of the ball while still airborne, the player may then land with the ball anywhere on the court. The player may not pass the ball to a teammate in the backcourt before landing.

30-2 **Example:** A1 in the backcourt passes the ball to A2 in the frontcourt. B1 jumps from the frontcourt, catches the ball while airborne and lands

(a) with both feet in the backcourt.

(b) straddling the centre line.

(c) straddling the centre line and then dribbles or passes the ball to the backcourt.

Interpretation: This is not a backcourt violation by team B. B1 established a new team B control of the ball while airborne and may land anywhere on the court. In all cases, B1 is legally in the backcourt.

30-3 **Example:** During the opening jump ball between A1 and B1, the ball is legally tapped. A2 jumps from the frontcourt, catches the ball while airborne and lands

(a) with both feet in the backcourt.

(b) straddling the centre line.

(c) straddling the centre line and then dribbles or passes the ball to the backcourt.

Interpretation: This is not a backcourt violation by A2. A2 established the first team A control of the ball while airborne and may land anywhere on the court. In all cases, A2 is legally in the backcourt.

30-4 **Example:** Thrower-in A1 in the frontcourt passes the ball to A2. A2 jumps from the frontcourt, catches the ball while airborne and lands

(a) with both feet in the backcourt.

第 30 条　球回后场

30-1　陈述　一名腾空的队员保持着与其离地前最后触及的比赛场地相同的状况。

当一名队员从其前场跳起，并仍在空中时获得了一个新的球队控制球时，该队员可以持球落在比赛场地上的任何地点。但该队员在落地前不可以将球传给位于其后场的同队队员。

30-2　举例　A1 在其后场将球传向位于其前场的 A2。B1 从其前场跳起，在空中拿球随后落回地面时：

（a）双脚位于其后场。

（b）骑跨中线。

（c）骑跨中线，随后运球或者传球到其后场。

解释　这不是 B 队的球回后场违例。B1 在空中时建立了一个新的 B 队控制球并可以落在比赛场地上的任何地点。上述所有情况下，B1 在其后场都是合法的。

30-3　举例　在 A1 和 B1 的开场跳球中，球被合法拍击。A2 从其前场跳起，在空中拿球随后落回地面时：

（a）双脚位于其后场。

（b）骑跨中线。

（c）骑跨中线，随后运球或者传球到其后场。

解释　这不是 A2 的球回后场违例。A2 在空中时建立了 A 队的首次控制球并可以落在比赛场地上的任何位置。上述所有情况下，A2 在其后场都是合法的。

30-4　举例　掷球入界队员 A1 在其前场将球传向 A2。A2 从其前场跳起，在空中拿球随后落回地面时：

（a）双脚位于其后场。

(b) straddling the centre line.

(c) straddling the centre line and then dribbles or passes the ball to the backcourt.

Interpretation: This is a backcourt violation by team A. Thrower-in A1 established team A control of the ball in the frontcourt before A2 caught the ball while airborne and landed in the backcourt.

30-5 **Example:** Thrower-in A1 in the backcourt passes the ball to A2. B1 jumps from the frontcourt and catches the ball while airborne. Before landing in the backcourt, B1 passes the ball to B2 in the backcourt.

Interpretation: This is a backcourt violation by team B. When B1 jumps from the frontcourt and gains a new team control while airborne B1 may land anywhere on the court. However, B1 may not pass the ball to a team-mate in the backcourt.

30-6 **Example:** During the opening jump ball between A1 and B1, the ball is legally tapped to A2 in the frontcourt. A2 jumps, catches the ball while airborne and before landing passes the ball to A1 in the backcourt.

Interpretation: This is a backcourt violation by team A. While airborne, A2 may land with the ball in the hands in the backcourt but A2 may not pass the ball to a team-mate in the backcourt.

30-7 **Statement:** A live ball is illegally returned to the backcourt when a team A player who is completely in the frontcourt causes the ball to touch the backcourt, after which a team A player is the first to touch the ball either in the frontcourt or the backcourt. However, it is legal when a team A player in the backcourt causes the ball to touch the frontcourt, after which a team A player is the first to touch the ball, either in the frontcourt or in the backcourt.

30-8 **Example:** A1 and A2 are both standing with both feet in their frontcourt close to the centre line. A1 bounce-passes the ball to A2. During the pass, the ball touches the team A backcourt, after which the ball touches A2 in the frontcourt.

Interpretation: This is a backcourt violation by team A.

（b）骑跨中线。

（c）骑跨中线，随后运球或者传球到其后场。

解释 这是A队的球回后场违例。A2在空中拿球并落回其后场之前，掷球入界队员A1已在其前场建立了A队控制球。

30-5 **举例** 掷球入界队员A1在其后场将球传向A2。B1从其前场跳起并在空中拿球，随后B1在落回其后场之前将球传给位于其后场的B2。

解释 这是B队的球回后场违例。B1从其前场跳起在空中时获得了一个新的球队控制球，B1可以落在比赛场地上的任何地点。然而，B1不可以传球给位于其后场的同队队员。

30-6 **举例** 在A1和B1的开场跳球中，球被A2合法拍到其前场。A2跳起在空中拿球，并在落回比赛场地前传球给位于其后场的A1。

解释 这是A队的球回后场违例。A2在空中时可以双手持球落回其后场，但A2不可以传球给位于其后场的同队队员。

30-7 **陈述** 当一名完全位于其前场的A队队员使球触及后场，之后任一A队队员在前场或者后场首先触及球时，该活球已非法回到后场。然而，一名在其后场的A队队员使球触及前场，之后任一A队队员在前场或者后场首先触及球，则是合法的。

30-8 **举例** A1和A2正双脚站在其前场靠近中线处。A1击地传球给A2。传球过程中，球触及了A队的后场，随后球触及到位于前场的A2。

解释 这是A队的球回后场违例。

30-9 **Example:** A1 standing with both feet in the backcourt close to the centre line bounce-passes the ball to A2 who is also standing with both feet in the backcourt close to the centre line. During the pass, the ball touches the team A frontcourt before A2 touches it.

Interpretation: This is not a backcourt violation by team A as no team A player with the ball was in the frontcourt. However, the 8-second period shall be stopped when the ball touched the team A frontcourt. A new 8-second period shall start as soon as A2 touches the ball in the backcourt.

30-10 **Example:** A1 in the backcourt passes the ball towards the frontcourt. The ball touches a referee standing on the court straddling the centre line. A2 still in the backcourt touches the ball.

Interpretation: This is not a backcourt violation by team A as no team A player had control of the ball in the frontcourt. However, the 8-second period shall be stopped when the ball touched the referee straddling the centre line. A new 8-second period shall start as soon as A2 touches the ball in the backcourt.

30-11 **Example:** Team A is in control of the ball in its frontcourt when the ball is simultaneously touched by A1 and B1. The ball then goes into the team A backcourt where A2 is the first to touch it.

Interpretation: This is a backcourt violation by team A.

30-12 **Example:** A1 dribbles from the backcourt to the frontcourt. A1 with both feet in the frontcourt still dribbles in the backcourt. The ball then touches A1's leg and bounces into the backcourt where A2 starts a dribble.

Interpretation: This is a legal play by team A. A1 has not yet established control of the ball in the frontcourt.

30-13 **Example:** A1 in the backcourt passes the ball to A2 in the frontcourt. A2 touches but does not control the ball, which returns to A1 still in the backcourt.

Interpretation: This is a legal play by team A. A2 has not yet established control of the ball in the frontcourt.

30-9 **举例** 正双脚站在其后场靠近中线处的 A1 击地传球给同样是双脚站在其后场靠近中线处的 A2。传球过程中，在 A2 触及球之前，球先触及了 A 队的前场。

解释 这不是 A 队的球回后场违例，因为 A 队的前场没有持球的 A 队队员。然而，当球触及 A 队的前场时，8 秒周期应停止计算。随后当 A2 在其后场触及球时，应开始计算一个新的 8 秒周期。

30-10 **举例** A1 在其后场向其前场传球。球触及了位于比赛场地内骑跨中线的裁判员。随后，位于其后场的 A2 触及球。

解释 这不是 A 队的球回后场违例，因为 A 队队员未在其前场控制过球。然而，当球触及骑跨中线的裁判员时，8 秒周期应停止计算。随后当 A2 在其后场触及球时，应开始计算一个新的 8 秒周期。

30-11 **举例** A 队在其前场控制球时，球被 A1 和 B1 同时触及。随后球回到 A 队的后场，被位于其后场的 A2 首先触及。

解释 这是 A 队的球回后场违例。

30-12 **举例** A1 从其后场运球至其前场的过程中双脚位于其前场但仍将球运在其后场。随后球触及了 A1 的腿后被反弹至 A1 的后场，在其后场的 A2 开始一次运球。

解释 A 队的比赛情况合法。A1 还没有在其前场建立控制球。

30-13 **举例** A1 在其后场传球给位于其前场的 A2。A2 触及了球但没有控制球，球随后回到了位于其后场的 A1 手中。

解释 这是 A 队的合法比赛。A2 还没有在其前场建立控制球。

30-14 **Example:** Thrower-in A1 in the frontcourt passes the ball to A2. A2 jumps from the frontcourt, catches the ball while airborne and lands on the court with the left foot in the frontcourt and with the right foot still in the air. A2 then puts the right foot into the backcourt.

Interpretation: This is a backcourt violation by team A. Thrower-in A1 had already established team A control in the frontcourt.

30-15 **Example:** A1 dribbles in the frontcourt close to the centre line when B1 taps the ball into the team A backcourt. A1 with both feet still in the frontcourt continues to dribble in the backcourt.

Interpretation: This is a legal play by team A. A1 was not the last player touching the ball in the frontcourt. A1 could even continue to dribble completely into the backcourt with a new 8-second period.

30-16 **Example:** A1 in the backcourt passes the ball to A2. A2 jumps from the frontcourt, catches the ball while airborne and lands

(a) with both feet in the backcourt.

(b) touching the centre line.

(c) straddling the centre line.

Interpretation: In all cases, this is a backcourt violation by team A. A2 established team A control in its frontcourt while airborne.

30-14 举例 掷球入界队员 A1 在其前场传球给 A2。A2 从其前场跳起并在空中拿球，然后，其左脚落回其前场时右脚仍在空中。最后，A2 右脚落回其后场。

解释 这是 A 队的球回后场违例。掷球入界队员 A1 已经在其前场建立了 A 队控制球。

30-15 举例 A1 在其前场靠近中线处运球时被 B1 将球拍至 A 队的后场。A1 的双脚仍然位于其前场但继续将球运在后场。

解释 A 队的比赛情况合法。A1 不是在其前场最后触及球的队员。A1 甚至可以完全回到其后场运球并获得一次新的 8 秒周期。

30-16 举例 A1 在其后场传球给 A2。A2 从其前场跳起并在空中拿球，落地时：

（a）双脚位于其后场。

（b）触及中线。

（c）骑跨中线。

解释 上述所有情况都是 A 队的球回后场违例。A2 在空中时已经建立了 A 队的前场控制球。

Article 31 Goaltending and Interference

31-1 **Statement:** When the ball is above the ring during a shot for a goal or a free-throw attempt, it is interference if a player reaches through the basket from below and touches the ball.

31-2 **Example:** During A1's last free throw

(a) before the ball touches the ring,

(b) after the ball touches the ring and still has the chance to enter the basket,

B1 reaches through the basket from below and touches the ball.

Interpretation: In both cases, this is an interference violation by B1. A1 shall be awarded 1 point.

(a) B1 shall be charged with a technical foul.

(b) B1 shall not be charged with a technical foul.

31-3 **Statement:** When the ball is above the ring during a pass or after it touches the ring, it is an interference if a player reaches through the basket from below and touches the ball.

31-4 **Example:** A1 on the court passes the ball above the ring when B1 reaches through the basket from below and touches the ball.

Interpretation: This is an interference violation by B1. A1 shall be awarded 2 or 3 points.

31-5 **Statement:** The ball touches the ring on a last unsuccessful free throw. If the ball is then legally touched by any player before it enters the basket, the free-throw becomes a 2-point goal.

31-6 **Example:** After A1's last free throw, the ball rebounds from the ring. B1 tries to tap the ball away but the ball enters the basket.

Interpretation: This is a legal play by B1 tapping the ball in the own basket. The team A captain on the court shall be awarded 2 points.

第 31 条　干涉得分和干扰得分

31-1　陈述　在一次投篮或罚球尝试中，当球在篮圈上方时，如果一名队员从下方伸手穿过球篮并触及球，这是干扰得分。

31-2　举例　在 A1 的最后一次罚球中：

（a）在球触及篮圈之前，

（b）在球触及篮圈后并仍然有机会进入球篮时，

B1 从下方伸手穿过球篮并触及球。

解释　在这两种情况下，B1 都发生了干扰得分违例。应判给 A1 得 1 分。

（a）应判 B1 一起技术犯规。

（b）不应判 B1 技术犯规。

31-3　陈述　在一次传球或球触及篮圈后，当球在篮圈上方时，如果一名队员从下方伸手穿过球篮并触及球，这是干扰得分。

31-4　举例　A1 在比赛场地上的传球在篮圈上方时，B1 从下方伸手穿过球篮并触及球。

解释　这是 B1 的干扰得分违例。应判给 A1 得 2 分或者 3 分。

31-5　陈述　在最后一次罚球中，球触及篮圈但未中篮。然后，如果球在进入球篮前被任一队员合法触及，该罚球就变为一次 2 分中篮。

31-6　举例　在 A1 的最后一次罚球后，球触及篮圈并弹起。B1 试图将球拍离，但球随即进入球篮。

解释　这起比赛情况中，B1 将球拍入本方球篮合法。应判给 A 队场上队长得 2 分。

31-7 **Statement:** After the ball touches the ring

- on a goal attempt,
- on a last unsuccessful free throw,
- after the game clock signal sounds for the end of the quarter or overtime

and the ball still has the chance to enter the basket, a foul is called. It is a violation if any player then touches the ball.

31-8 **Example:** After A1's last free throw, the ball rebounds from the ring. During the rebound, B2 fouls A2. This is the third team B foul in the quarter. The ball still has the chance to enter the basket and is touched by

(a) A3.

(b) B3.

Interpretation: In both cases, this is an interference violation by A3 or B3.

(a) No point shall be awarded. Both throw-in penalties shall cancel each other. The game shall be resumed with an alternating possession throw-in from behind the endline nearest to where the foul occurred, except from directly behind the backboard.

(b) A1 shall be awarded 1 point. As a result of B2's foul, the game shall be resumed with a team A throw-in from behind team B's endline nearest to where the foul occurred, except from directly behind the backboard.

31-9 **Example:** After A1's last free throw, the ball rebounds from the ring. During the rebound, B2 fouls A2. This is the fifth team B foul in the quarter. The ball still has the chance to enter the basket and is touched by

(a) A3.

(b) B3.

Interpretation: In both cases, this is an interference violation by A3 or B3.

31-7 **陈述** 在下列情况中：

- 一次投篮尝试，
- 最后一次罚球未中篮，
- 结束一节或决胜期的比赛计时钟信号响后，

球触及篮圈后，并且球仍然有机会进入球篮时判了一起犯规。随后如果有任一队员触及球，则是一起违例。

31-8 **举例** A1 的最后一次罚球后，球触及篮圈并弹起。在抢篮板球中，B2 对 A2 犯规。这是该节 B 队的第 3 次全队犯规。球在仍然有机会进入球篮时，被下述队员触及。

（a）A3。

（b）B3。

解释 在这两种情况下，A3 或 B3 发生了一起干扰得分违例。

（a）不应判给得分。两个掷球入界的罚则应相互抵消。应由拥有下一次交替拥有掷球入界权的球队在端线后最靠近发生犯规的地点执行掷球入界继续比赛，篮板正后方除外。

（b）应判给 A1 得 1 分。作为 B2 犯规的结果，应由 A 队在 B 队的端线后最靠近发生犯规的地点执行掷球入界继续比赛，篮板正后方除外。

31-9 **举例** A1 的最后一次罚球后，球触及篮圈并弹起。在抢篮板球中，B2 对 A2 犯规。这是该节 B 队的第 5 次全队犯规。球在仍然有机会进入球篮时，被下述队员触及。

（a）A3。

（b）B3。

解释 在这两种情况下，A3 或 B3 发生了一起干扰得分违例。

(a) No point shall be awarded.

(b) A1 shall be awarded 1 point.

In both cases, as a result of B2's foul, A2 shall attempt 2 free throws. The game shall continue as after any last free throw.

31-10 **Example:** After A1's last free throw, the ball rebounds from the ring. During the rebound, A2 fouls B2. This is the fifth team A foul in the quarter. The ball still has the chance to enter the basket and is touched by

(a) A3.

(b) B3.

Interpretation: In both cases, this is an interference violation by A3 or B3.

(a) No point shall be awarded.

(b) A1 shall be awarded 1 point.

In both cases, as a result of A2's foul, B2 shall attempt 2 free throws. The game shall continue as after any last free throw.

31-11 **Example:** After A1's last free throw, the ball rebounds from the ring. During the rebound, a double foul between B2 and A2 occurs. The ball still has the chance to enter the basket and is touched by

(a) A3.

(b) B3.

Interpretation: In both cases, this is an interference violation by A3 or B3. The foul shall be entered on the scoresheet against each offender.

(a) No point shall be awarded. The game shall be resumed with an alternating possession throw-in from behind the endline nearest to where the double foul occurred, except from directly behind the backboard.

（a）不应判给得分。

（b）应判给 A1 得 1 分。

在这两种情况下，作为 B2 犯规的结果，应由 A2 执行 2 次罚球。应如同任何最后一次罚球后那样继续比赛。

31-10 **举例** A1 的最后一次罚球后，球触及篮圈并弹起。在抢篮板球中，A2 对 B2 犯规。这是该节 A 队的第 5 次全队犯规。球在仍然有机会进入球篮时，被下述队员触及。

（a）A3。

（b）B3。

解释 在这两种情况下，A3 或 B3 发生了一起干扰得分违例。

（a）不应判给得分。

（b）应判给 A1 得 1 分。

在这两种情况下，作为 A2 犯规的结果，应由 B2 执行 2 次罚球。应如同任何最后一次罚球后那样继续比赛。

31-11 **举例** A1 的最后一次罚球后，球触及篮圈并弹起。在抢篮板球中，发生了 B2 和 A2 之间的双方犯规。球在仍然有机会进入球篮时，被下述队员触及。

（a）A3。

（b）B3。

解释 在这两种情况下，A3 或 B3 发生了一起干扰得分违例。应将该双方犯规登记在记录表上相关犯规队员的名下。

（a）不应判给得分。应由拥有下一次交替拥有掷球入界权的球队在端线后最靠近发生双方犯规的地点执行掷球入界继续比赛，篮板正后方除外。

(b) A1 shall be awarded 1 point. The game shall be resumed with a team B throw-in from any place behind its endline as after any successful last free throw.

31-12 **Example:** A1 attempts a shot for a goal. The ball rebounds from the ring and still has the chance to enter the basket when the game clock signal sounds for the end of the third quarter. The ball is then touched by

(a) A2. The ball enters the basket.

(b) B2. The ball enters the basket.

(c) A2. The ball does not enter the basket.

(d) B2. The ball does not enter the basket.

Interpretation: In all cases, this is an interference violation by A2 or B2. After the game clock signal sounds for the end of the quarter, no player shall touch the ball after it touches the ring and still has a chance to enter the basket.

(a) A1's goal shall not count.

(b) A1's goal shall count for 2 or 3 points.

(c) The quarter has ended.

(d) A1's goal shall count for 2 or 3 points.

In all cases, the third quarter has ended. The game shall be resumed with an alternating possession throw-in from the centre line extended.

31-13 **Statement:** If during a shot for a goal a player touches the ball on its flight to the basket, all restrictions related to goaltending and interference shall apply.

31-14 **Example:** A1 attempts a shot for a 2-point goal. The ball on its upward flight is touched by A2 or B2. On its downward flight to the basket the ball is touched by

(a) A3.

(b) B3.

（b）应判给 A1 得 1 分。如同任何成功的最后一次罚球后一样，应由 B 队在其端线后的任何地点执行掷球入界继续比赛。

31-12 举例 A1 尝试投篮。球从篮圈上弹起且仍然有机会进入球篮时，结束第 3 节的比赛计时钟信号响。随后球被：

（a）A2 触及，球进入球篮。

（b）B2 触及，球进入球篮。

（c）A2 触及，球未进入球篮。

（d）B2 触及，球未进入球篮。

解释 上述所有情况下，A2 或 B2 发生了一起干扰得分违例。在结束该节的比赛计时钟信号响后，不得有队员在球触及篮圈后并仍然有机会进入球篮时去触及球。

（a）A1 的中篮不应计得分。

（b）A1 的中篮应计 2 分或者 3 分。

（c）该节结束。

（d）A1 的中篮应计 2 分或者 3 分。

上述所有情况下，第 3 节已经结束。应在中线延长线处以交替拥有掷球入界继续比赛。

31-13 陈述 在一次投篮中，如果一名队员触及飞向球篮的球，涉及干涉得分和干扰得分的所有限制应适用。

31-14 举例 A1 尝试 2 分投篮。球在向上飞行时被 A2 或 B2 触及。在球下落飞向球篮时，被下述队员触及。

（a）A3。

（b）B3。

Interpretation: This is a legal play when A2 or B2 touch the ball on its upward flight. It is a goaltending violation when A3 or B3 touch the ball on its downward flight.

(a) Team B shall be awarded a throw-in from the free-throw line extended.

(b) A1 shall be awarded 2 points.

31-15 **Example:** The ball is in the air on A1's shot for a goal when B1 fouls A1. Then B2 legally touches the ball on its upward flight. The ball enters the basket.

Interpretation: The goal shall not count. After a referee blows the whistle, with B2's touch the ball becomes dead immediately.

31-16 **Example:** A1 attempts a shot for a goal. The ball is touched by A2 or B2 at its highest point, above the level of the ring.

Interpretation: This is a legal play by A2 or B2. The ball is illegally touched only after it has reached its highest point and started its downward flight.

31-17 **Statement:** It is an interference violation when a player causes the basket to vibrate or grasps the basket (ring and/or net) in such a way that it causes the ball to take an unnatural bounce or to change direction, thus the ball is prevented from entering the basket or is caused to enter the basket.

31-18 **Example:** A1 attempts a shot for a 3-point goal close to the end of the game. The ball is in the air when the game clock signal sounds for the end of the game. After the signal

(a) B1 causes the basket to vibrate in such a way that it causes the ball to take an unnatural bounce or to change direction, thus the ball is prevented from entering the basket.

(b) A2 causes the basket to vibrate in such a way that it causes the ball to change direction, thus the ball is caused to enter the basket.

Interpretation: Even after the game clock signal sounds for the end of the game, the ball remains live. This is an interference violation by

解释 这起比赛情况中，A2 或 B2 触及向上飞行的球合法。但 A3 或 B3 触及下落飞行的球则是一起干涉得分违例。

（a）应将球判给 B 队在罚球线延长线处执行掷球入界。

（b）应判给 A1 得 2 分。

31-15 **举例** A1 投篮离手的球在空中时，B1 对 A1 犯规。随后球在向上飞行时被 B2 合法触及。球进入球篮。

解释 中篮不应计得分。在裁判员鸣哨后，当球被 B2 触及时，球立即成为死球。

31-16 **举例** A1 尝试投篮。球在篮圈水平面以上位于最高点时被 A2 或 B2 触及。

解释 A2 或 B2 的比赛情况合法。只有在球已到达它的最高点并开始下落后被触及，才是非法的。

31-17 **陈述** 当一名队员使球篮颤动或者抓住球篮（篮圈和 / 或篮网）的行为造成了球被非自然地反弹或改变方向，并已阻碍了球进入球篮或已使球进入球篮时，一起干扰得分违例发生。

31-18 **举例** A1 在临近比赛结束时尝试 3 分投篮。球在空中时，结束比赛的计时钟信号响起。在信号之后，

（a）B1 使球篮颤动的行为造成了球被非自然地反弹或改变方向，并已阻碍了球进入球篮。

（b）A2 使球篮颤动的行为造成了球改变方向，并已使球进入球篮。

解释 即使是在结束比赛的计时钟信号响起后，球仍然是活球。这是：

(a) B1. A1 shall be awarded 3 points.

(b) A2. A1's goal shall not count.

31-19 **Statement:** It is an interference violation if a defensive or offensive player, during a shot for a goal, touches the basket (ring or net) or the backboard while the ball is in contact with the ring and still has a chance to enter the basket.

Diagram 3 Ball is in contact with the ring

31-20 **Example:** After A1's shot for a goal, the ball rebounds from the ring and then lands on the ring. B1 touches the basket or backboard while the ball is on the ring.

Interpretation: This is an interference violation by B1. The interference restrictions apply when the ball has still the chance to enter the basket.

31-21 **Example:** A1's shot for a goal is on its downward flight and completely above the level of the ring when the ball is simultaneously touched by A2 and B2. The ball then

(a) enters the basket.

(b) does not enter the basket.

Interpretation: This is a goaltending violation by A2 and B2. In both cases, no points shall be awarded. The game shall be resumed with an alternating possession throw-in.

31-22 **Statement:** It is an interference violation when a player grasps the basket (ring or net) to play the ball.

（a）B1 的干扰得分违例。应判给 A1 得 3 分。

（b）A2 的干扰得分违例。A1 的中篮不应计得分。

31-19 **陈述** 在一次投篮中，当球正触及篮圈并仍然有机会进入球篮时，如果一名防守队员或进攻队员触及球篮（篮圈或篮网）或篮板，该队员就发生了一起干扰得分违例。

图 3 球正触及篮圈

31-20 **举例** A1 投篮后，球从篮圈上弹起后又落在篮圈上。当球在篮圈上时，B1 触及球篮或者篮板。

解释 这是 B1 的干扰得分违例。只要球仍然有机会进入球篮，干扰得分的限制就适用。

31-21 **举例** A1 投篮，球在下落飞行并完全在篮圈水平面以上时被 A2 和 B2 同时触及。球随后：

（a）进入球篮。

（b）未进入球篮。

解释 这是 A2 和 B2 的干涉得分违例。在这两种情况下，都不应判给得分。应由交替拥有掷球入界继续比赛。

31-22 **陈述** 如果一名队员抓住球篮（篮圈或篮网）打球，这是一起干扰得分违例。

31-23 **Example:** A1 attempts a shot for a goal. The ball rebounds from the ring when

(a) A2 grasps the ring and taps the ball into the basket.

(b) A2 grasps the ring when the ball has the chance to enter the basket. The ball enters the basket.

(c) B2 grasps the ring and taps the ball away from the basket.

(d) B2 grasps the ring when the ball has still the chance to enter the basket. The ball does not enter the basket.

Interpretation: In all cases, this is an interference violation by A2 or B2.

(a) and (b) No points shall be awarded. The game shall be resumed with a team B throw-in from the free-throw line extended.

(c) and (d) A1 shall be awarded 2 or 3 points. The game shall be resumed with a team B throw-in from behind its endline as after any successful goal.

31-24 **Statement:** It is an interference violation if a defensive player touches the ball while the ball is within the basket.

Diagram 4 Ball is within the basket

31-25 **Example:** A1 attempts a shot for a 2-point goal. The ball turns around the ring with its slightest part within the basket when

(a) B1 touches the ball.

(b) A2 touches the ball.

31-23 举例 A1 尝试投篮。球从篮圈上弹起，此时：

（a）A2 抓住篮圈并将球拍入球篮。

（b）A2 在球有机会进入球篮时抓住篮圈。球进入球篮。

（c）B2 抓住篮圈并将球拍离球篮。

（d）B2 在球仍然有机会进入球篮时抓住篮圈。球未进入球篮。

解释 上述所有情况下，A2 或 B2 发生了一起干扰得分违例。

（a）和（b）不应判给得分。应由 B 队在罚球线延长线处执行掷球入界继续比赛。

（c）和（d）应判给 A1 得 2 分或 3 分。应由 B 队按任何中篮后在其端线后执行掷球入界那样继续比赛。

31-24 陈述 当球在球篮中时，如果一名防守队员触及球，是干扰得分违例。

图 4 球在球篮中

31-25 举例 A1 尝试 2 分投篮。当球在篮圈上滚动并有极少部分的球体在球篮中时：

（a）B1 触及了球。

（b）A2 触及了球。

Interpretation: The ball is within the basket when the slightest part of the ball is within and below the level of the ring.

(a) This is an interference violation by B1. A1 shall be awarded 2 points.

(b) This is a legal play by A2. An offensive player may touch the ball.

31-26 **Example:** A1 attempts a shot for a 2-point goal. The game clock signal sounds for the end of the quarter while the ball turns around the ring with its slightest part within the basket. After the game clock sounds

(a) A2

(b) B2

touches the ball.

Interpretation: This is an interference violation by

(a) A2. The goal, if made, shall not count.

(b) B2. A1 shall be awarded 2 points.

After the game clock signal sounds for the end of the quarter the ball becomes dead immediately when it is touched by a player from either team.

31-27 **Example:** A1 attempts a last free throw. The ball rebounds from the ring, touches the backboard and then turns around the ring with its slightest part within the basket. Then

(a) B2

(b) A2

touches the ball while still on the ring.

Interpretation:

(a) This is an interference violation by B2.

(b) This is a legal play by A2.

In both cases, A1 shall be awarded 1 point.

解释 当有极少部分的球体在球篮中并在篮圈水平面以下时，就是球在球篮中。

（a）这是 B1 的干扰得分违例。应判给 A1 得 2 分。

（b）A2 的比赛情况合法。进攻队员可以触及球。

31-26 **举例** A1 尝试 2 分投篮。当球在篮圈上滚动并有极少部分的球体在球篮中时，结束该节的比赛计时钟信号响。比赛计时钟信号响后：

（a）A2 触及了球。

（b）B2 触及了球。

解释 这是：

（a）A2 的干扰得分违例。如中篮不应计得分。

（b）B2 的干扰得分违例。应判给 A1 得 2 分。

在结束该节的比赛计时钟信号响后，当任一队的队员触及球时，球立即成为死球。

31-27 **举例** A1 尝试最后一次罚球。球从篮圈上弹起，触及了篮板之后在篮圈上滚动并有极少部分的球体在球篮中。随后，当球还在篮圈上时，被：

（a）B2 触及。

（b）A2 触及。

解释

（a）这是 B2 的干扰得分违例。

（b）A2 的比赛情况合法。

在这两种情况下，应判给 A1 得 1 分。

Article 33 Contact: General principles

33-1 **Statement:** The cylinder principle applies to all players, regardless of whether they are defensive or offensive players.

33-2 **Example:** A1 is in the air on the shot for a 3-point goal. A1 extends the leg which contacts the defensive player B1.

Interpretation: This is a foul by A1 for moving the leg outside the boundaries of the cylinder and contacting the defensive player B1.

33-3 **Statement:** The purpose of the no-charge semi-circle rule (Article 33.10) is to not reward a defensive player who takes a position under the own basket in an attempt to draw a charging foul against an offensive player who is in control of the ball and drives to the basket.

For the no-charge semi-circle rule the following criteria shall apply:

(a) The defensive player shall have one foot or both feet in contact with the semi-circle area (Diagram 5). The semi-circle line is part of tho semi-circle area.

(b) The offensive player shall drive to the basket over the semi-circle line and attempt a shot for a goal or a pass while airborne.

The no-charge semi-circle rule criteria shall not apply and any contact shall be judged according to the rules, e. g. cylinder principle, charge/ block principle:

(a) For all play situations outside the no-charge semi-circle area or for plays developing from the area between the semi-circle area and the endline.

(b) For all rebounding play situations when, after a shot, the ball rebounds and illegal contact occurs.

(c) For any illegal use of the hands, arms, legs or body by either the offensive or defensive player.

Diagram 5 Position of a player inside/outside the no-charge semi-circle area

第 33 条　身体接触：一般原则

33-1　陈述　圆柱体原则适用于所有的队员，无论是防守队员还是进攻队员。

33-2　举例　A1 在空中尝试 3 分投篮，然后 A1 伸腿去触及了防守队员 B1。

解释　A1 将腿伸出其圆柱体的界限并触及了防守队员 B1，这是 A1 的一起犯规。

33-3　陈述　无撞人半圆区规则（规则第 33.10 款）的目的，不是鼓励防守队员去占据其本方篮下的位置并以此试图让正控制球并突破上篮的进攻队员发生撞人犯规。

无撞人半圆区规则应适用于下列情况。

（a）防守队员单脚或双脚触及半圆区（图 5）。该半圆线是半圆区的一部分。

（b）进攻队员应突破上篮并腾空越过半圆区线，并且在空中尝试投篮或者传球。

无撞人半圆区规则不适用于下列情况，任何接触都应依据相关的规则来判定（例如：圆柱体原则，撞人 / 阻挡原则）。

（a）对所有无撞人半圆区外出现的比赛情况，或从半圆区和端线之间区域向半圆区内发展的比赛情况。

（b）对所有抢篮板球的比赛情况，也就是当投篮之后，球弹起后发生的非法接触情况。

（c）对任一进攻队员或防守队员非法用手、臂、腿或者身体的情况。

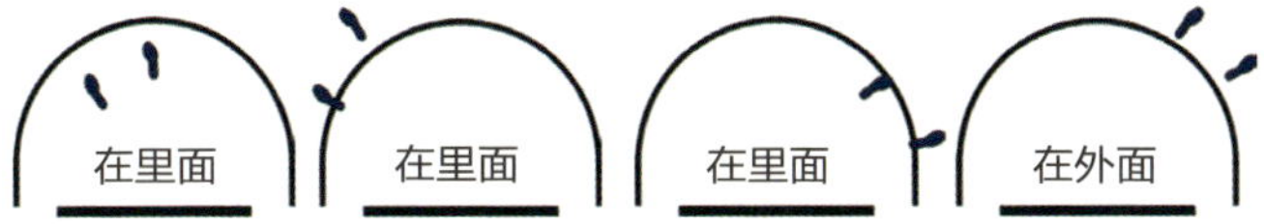

图 5　队员在无撞人半圆区（内 / 外）的位置

33-4 **Example:** A1 attempts a jump shot that starts from outside the semi-circle area. A1 charges into B1 who is in contact with the semi-circle area.

Interpretation: This is a legal play by A1. The no-charge semi-circle rule shall apply.

33-5 **Example:** A1 dribbles along the endline and, after reaching the area behind the backboard, jumps on the court towards the free-throw line. A1 charges into B1 who is in a legal guarding position in contact with the semi-circle area.

Interpretation: This is a team control foul by A1. The no-charge semi-circle rule shall not apply. A1 entered the no-charge semi-circle area from the court directly behind the backboard and its extended imaginary line.

33-6 **Example:** A1's shot for a goal rebounds from the ring. A2 jumps, catches the ball and then charges into B1 who is in a legal guarding position in contact with the semi-circle area.

Interpretation: This is a team control foul by A2. The no-charge semi-circle rule shall not apply.

33-7 **Example:** A1 drives to the basket in the act of shooting. Instead of ending the drive with a shot for a goal, A1 passes the ball to A2 who is directly following A1. A1 then charges into B1 who is in contact with the no-charge semi-circle area. At approximately the same time, A2 with the ball in the hands is on a direct drive to the basket in an attempt to score.

Interpretation: This is a team control foul by A1. The no-charge semi-circle rule shall not apply. A1 illegally uses the body to clear the way for A2 to the basket.

33-8 **Example:** A1 drives to the basket in the act of shooting. While A1 is airborne, instead of ending the drive with a shot for a goal, A1 passes the ball to A2 who is standing in the corner of the court. A1 then charges into B1 who is in contact with the no-charge semi-circle area.

Interpretation: This is a legal play by A1. The no-charge semi-circle rule shall apply.

33-4 **举例** A1 从半圆区外尝试跳投。A1 随后撞到了触及半圆区的 B1。

解释 A1 的比赛情况合法。无撞人半圆区规则应适用。

33-5 **举例** A1 沿着端线运球，并在到达篮板后方区域后在比赛场地上朝着罚球线的方向跳起并撞到了触及半圆区且处于合法防守位置的 B1。

解释 这是 A1 的控制球队犯规。无撞人半圆区规则不适用。A1 是从篮板正后方及其延伸假想线的比赛场地区域进入到无撞人半圆区域的。

33-6 **举例** A1 投篮，球从篮圈上弹起。A2 跳起拿球，并随即撞到了触及半圆区并处于合法防守位置的 B1。

解释 这是 A2 的控制球队犯规。无撞人半圆区规则不适用。

33-7 **举例** A1 突破上篮时做出投篮动作。A1 并没有以投篮来结束其突破，而是将球传给紧随其后的 A2。随后 A1 撞到了触及无撞人半圆区的 B1。几乎同时，A2 双手持球直接突破上篮尝试得分。

解释 这是 A1 的控制球队犯规。无撞人半圆区规则不适用。A1 非法用身体为 A2 清空了投篮路径。

33-8 **举例** A1 突破上篮时做出投篮动作。A1 在腾空时并没有以投篮来结束其突破，而是将球传给正站在比赛场地角落的 A2。随后 A1 撞到了触及无撞人半圆区的 B1。

解释 A1 的比赛情况合法。无撞人半圆区规则应适用。

33-9 **Example:** A1 drives to the basket in the act of shooting. A1 uses the arm to push away B1 who is in contact with the no-charge semi-circle area, before releasing the ball for a shot for goal.

Interpretation: This is a team control foul by A1. The no-charge semi-circle rule shall not apply as A1 illegally uses the arm.

33-10 **Example:** A1 attempts a jump shot that starts from outside the no-charge semi-circle area and contacts B1 who is in the air after jumping vertically from the semi-circle area.

Interpretation: This is a legal play by B1. The no-charge semi-circle rule shall not apply as B1 does not have one foot or both feet in contact with the semi-circle area when the contact with A1 occurs. Any contact shall be judged according to the rules.

33-11 **Statement:** A personal foul is a player's illegal contact with an opponent. The player causing the illegal contact with the opponent shall be penalised accordingly.

33-12 **Example:** A1 attempts a shot for a goal. B1 pushes team-mate B2 who then causes an illegal contact with A1 in the act of shooting. The ball enters the basket.

Interpretation: A1 shall be awarded 2 or 3 points. B2 has contacted A1 and shall be charged with the foul. A1 shall attempt 1 free throw. The game shall continue as after any last free throw.

33-13 **Example:** A1 attempts a shot for a goal. B2 pushes A2 who then causes an unnecessary contact with team-mate A1. The ball enters the basket. This is the third team B foul in the quarter.

Interpretation: A1 shall be awarded 2 or 3 points. Team A shall be awarded a throw-in from the place nearest to where B2's personal foul occurred.

33-9 **举例** A1 突破上篮时做出投篮动作。A1 在投篮的球离手之前，用手臂推开了触及无撞人半圆区的 B1。

解释 这是 A1 的控制球队犯规。无撞人半圆区规则不适用，因为 A1 非法使用了手臂。

33-10 **举例** A1 从无撞人半圆区外尝试跳投，并与在半圆区内垂直跳起的 B1 发生了接触。

解释 B1 的比赛情况合法。无撞人半圆区规则不适用。因为在与 A1 发生接触时，B1 没有以单脚或双脚触及半圆区。发生的任何接触应根据规则判定。

33-11 **陈述** 侵人犯规是一名队员与一名对方队员的非法身体接触。造成与对方队员非法身体接触的队员应受到相应的处罚。

33-12 **举例** A1 尝试投篮，B1 推同队队员 B2 并导致 B2 非法触及了正在做投篮动作的 A1，球进入球篮。

解释 应判给 A1 得 2 分或 3 分。B2 触及了 A1，应被判为犯规。应由 A1 执行 1 次罚球，应如同任何最后一次罚球后那样继续比赛。

33-13 **举例** A1 尝试投篮，B2 推 A2 并导致 A2 与其同队队员 A1 发生了不必要的接触，球进入球篮。这是该节 B 队的第 3 次全队犯规。

解释 应判给 A1 得 2 分或 3 分。应判给 A 队在最靠近 B2 发生侵人犯规的地点执行掷球入界。

Article 34 Personal foul

34-1 **Statement:** The game clock shows 2:00 or less in the fourth quarter or in each overtime and the ball is in the hands of the referee or at the disposal of the thrower-in. If at this time a defensive player illegally contacts an offensive player on the court, this is a throw-in foul unless the contact meets the criteria of an unsportsmanlike foul. The player who was fouled shall attempt 1 free throw with no line-up, regardless of the number of the team fouls in the fourth quarter. The game shall be resumed with a throw-in by the non-offending team from the place nearest to the infraction.

34-2 **Example:** With 1:31 on the game clock in the fourth quarter, before thrower-in A1 releases the ball, B2 illegally contacts A2 on the court. A throw-in foul is called against B2.

Interpretation: Regardless of the number of team B fouls in the fourth quarter, A2 shall attempt 1 free throw with no line-up. The game shall be resumed with a team A throw-in from the place nearest to where B2's foul occurred. If in the

(a) backcourt, team A shall have 24 seconds on the shot clock.

(b) frontcourt, team A shall have the time remaining if 14 seconds or more are shown on the shot clock and 14 seconds on the shot clock, if 13 seconds or less are shown on the shot clock.

34-3 **Example:** With 1:24 on the game clock in the fourth quarter, after B1's successful goal or free throw, thrower-in A1 has the ball in the hands behind the endline. Before A1 releases the ball, B2 illegally contacts A2 on the court. This is the fifth team B foul.

Interpretation: Unless B2's contact against A2 meets the criteria of an unsportsmanlike foul, it is a throw-in foul. Regardless of the number of team B fouls in the fourth quarter, A2 shall attempt 1 free throw with no line-up. The game shall be resumed with a team A throw-in from the place nearest to where B2's foul occurred except from directly behind the backboard. The team A thrower-in shall not have the right to move along the endline from the designated throw-in place or to pass the ball to a team-mate behind the endline before releasing the ball on to the court, as after a successful basket or last free throw.

第 34 条　侵人犯规

34-1　陈述　在第 4 节或每一决胜期比赛计时钟显示 2:00 或更少，并且球在裁判员手中，或掷球入界队员可处理球时。如果此时一名比赛场地上的防守队员非法触及了一名进攻队员，这是一起掷球入界时的犯规，除非该接触达到了一起违反体育运动精神的犯规的标准。无论违犯队在第 4 节的全队犯规是几次，应判给被犯规的队员执行 1 次不占位的罚球。应由非违犯队在最靠近犯规的地点执行掷球入界继续比赛。

34-2　举例　第 4 节，比赛计时钟显示 1:31 时，在掷球入界队员 A1 球离手之前，B2 在比赛场地上非法触及了 A2。B2 被判一起掷球入界时的犯规。

解释　无论 B 队在第 4 节的全队犯规是几次，A2 应执行 1 次不占位的罚球。应由 A 队在最靠近 B2 发生犯规的地点执行掷球入界继续比赛。如果该掷球入界的地点是在：

（a）后场，A 队应拥有 24 秒进攻时间。

（b）前场，如果进攻计时钟显示 14 秒或更多，则 A 队应拥有进攻计时钟显示的剩余时间；如果进攻计时钟显示 13 秒或更少，则 A 队应拥有 14 秒进攻时间。

34-3　举例　第 4 节，比赛计时钟显示 1:24 时，在 B1 中篮或罚球成功后，位于端线后的掷球入界队员 A1 双手持球。在 A1 球离手之前，B2 在比赛场地上非法触及了 A2。这是 B 队的第 5 次全队犯规。

解释　这是一起掷球入界时的犯规，除非 B2 对 A2 的接触达到了一起违反体育运动精神的犯规的标准。无论 B 队在第 4 节的全队犯规是几次，A2 应执行 1 次不占位的罚球。应由 A 队在最靠近 B2 发生犯规的地点执行掷球入界继续比赛，篮板正后方除外。如同任何中篮或最后一次罚球成功后那样，A 队的掷球入界队员在将球掷入比赛场地球离手前，无权从指定的掷球入界地点沿着端线移动或者在端线后将球传给同队队员。

34-4 **Example:** With 58 seconds on the game clock in the fourth quarter, before thrower-in A1 releases the ball, B2 illegally contacts A2 on the court.

Interpretation: Unless B2's contact against A2 meets the criteria of an unsportsmanlike foul, it is a throw-in foul. A2 shall be awarded 1 free throw with no line-up. The game shall be resumed with a team A throw-in from the place nearest to where B2's foul occurred.

34-5 **Example:** With 55 seconds on the game clock in the fourth quarter, before thrower-in A1 releases the ball, B2 contacts A2 on the court in a manner which meets the criteria of an unsportsmanlike foul. An unsportsmanlike foul is called against B2.

Interpretation: A2 shall attempt 2 free throws with no line-up. The game shall be resumed with a team A throw-in from the throw-in line in its frontcourt. Team A shall have 14 seconds on the shot clock.

34-6 **Example:** With 54 seconds on the game clock in the fourth quarter, before thrower-in A1 releases the ball, B2 illegally contacts A2 on the court. A throw-in foul is called against B2. A2 is then charged with a technical foul.

Interpretation: The game shall be resumed with 1 free throw for any team B player, followed by 1 free throw for A2 and a team A throw-in from the place nearest to where B2's foul occurred. If in the backcourt, team A shall have 24 seconds on the shot clock. If in the frontcourt, team A shall have 14 seconds on the shot clock, if 13 seconds or less are shown on the shot clock and the time remaining if 14 seconds or more are shown on the shot clock.

34-7 **Example:** With 53 seconds on the game clock in the fourth quarter, before thrower-in A1 releases the ball, A2 contacts B2 on the court. A team control foul is called against A2.

Interpretation: Team A did not gain an advantage by A2's team control foul. A2 shall be charged with a personal foul unless there is a contact which meets the criteria of an unsportsmanlike foul or a disqualifying foul. The game shall be resumed with a team B throw-in from the place nearest to where A2's foul occurred.

34-4 **举例** 第 4 节，比赛计时钟显示 58 秒时，在掷球入界队员 A1 球离手之前，B2 在比赛场地上非法触及了 A2。

解释 这是一起掷球入界时的犯规，除非 B2 对 A2 的接触达到了一起违反体育运动精神的犯规的标准。A2 应执行 1 次不占位的罚球。应由 A 队在最靠近 B2 发生犯规的地点执行掷球入界继续比赛。

34-5 **举例** 第 4 节，比赛计时钟显示 55 秒时，在掷球入界队员 A1 球离手之前，B2 在比赛场地上触及了 A2，该行为达到了一起违反体育运动精神的犯规的标准。B2 被判一起违反体育运动精神的犯规。

解释 A2 应执行 2 次不占位的罚球。应由 A 队在其前场的掷球入界线处执行掷球入界继续比赛。A 队应拥有 14 秒进攻时间。

34-6 **举例** 第 4 节，比赛计时钟显示 54 秒时，在掷球入界队员 A1 球离手之前，B2 在比赛场地上非法触及了 A2。B2 被判一起掷球入界时的犯规。随后 A2 被判一起技术犯规。

解释 应由 B 队任一队员执行 1 次罚球，随后应由 A2 执行 1 次罚球；应由 A 队在最靠近 B2 发生犯规的地点执行掷球入界继续比赛。如果在后场，A 队应拥有 24 秒进攻时间。在前场，如果进攻计时钟显示 13 秒或更少，则 A 队应拥有 14 秒进攻时间；如果进攻计时钟显示 14 秒或更多，则 A 队应拥有进攻计时钟显示的剩余时间。

34-7 **举例** 第 4 节，比赛计时钟显示 53 秒时，在掷球入界队员 A1 球离手之前，A2 在比赛场地上触及了 B2。宣判 A2 一起控制球队犯规。

解释 A 队并未因 A2 的控制球队犯规而获益。应判 A2 一起侵人犯规，除非该接触达到了一起违反体育运动精神的犯规或取消比赛资格的犯规的标准。应由 B 队在最靠近 A2 发生犯规的地点执行掷球入界继续比赛。

34-8 **Example:** With 51 seconds on the game clock in the fourth quarter and with the score A 83 – B 80, thrower-in A1 has the ball in the hands when B2 contacts A2 in a different area of the court from where the throw-in is administered. B2 is charged with a foul against A2.

Interpretation: Unless B2's contact against A2 meets the criteria of an unsportsmanlike foul, it is a throw-in foul. A2 shall attempt 1 free throw with no line-up. The game shall be resumed with a team A throw-in from the place nearest to where B2's foul occurred.

34-9 **Example:** With 48 seconds on the game clock in the fourth quarter and with the score A 83 – B 80, the ball has left thrower-in A1's hands when B2 contacts A2 in a different area of the court to where the throw-in is administered. B2 is charged with a foul on A2.

Interpretation: This is not a throw-in foul as the ball has already left the hands of the thrower-in A1. Unless B2's contact against A2 meets the criteria of an unsportsmanlike foul or a disqualifying foul, it is a personal foul and shall be penalised accordingly.

34-8 **举例** 第 4 节，比赛计时钟显示 51 秒时，比分 A83 – B80，掷球入界队员 A1 双手持球，B2 在比赛场地上和执行掷球入界地点不同的区域触及了 A2。B2 被判对 A2 犯规。

解释 这是一起掷球入界时的犯规，除非 B2 对 A2 的接触达到了一起违反体育运动精神的犯规的标准。A2 应执行 1 次不占位的罚球。应由 A 队在最靠近 B2 发生犯规的地点执行掷球入界继续比赛。

34-9 **举例** 第 4 节，比赛计时钟显示 48 秒时，比分 A83 – B80，球已离开掷球入界队员 A1 的手，B2 在比赛场地上和执行掷球入界地点不同的区域触及了 A2。B2 被判对 A2 犯规。

解释 这不是一起掷球入界时的犯规，因为球已离开掷球入界队员 A1 的手。这是一起侵人犯规并应执行相应的罚则，除非 B2 对 A2 的接触达到了一起违反体育运动精神的犯规或取消比赛资格的犯规的标准。

Article 35 Double foul

35-1 **Statement:** A foul may be a personal foul, an unsportsmanlike foul, a disqualifying foul or a technical foul. To be considered as a double foul, both fouls must be player's fouls between the same 2 opponents and must be in the same category, either both are personal fouls or both are any combination of the unsportsmanlike fouls and disqualifying fouls. No free throw shall be awarded irrespective of the team fouls of the teams. The double foul must involve physical contact, therefore the technical fouls are not a part of a double foul as they are non-contact fouls.

If both fouls, occurred at approximately the same time, are not of the same category (personal or unsportsmanlike/disqualifying), it is not a double foul. The penalties shall not cancel each other. The personal foul shall always be considered as having occurred first and the unsportsmanlike/disqualifying fouls as having occurred second.

35-2 **Example:** A1 dribbles when A2 and B2 are charged with technical fouls.

Interpretation: Technical fouls are not part of a double foul. The penalties shall cancel each other. The game shall be resumed with a team A throw-in from the place nearest to where the ball was located when the first technical foul occurred. Team A shall have the time remaining on the shot clock.

35-3 **Example:** Dribbler A1 and B1 foul each other at approximately the same time. This is the second team A foul and the fifth team B foul in the quarter.

Interpretation: Both fouls are of the same category (personal fouls), therefore it is a double foul. The different number of team fouls in the quarter is not relevant. The game shall be resumed with a team A throw-in from the place nearest to where the double foul occurred. Team A shall have the time remaining on the shot clock.

35-4 **Example:** A1, with the ball still in the hands in the act of shooting, and B1 foul each other (both personal fouls) at approximately the same time.

第 35 条 双方犯规

35-1 **陈述** 一起犯规可能是侵人犯规、违反体育运动精神的犯规、取消比赛资格的犯规或是技术犯规。要视为一起双方犯规，两起犯规必须是同样的两名互为对方的队员之间的犯规，还必须是相同种类的，要么两起都是侵人犯规，或者两起犯规是违反体育运动精神的犯规和取消比赛资格的犯规的任意组合。无论双方球队的全队犯规次数是多少，都不应判给罚球。双方犯规必须包含身体接触，因此，技术犯规不是双方犯规的一部分，因为它是非身体接触的犯规。

如果两起犯规几乎同时发生，但种类不同（侵人的或违反体育运动精神的 / 取消比赛资格的），这不是一起双方犯规。罚则不能相互抵消。侵人犯规应总是被视为发生在先的，而违反体育运动精神的 / 取消比赛资格的犯规应总是被视为发生在后的。

35-2 **举例** A1 运球时，A2 和 B2 被判了技术犯规。

解释 技术犯规不是双方犯规的一部分。这两起犯规的罚则应相互抵消。应由 A 队在最靠近发生第 1 起技术犯规时球所在位置的地点执行掷球入界继续比赛。A 队应拥有剩余的进攻时间。

35-3 **举例** 运球队员 A1 和 B1 几乎同时相互犯规。这是该节 A 队的第 2 次全队犯规，B 队的第 5 次全队犯规。

解释 两起犯规是相同种类的犯规（侵人犯规），因此这是一起双方犯规。与两队在该节中不同的全队犯规次数无关。应由 A 队在最靠近发生双方犯规的地点执行掷球入界继续比赛。A 队应拥有剩余的进攻时间。

35-4 **举例** A1 正在做投篮动作且球仍在手中时，A1 和 B1 几乎同时相互犯规（两起都是侵人犯规）。

Interpretation: Both fouls are of the same category therefore it is a double foul.

If A1's shot is successful, the goal shall not count. The game shall be resumed with a team A throw-in from the free-throw line extended.

If A1's shot is unsuccessful, the game shall be resumed with a team A throw-in from the place nearest to where the double foul occurred.

In both cases, team A shall have the time remaining on the shot clock.

35-5 **Example:** A1's shot for a goal is in the air when A1 and B1 foul each other (both personal fouls) at approximately the same time.

Interpretation: Both fouls are of the same category therefore it is a double foul.

If A1's shot is successful, the goal shall count. The game shall be resumed with a team B throw-in from behind its endline as after any successful goal.

If A1's shot is unsuccessful, this is a jump ball situation. The game shall be resumed with an alternating possession throw-in.

35-6 **Example:** Team A has 2 team fouls and team B has 3 team fouls in the quarter. Then

(a) while A2 dribbles, A1 and B1 are pushing each other at the post position.

(b) during a rebound, A1 and B1 are pushing each other.

(c) while A1 is receiving a pass from A2, A1 and B1 are pushing each other.

Interpretation: In all cases, this is a double foul. The game shall be resumed with

(a) and (c) a team A throw-in from the place nearest to where the double foul occurred.

(b) an alternating possession throw-in.

解释 两起犯规是相同种类的犯规，因此这是一起双方犯规。

如果 A1 投篮成功，不应计得分。应由 A 队在罚球线延长线处执行掷球入界继续比赛。

如果 A1 投篮未成功，应由 A 队在最靠近发生双方犯规的地点执行掷球入界继续比赛。

在这两种情况下，A 队应拥有剩余的进攻时间。

35-5 **举例** A1 投篮的球在空中时，A1 和 B1 几乎同时相互犯规（两起都是侵人犯规）。

解释 两起犯规是相同种类的犯规，因此这是一起双方犯规。

如果 A1 投篮成功，应计得分。应由 B 队按任何中篮后在其端线后执行掷球入界那样继续比赛。

如果 A1 投篮未成功，这是一次跳球情况。应由交替拥有掷球入界继续比赛。

35-6 **举例** 一节比赛中，A 队 2 次全队犯规，B 队 3 次全队犯规。然后：

（a）A2 运球时，A1 和 B1 在低位的攻防中相互推搡。

（b）在抢篮板球中，A1 和 B1 相互推搡。

（c）A1 在接 A2 的传球中，A1 和 B1 相互推搡。

解释 上述所有情况都是双方犯规。应按如下方式继续比赛。

（a）和（c） 由 A 队在最靠近发生双方犯规的地点执行掷球入界。

（b） 执行交替拥有掷球入界。

35-7 **Example:** B1 is charged with a personal foul for pushing dribbler A1. This is the third team B foul in the quarter. At approximately the same time, A1 is charged with an unsportsmanlike foul for hitting B1 with an elbow.

Interpretation: The two fouls are not of the same category (personal foul and unsportsmanlike foul), therefore it is not a double foul. The penalties shall not cancel each other. The personal foul shall always be considered as having occurred first. The throw-in penalty for team A shall be cancelled as there is a further foul penalty to be administered. B1 shall attempt 2 free throws with no line-up. The game shall be resumed with a team B throw-in from the throw-in line in its frontcourt. Team B shall have 14 seconds on the shot clock.

35-8 **Example:** B1 is charged with a personal foul for pushing dribbler A1. This is the fifth team B foul in the quarter. At approximately the same time, A1 is charged with an unsportsmanlike foul for hitting B1 with an elbow.

Interpretation: The 2 fouls are not of the same category (personal foul and unsportsmanlike foul), therefore it is not a double foul. The penalties shall not cancel each other. The personal foul shall always be considered as having occurred first. A1 shall attempt 2 free throws with no line-up. B1 shall attempt 2 free throws with no line-up. The game shall be resumed with a team B throw-in from the throw-in line in its frontcourt. Team B shall have 14 seconds on the shot clock.

35-9 **Example:** Dribbler A1 is charged with a team control personal foul against B1. This is the fifth team A foul in the quarter. At approximately the same time, B1 is charged with an unsportsmanlike foul for hitting A1 with an elbow.

Interpretation: The 2 fouls are not of the same category (personal foul and unsportsmanlike foul), therefore it is not a double foul. The penalties shall not cancel each other. The personal foul shall always be considered as having occurred first. The throw-in penalty for a team B possession shall be cancelled as there is a further foul penalty to be administered. A1 shall attempt 2 free throws with no line-up. The game shall be resumed with a team A throw-in from the throw-in line in its frontcourt. Team A shall have 14 seconds on the shot clock.

35-7 **举例** B1 因推运球队员 A1 被判侵人犯规。这是该节 B 队的第 3 次全队犯规。几乎同时，A1 肘击 B1 被判违反体育运动精神的犯规。

解释 两起犯规种类不同（侵人犯规和违反体育运动精神的犯规），因此这不是一起双方犯规。这两起犯规的罚则不应相互抵消。侵人犯规应总是被视为发生在先的。因有进一步的罚则要执行，A 队掷球入界的罚则应被取消。B1 应执行 2 次不占位的罚球。应由 B 队在其前场的掷球入界线处执行掷球入界继续比赛。B 队应拥有 14 秒进攻时间。

35-8 **举例** B1 因推运球队员 A1 被判侵人犯规。这是该节 B 队的第 5 次全队犯规。几乎同时，A1 肘击 B1 被判违反体育运动精神的犯规。

解释 两起犯规种类不同（侵人犯规和违反体育运动精神的犯规），因此这不是一起双方犯规。这两起犯规的罚则不应相互抵消。侵人犯规应总是被视为是发生在先的。A1 应执行 2 次不占位的罚球。B1 应执行 2 次不占位的罚球。应由 B 队在其前场的掷球入界线处执行掷球入界继续比赛。B 队应拥有 14 秒进攻时间。

35-9 **举例** 运球队员 A1 被判对 B1 发生一起控制球队的侵人犯规。这是该节 A 队的第 5 次全队犯规。几乎同时，B1 肘击 A1 被判一起违反体育运动精神的犯规。

解释 两起犯规种类不同（侵人犯规和违反体育运动精神的犯规），因此这不是一起双方犯规。这两起犯规的罚则不应相互抵消。侵人犯规应总是被视为发生在先的。因有进一步的罚则要执行，B 队掷球入界权的罚则应被取消。A1 应执行 2 次不占位的罚球。应由 A 队在其前场的掷球入界线处执行掷球入界继续比赛。A 队应拥有 14 秒进攻时间。

35-10 **Example:** A1 dribbles when at approximately the same time A1 and B1 foul each other.

(a) Both fouls are personal fouls.

(b) Both fouls are unsportsmanlike fouls.

(c) A1's foul is an unsportsmanlike foul and B1's foul is a disqualifying foul.

(d) A1's foul is a disqualifying foul and B1's foul is an unsportsmanlike foul.

Interpretation: In all cases, the 2 fouls are of the same category (personal fouls or unsportsmanlike/disqualifying fouls), therefore it is a double foul. The game shall be resumed with a team A throw-in from the place nearest to where the double foul occurred. Team A shall have the time remaining on the shot clock.

35-10 **举例** A1 运球时，A1 和 B1 几乎同时相互犯规。

（a）两起犯规都是侵人犯规。

（b）两起犯规都是违反体育运动精神的犯规。

（c）A1 的犯规是违反体育运动精神的犯规，B1 的犯规是取消比赛资格的犯规。

（d）A1 的犯规是取消比赛资格的犯规，B1 的犯规是违反体育运动精神的犯规。

解释 上述每个情况下的两起犯规种类都相同（侵人犯规或违反体育运动精神的 / 取消比赛资格的犯规），因此这是一起双方犯规。应由 A 队在最靠近发生双方犯规的地点执行掷球入界继续比赛。A 队应拥有剩余的进攻时间。

Article 36 Technical foul

36-1 **Statement:** A warning is given to a player for an action or behaviour which, if repeated, may lead to a technical foul. That warning shall also be communicated to the head coach of that team and shall apply to any member of that team for any similar actions for the remainder of the game. A warning shall be given only when the ball becomes dead and the game clock is stopped.

36-2 **Example:** A1 is given a warning for interfering with a throw-in or for any other action which, if repeated, may lead to a technical foul.

Interpretation: A1's warning shall also be communicated to the team A head coach and shall apply to all team A members for similar actions, for the remainder of the game.

36-3 **Statement:** While a player is in the act of shooting, opponents shall not be permitted to disconcert that player by actions such as placing hands close to the shooter's eyes, shouting loudly, stamping feet heavily or clapping hands close to the shooter. To do so may result in a technical foul if the shooter is disadvantaged by the action, or a warning may be given if the shooter is not disadvantaged.

36-4 **Example:** A1 is in the act of shooting for a goal with the ball still in the hands when B1 waves the hands in front of A1's eyes or distracts A1 by shouting loudly or stamping the feet heavily on the court. A1's shot for a goal is then

(a) successful.

(b) unsuccessful.

Interpretation:

(a) A1's goal shall count. B1 shall be given a warning, which shall also be communicated to the team B head coach. The game shall be resumed with a team B throw-in from behind its endline.

If any team B member had already been given a warning for similar behaviour, B1 shall be charged with a technical foul. Any team A player shall attempt 1 free throw with no line-up.

第 36 条　技术犯规

36-1　**陈述**　裁判员对某队员的某种动作或行为给予警告，如果该队员重复这种动作或行为，裁判员就可以宣判一起技术犯规。裁判员还应将该警告通知该队主教练，且该警告在剩下的比赛中对出现类似行为的该队任何成员均适用。警告应只在球成死球且比赛计时钟停止时给予。

36-2　**举例**　A1 因为干扰掷球入界，或因为做出了任何其他重复出现就会导致一起技术犯规的行为，已被给予一次警告。

解释　给予 A1 的警告也应通知 A 队主教练，且该警告在剩下的比赛中对出现类似行为的 A 队所有成员均适用。

36-3　**陈述**　当一名队员正在做投篮动作时，不允许对方队员用诸如将手贴近投篮队员的眼睛、大声叫喊、靠近投篮队员时用力跺脚或拍手等行为来妨碍投篮队员。如果投篮队员因此被置于不利，可导致一起技术犯规。如果投篮队员未因此被置于不利，可给予一次警告。

36-4　**举例**　A1 正在做投篮动作，且球仍在手中时，B1 将手放在 A1 眼前晃动，或大声喊叫或在比赛场地上用力跺脚来扰乱 A1。随后，A1 的投篮：

（a）成功。

（b）不成功。

解释

（a）A1 的中篮应记得分。应给予 B1 一次警告，还应通知 B 队主教练。应由 B 队在其端线后执行掷球入界继续比赛。

如果 B 队任一成员因为类似行为已经被给予一次警告，则应判 B1 一起技术犯规。应由 A 队任一队员执行 1 次不占位的罚球。

(b) B1 shall be charged with a technical foul. Any team A player shall attempt 1 free throw with no line-up. The game shall be resumed with a team A throw-in from the place nearest to where the ball was located when B1's technical foul occurred.

36-5 **Statement:** When the referees recognise that more than 5 players of the same team are on the court simultaneously while the game clock is running, at least 1 player must have re-entered or remained on the court illegally.

The error must be corrected immediately without placing the opponents at a disadvantage.

Whatever occurred during the period between the illegal participation and the game being stopped when the illegal participation is recognised shall remain valid.

At least 1 player shall be removed from the game and a technical foul shall be charged against the head coach of that team, entered as a 'B_1'. The head coach is responsible for ensuring that all the substitutions are applied correctly.

36-6 **Example:** With the game clock running, team A has 6 players on the court. When it is recognised

(a) team B (with 5 players)

(b) team A (with more than 5 players)

has control of the ball.

Interpretation:

The game shall be stopped immediately, unless team B is placed at a disadvantage. One team A player, as indicated by the head coach, shall be removed from the game. The team A head coach shall be charged with a technical foul, entered as a 'B_1' .

36-7 **Example:** With the game clock running, team A has 6 players on the court. This is recognised after

(a) A1 is charged with a team control foul.

（b）应判 B1 一起技术犯规。应由 A 队任一队员执行 1 次不占位的罚球。应由 A 队在最靠近 B1 发生技术犯规时球所在位置的地点执行掷球入界继续比赛。

36-5 陈述 比赛计时钟运行时，如果裁判员确认同一队同时有 5 名以上的队员在比赛场地上，至少一名队员必定是非法地重新进入或留在了比赛场地上。

只要不置对方于不利，该错误必须立即得以纠正。

从非法参赛至非法参赛被确认并停止比赛期间所发生的一切应保留有效。

至少一名队员应离开比赛场地，并应登记该队主教练一起技术犯规，登记为“B_1”。确保每一次替换被正确实施是主教练的责任。

36-6 举例 比赛计时钟运行时，A 队有 6 名队员在比赛场地上。在该情况被确认时：

（a）（有 5 名队员的）B 队在控制球。

（b）（有多于 5 名队员的）A 队在控制球。

解释 比赛应立即停止，除非 B 队将被置于不利。A 队主教练应指示一名 A 队队员离场。应登记 A 队主教练一起技术犯规，登记为“B_1”。

36-7 举例 比赛计时钟运行时，A 队有 6 名队员在比赛场地上。该情况在出现下列情况后被确认。

（a）A1 被判控制球队犯规。

(b) A1 scores a goal.

(c) B1 fouls A1 during an unsuccessful shot for a goal.

(d) team A's sixth player has left the court.

Interpretation:

In all cases, the team A head coach shall be charged with a technical foul, entered as a 'B_1' .

In (a), (b) and (c) one team A player, as indicated by the head coach, shall be removed from the game. Any team B player shall attempt 1 free throw with no line-up.

The game shall be resumed

(a) with a team B throw-in from the place nearest to A1's foul.

(b) with a team B throw-in from behind its endline as after any successful goal.

(c) with A1 attempting 2 or 3 free throws.

(d) from the place nearest to where the game was stopped. If neither team had control of the ball nor was entitled to the ball, a jump ball situation occurred.

36-8 **Statement:** After being charged with a fifth personal foul or technical foul or unsportsmanlike foul, a player becomes an excluded player and may sit on the team bench.

When the referees recognise that an excluded player is on the court while the game clock is running, that player must have remained or re-entered on the court illegally.

The error must be corrected immediately without placing the opponents at a disadvantage.

Whatever occurred during the period between the illegal participation and the game being stopped when the illegal participation is recognised shall remain valid.

（b）A1 中篮得分。

（c）A1 在投篮中被 B1 犯规，球未中篮。

（d）A 队的第 6 名队员已离开了比赛场地。

解释

上述所有情况都应登记A队主教练一起技术犯规，登记为“B_1”。

在（a）（b）和（c）中，A 队主教练应指示一名 A 队队员离场。应由 B 队任一队员执行 1 次不占位的罚球。

应按如下方式继续比赛。

（a）由 B 队在最靠近 A1 发生犯规的地点执行掷球入界。

（b）由 B 队在其端线后执行掷球入界，如同任何中篮后那样继续比赛。

（c）由 A1 执行 2 次或 3 次罚球。

（d）在最靠近比赛被停止的地点，如果既没有球队控制球，也没有球队拥有球权，一次跳球情况发生。

36-8 **陈述** 当队员在被登记了第 5 次侵人犯规、技术犯规或违反体育运动精神的犯规后，就成为一名出局的队员，该出局的队员可以坐在该队球队席上。

比赛计时钟运行时，当裁判员确认一名出局的队员在比赛场地上时，该出局的队员必定是非法地重新进入或留在了比赛场地上。

只要不置对方于不利，该错误必须立即得以纠正。

从非法参赛至非法参赛被确认并停止比赛期间所发生的一切应保留有效。

The excluded player shall be removed from the game and a technical foul shall be charged against the head coach of that team, entered as a 'B_1'. The head coach is responsible for ensuring that only eligible players are on the court during the game clock running periods of the game.

36-9 **Example:** With the game clock running, excluded player B1 is on the court. B1's illegal participation is recognised when the ball is

(a) live again while team A is in control of the ball.

(b) live again while team B is in control of the ball.

(c) dead again with B1 still being in the game.

Interpretation:

The game shall be stopped immediately, unless team A is placed in disadvantage. B1 shall be removed from the game. The team B head coach shall be charged with a technical foul, entered as a 'B_1' .

36-10 **Example:** With the game clock running, excluded player A1 is on the court. A1's illegal participation is recognised after

(a) A1 scores a goal.

(b) A1 fouls B1.

(c) B1 fouls dribbler A1. This is the fifth team B foul in the quarter.

Interpretation:

The game shall be stopped immediately. A1 shall be removed from the game. The team A head coach shall be charged with a technical foul, entered as a 'B_1'.

(a) A1's goal shall count.

(b) A1's foul is a player foul. It shall be entered on the scoresheet in the space after the fifth foul.

(c) A1's substitute shall attempt 2 free throws.

出局的队员应离开比赛场地，该队主教练应被判一起技术犯规，登记为“B_1”。主教练应确保在比赛计时钟运作时，只有有参赛资格的队员在比赛场地上。

36-9 **举例** 比赛计时钟运行时，出局的队员 B1 在比赛场地上。B1 的非法参赛被确认于:

（a）球再次成为活球，A 队控制球时。

（b）球再次成为活球，B 队控制球时。

（c）球再次成为死球，B1 仍在比赛时。

解释

比赛应立即停止，除非 A 队将被置于不利。B1 应离开比赛场地。应登记 B 队主教练一起技术犯规，登记为“B_1”。

36-10 **举例** 比赛计时钟运行时，出局的队员 A1 在比赛场地上。A1 的非法参赛在出现下列情况后被确认。

（a）A1 中篮得分。

（b）A1 对 B1 犯规。

（c）B1 对运球队员 A1 犯规，这是该节 B 队的第 5 次全队犯规。

解释

应立即停止比赛。A1 应离开比赛场地。应登记 A 队主教练一起技术犯规，登记为“B_1”。

（a）A1 的中篮应计得分。

（b）A1 的犯规是一起队员的犯规，应被登记在记录表上 A1 第 5 次犯规后的空白处。

（c）替换 A1 的队员应执行 2 次罚球。

36-11 **Example:** With 7 seconds on the game clock in the fourth quarter and with the score A 70 – B 70, A1 is charged with a fifth personal foul and becomes an excluded player. After the following time-out, team A gains control of the ball and A1 scores a goal. A1's illegal participation is now recognised with 1 second remaining on the game clock.

Interpretation: A1's goal shall count. The team A head coach shall be charged with a technical foul, entered as a 'B_1'. Any team B player shall attempt 1 free throw with no line-up. The game shall be resumed with a team B throw-in from behind its endline with 1 second remaining on the game clock.

36-12 **Statement:** Whenever a player fakes being fouled, the following procedure shall apply:

- Without stopping the game, the referee signals the fake by showing twice the 'lower-the-forearm' signal.
- When the game is stopped the next time for any reason, a warning shall be communicated to the player and the head coach of the team. Each team is entitled to 1 'fake being fouled' warning.
- When the next time any player of that team fakes being fouled, a technical foul shall be called. This also applies when the game was not stopped to communicate the earlier warning to any player or head coach of that team.
- When an excessive fake without any contact occurs, a technical foul may be called immediately without a warning being given.
- All faking to be fouled situations shall be addressed, regardless of whether fouls or violations are called or not in the same situation.
- A player may be charged with both a foul and a 'fake a foul warning' on any play, or the player who is fouled may also be charged with a 'fake a foul warning'.

36-13 **Example:** B1 defends dribbler A1. A1 pushes B1 and A1 makes a sudden move with the head trying to give an impression of being fouled by B1. The referee calls an offensive foul against A1.

36-11 **举例** 第 4 节，比赛计时钟显示 7 秒时， 比分 A70 – B70，A1 被登记了第 5 次犯规后成为一名出局的队员。在随后的暂停结束后，A 队获得控制球并由 A1 中篮得分。此时 A1 的非法参赛被确认，比赛计时钟还剩余 1 秒。

解释 A1 的中篮应计得分。应登记 A 队主教练一起技术犯规，登记为“B_1”。应由 B 队任一队员执行 1 次不占位的罚球。应由 B 队在其端线后执行掷球入界继续比赛，比赛计时钟剩余 1 秒。

36-12 **陈述** 当一名队员骗取犯规时，裁判员应执行如下程序。

- 在不停止比赛的情况下，裁判员做两次“下压前臂”的手势以示意骗取犯规。
- 当比赛因任何原因在下一次被停止时，裁判员应立即将该警告通知该队员和该队主教练。每队各有一次因“骗取犯规”而被警告的机会。
- 当下一次该队队员出现骗取犯规时，裁判员应宣判一起技术犯规。这同样适用于先前应对该队任一队员或主教练给予警告，却没有出现比赛停止的情况。
- 当出现没有发生身体接触的过分的骗取犯规时，裁判员不必警告便可以立即宣判一起技术犯规。
- 所有的骗取犯规情况都应被处理，无论在同一比赛情况中是否宣判了犯规或违例。
- 在任一比赛情况中，一名队员可能被登记一次犯规并被给予一次“骗取犯规警告”，或者，一名被犯规的队员可能同时被给予一次“骗取犯规警告”。

36-13 **举例** B1 防守运球队员 A1。A1 推 B1，并且 A1 突然甩头，试图制造出被 B1 犯规的假象。裁判员宣判了 A1 一起进攻犯规。

Interpretation: In addition to the offensive foul against A1, the referee shall charge A1 with a fake warning (if the team's first fake warning) or a technical foul (if the team's second fake warning).

36-14 **Example:** B1 defends dribbler A1. B1 pushes A1 and A1 makes a sudden move with the head trying to give an impression of being fouled by B1. The referee calls a defensive foul against B1.

Interpretation: In addition to the defensive foul against B1, the referee shall charge A1 with a fake warning (if the team's first fake warning) or a technical foul (if the team's second fake warning).

36-15 **Example:** B1 defends dribbler A1. A1 makes a sudden move with the head trying to give an impression of being fouled by B1. The referee shows twice the 'lower-the-forearm' signal. Later in the game, within the same game clock running period,

(a) A1 falls on the court trying to give an impression of being pushed by B1.

(b) B2 falls on the court trying to give an impression of being pushed by A2.

Interpretation:

(a) The referee already gave a warning to A1 for the first fake with the head, showing A1 twice the 'lower-the-forearm' signal. A1 shall be charged with a technical foul for the second fake by falling on the court, even though the game was not stopped to communicate the warning for A1's first fake to either A1 or to the team A head coach.

(b) The referee shall charge B2 with the first fake warning by showing B2 twice the 'lower-the-forearm' signal. The warning shall be communicated to B2 and the team B head coach, when the game clock shall be stopped the next time for any reason. As this is the first stoppage of the game after A1's fake, that warning shall also be communicated to the team A head coach.

解释 除了登记 A1 的进攻犯规之外，裁判员应给予 A1 一次骗取犯规警告（如果这是该队的第 1 次骗取犯规警告）或登记一次技术犯规（如果这是该队的第 2 次骗取犯规警告）。

36-14 **举例** B1 防守运球队员 A1。B1 推 A1，并且 A1 突然甩头，试图制造出被 B1 犯规的假象。裁判员宣判了 B1 一起防守犯规。

解释 除了登记 B1 的防守犯规之外，裁判员应给予 A1 一次骗取犯规警告（如果这是该队的第 1 次骗取犯规警告）或登记一次技术犯规（如果这是该队的第 2 次骗取犯规警告）。

36-15 **举例** B1 防守运球队员 A1。A1 突然甩头，试图制造出被 B1 犯规的假象。裁判员向 A1 做了两次“下压前臂”的手势。在之后同一个比赛计时钟运行的时段中，

（a）A1 跌倒在比赛场地上，试图制造出被 B1 推倒的假象。

（b）B2 跌倒在比赛场地上，试图制造出被 A2 推倒的假象。

解释

（a）裁判员已经向 A1 示意过两次“下压前臂”的手势对 A1 用甩头方式第一次骗取犯规给予过警告。即使没有出现比赛停止，使裁判员就 A1 的第一次骗取犯规对 A1 和 A 队主教练给予警告，也应对 A1 第 2 次假装跌倒在比赛场地上的行为宣判一起技术犯规。

（b）裁判员应向 B2 示意两次“下压前臂”的手势，对其给予第 1 次骗取犯规警告。当比赛计时钟因任何原因在下一次被停止时，应将该警告通知 B2 和 B 队主教练。因为这是 A1 骗取犯规后的首次比赛中断，所以也应将 A1 的警告通知 A 队主教练。

36-16 **Example:** B1 defends dribbler A1. B1 falls down trying to give an impression of being fouled by A1. At the same time, A1 makes a sudden move with the head trying to give an impression of being fouled by B1.

Interpretation: The referee charges both A1 and B1 with a fake warning (if the team's first fake warning) or a technical foul (if the team's second fake warning).

36-17 **Statement:** Serious injury may occur by excessive swinging of elbows, especially in the rebounding and closely guarded player situations. If such actions result in contact, then a personal foul, an unsportsmanlike foul or even a disqualifying foul may be called. If the actions do not result in contact, a technical foul may be called.

36-18 **Example:** A1 rebounds the ball and is immediately closely guarded by B1. Without contacting B1, A1 excessively swings the elbows to intimidate B1 or to clear enough space to pivot, pass or dribble.

Interpretation: A1's action does not conform to the spirit and intent of the rules. A1 may be charged with a technical foul.

36-19 **Statement:** A player who has committed 2 technical fouls or 2 unsportsmanlike fouls or 1 unsportsmanlike foul and 1 technical foul shall be game disqualified automatically.

A head coach who has committed 2 technical fouls ('C') because of the personal unsportsmanlike behaviour or 3 technical fouls, either all of them ('B') or one of them ('C') shall be game disqualified automatically.

When any persons are game disqualified, they shall leave the game immediately (taking no more than 30 seconds) and shall go to and remain in the team's dressing room for the duration of the game or shall leave the building.

36-20 **Example:** In the first half, A1 is charged with a first technical foul for hanging on the ring. In the second half, A1 is charged with a second technical foul for an unsportsmanlike behaviour.

36-16 **举例** B1 防守运球队员 A1。B1 倒地，试图制造出被 A1 犯规的假象。同时，A1 突然甩头，试图制造出被 B1 犯规的假象。

解释 裁判员应给予 A1 和 B1 各一次骗取犯规警告（如果这是该队的第 1 次骗取犯规警告）或登记一次技术犯规（如果这是该队的第 2 次骗取犯规警告）。

36-17 **陈述** 过分挥肘可能导致严重受伤，尤其在抢篮板球和严密防守队员的情况下。如果这样的动作造成接触，就可以宣判一起侵人犯规、违反体育运动精神的犯规，甚至是取消比赛资格的犯规。如果这样的动作没有造成接触，可以宣判一起技术犯规。

36-18 **举例** A1 在抢到篮板球后立即被 B1 严密防守。在没有触及 B1 的情况下，A1 过分挥肘以威胁 B1 或以此清理出足够的空间来旋转、传球或运球。

解释 A1 的动作不符合规则的精神和意图。可以宣判 A1 一起技术犯规。

36-19 **陈述** 一名队员已发生了 2 次技术犯规或 2 次违反体育运动精神的犯规，或一次技术犯规和一次违反体育运动精神的犯规时，应被自动取消本场比赛资格。

一名主教练因其自身违反体育运动精神的行为已发生了 2 次技术犯规（“C”），或已发生了 3 次技术犯规（3 次全部是“B”，或者其中一次是“C”）时，应被自动取消本场比赛资格。

任何被取消本场比赛资格的人员都应立即离开比赛（在 30 秒内）且应去该队的更衣室，并在比赛期间留在那里，或者应离开体育馆。

36-20 **举例** A1 在上半时因为悬挂在篮圈上被判第 1 起技术犯规，A1 在下半时又因为违反体育运动精神的行为被判第 2 起技术犯规。

Interpretation: A1 shall be game disqualified automatically. Only A1's second technical foul is to be penalised and no additional penalty for the disqualification shall be administered. The timer must notify a referee immediately when A1 is charged with 2 technical fouls and that A1 should be game disqualified automatically.

36-21 **Statement:** After being charged with a fifth personal foul, technical foul or unsportsmanlike foul, a player becomes an excluded player. After a fifth foul, any further technical fouls against the player shall be charged against that player's head coach, entered as a 'B_1'.

The excluded player is not a disqualified player and may stay in the team bench area.

36-22 **Example:** In the first quarter, B1 is charged with

(a) a technical foul.

(b) an unsportsmanlike foul.

In the fourth quarter, B1 is charged with a fifth foul. This is the second team B foul in the quarter. While going to the team bench, B1 is assessed a technical foul.

Interpretation: In both cases, B1 shall not be disqualified. With the fifth foul B1 becomes an excluded player. Any further technical fouls by B1 shall be charged against B1's head coach, entered as a 'B_1'. Any team A player shall attempt 1 free throw with no line-up. The game shall be resumed with a team A throw-in from the place nearest to where the ball was located when B1's last technical foul occurred.

36-23 **Example:** B1 fouls dribbler A1. This is B1's fifth personal foul and the second team B foul in the quarter. While going to the team bench, B1 is assessed a disqualifying foul.

解释 A1 应被自动取消本场比赛资格。应只处罚 A1 的第 2 起技术犯规，不再额外执行该取消比赛资格的罚则。当 A1 已被判 2 起技术犯规而应被自动取消本场比赛资格时，计时员必须立即通知裁判员。

36-21 **陈述** 当队员在被登记了第 5 次侵人犯规、技术犯规或违反体育运动精神的犯规后，就成为一名出局的队员。在其第 5 次犯规后，该队员再有任何的技术犯规都应登记在其主教练名下，登记为“B_1”。

该出局的队员不是一名被取消比赛资格的队员，可以留在其球队席区域内。

36-22 **举例** 第 1 节，B1 被登记了：

（a）一起技术犯规。

（b）一起违反体育运动精神的犯规。

第 4 节，B1 被登记了第 5 次犯规。这是该节 B 队的第 2 次全队犯规。B1 在回其球队席的途中被判了一起技术犯规。

解释 在这两种情况下，B1 不应被取消比赛资格。B1 在被登记第 5 次犯规时成为一名出局的队员。B1 再有任何的技术犯规应登记在 B1 的主教练名下并登记为“B_1”。应由 A 队任一队员执行 1 次不占位的罚球。应由 A 队在最靠近 B1 发生最后一次技术犯规时球所在位置的地点执行掷球入界继续比赛。

36-23 **举例** B1 对运球队员 A1 犯规，这是 B1 的第 5 次犯规，也是该节 B 队的第 2 次全队犯规。B1 在回其球队席的途中被判了一起取消比赛资格的犯规。

Interpretation: B1 is disqualified and shall go to the dressing room or if B1 so wishes, B1 shall leave the building. B1's disqualifying foul shall be entered on the scoresheet against B1 as a 'D' in the space after B1's fifth foul and against the team B head coach as a 'B_2'. Any team A player shall attempt 2 free throws with no line-up. The game shall be resumed with a team A throw-in from the throw-in line in its frontcourt. Team A shall have 14 seconds on the shot clock.

36-24 **Example:** B1 fouls dribbler A1. This is B1's fifth personal foul and the fifth team B foul in the quarter. While going to the team bench, B1 is assessed a disqualifying foul.

Interpretation: B1 is disqualified and shall go to the dressing room or if B1 so wishes, B1 shall leave the building. B1's disqualifying foul shall be entered on the scoresheet against B1 as a 'D' and against the team B head coach as a 'B_2'. A1 shall attempt 2 free throws with no line-up. Any team A player then shall attempt 2 free throws with no line up. The game shall be resumed with a team A throw-in from the throw-in line in its frontcourt. Team A shall have 14 seconds on the shot clock.

36-25 **Example:** In the first half, A1 is charged with a technical foul for delaying the game. In the second half, A1 is charged with a foul against B1 for a contact which meets the criteria of an unsportsmanlike foul.

Interpretation: The timer must notify a referee immediately when a player is charged with 1 technical foul and 1 unsportsmanlike foul and that A1 shall be game disqualified automatically. Only A1's unsportsmanlike foul is to be penalised and no additional penalty for A1's disqualification shall be administered. B1 shall attempt 2 free throws with no line-up. The game shall be resumed with a team B throw-in from the throw-in line in its frontcourt. Team B shall have 14 seconds on the shot clock.

36-26 **Example:** In the first half, A1 is charged with an unsportsmanlike foul for an unnecessary contact in stopping the progress of the offensive team in transition. In the second half, A2 dribbles in the backcourt when A1 is charged with a technical foul for faking being fouled away from the ball.

解释 B1 被取消比赛资格后应回到其球队更衣室，或者如果 B1 愿意的话，B1 应离开体育馆。B1 被取消比赛资格的犯规应被登记在记录表上 B1 名下，其第 5 次犯规后面的空间处，登记为“D”，并在 B 队主教练名下登记“B_2”。应由 A 队任一队员执行 2 次不占位的罚球。应由 A 队在其前场的掷球入界线处执行掷球入界继续比赛。A 队应拥有 14 秒进攻时间。

36-24 **举例** B1 对运球队员 A1 犯规，这是 B1 的第 5 次犯规，也是该节 B 队的第 5 次全队犯规。B1 在回其球队席的途中被判了一起取消比赛资格的犯规。

解释 B1 被取消比赛资格后应回到其球队更衣室，或者如果 B1 愿意的话，B1 应离开体育馆。B1 被取消比赛资格的犯规应被登记在记录表上 B1 名下，登记为“D”，并在 B 队主教练名下登记“B_2”。应由 A1 执行 2 次不占位的罚球。应由 A 队任一队员执行 2 次不占位的罚球。应由 A 队在其前场的掷球入界线处执行掷球入界继续比赛。A 队应拥有 14 秒进攻时间。

36-25 **举例** A1 在上半时因为延误比赛被判一起技术犯规，A1 在下半时又因为对 B1 的一次接触达到了标准而被判一起违反体育运动精神的犯规。

解释 当一名队员被判一起技术犯规和一起违反体育运动精神的犯规要自动被取消比赛资格时，计时员必须立即通知裁判员。A1 应被自动取消本场比赛资格。应只处罚 A1 的违反体育运动精神的犯规，不再额外执行该取消比赛资格的罚则。应由 B1 执行 2 次不占位的罚球。应由 B 队在其前场的掷球入界线处执行掷球入界继续比赛。B 队应拥有 14 秒进攻时间。

36-26 **举例** A1 在上半时因为采用不必要的身体接触阻止进攻队的攻防转换而被判一起违反体育运动精神的犯规。在下半时，A2 在其后场运球时，A1 又因为在无球情况下骗取犯规被判一起技术犯规。

Interpretation: The timer must notify a referee immediately when a player is charged with 1 unsportsmanlike foul and 1 technical foul and that A1 shall be game disqualified automatically. Only A1's technical foul is to be penalised and no additional penalty for A1's disqualification shall be administered. Any team B player shall attempt 1 free throw with no line-up. The game shall be resumed with a team A throw-in from the place nearest to where the ball was located when A1's technical foul was called. Team A shall have the time remaining on the shot clock.

36-27 **Statement:** A player head coach shall be game disqualified automatically when charged with the following fouls:

- 2 technical fouls as a player.
- 2 unsportsmanlike fouls as a player.
- 1 unsportsmanlike foul and 1 technical foul as a player.
- 1 technical foul as a head coach, entered as a 'C_1' and 1 unsportsmanlike foul or technical foul as a player.
- 1 technical foul as a head coach, entered as a 'B_1' or 'B_2', 1 technical foul as a head coach, entered as a 'C_1' and 1 unsportsmanlike foul or technical foul as a player.
- 2 technical fouls as a head coach, entered as a 'B_1' or 'B_2' and 1 unsportsmanlike foul or technical foul as a player.
- 2 technical fouls as a head coach, entered as a 'C_1'.
- 1 technical foul as a head coach, entered as a 'C_1' and 2 technical fouls as a head coach, entered as a 'B_1' or 'B_2'.
- 3 technical fouls as a head coach, entered as a 'B_1' or 'B_2'.

Whenever a player head coach is game disqualified automatically a 'GD' shall be entered in the scoresheet behind the foul which led to the automatic disqualification. The player designated as the new captain shall become the new player head coach.

解释 当一名队员被判一起违反体育运动精神的犯规和一起技术犯规要自动被取消比赛资格时，计时员必须立即通知裁判员。A1 应被自动取消本场比赛资格。应只处罚 A1 的技术犯规，不再额外执行该取消比赛资格的罚则。应由 B 队任一队员执行 1 次不占位的罚球。应由 A 队在最靠近 A1 宣判技术犯规时球所在位置的地点执行掷球入界继续比赛。A 队应拥有剩余的进攻时间。

36-27 陈述 当一名队员兼主教练被登记了如下犯规时，应被自动取消本场比赛资格。

- 作为队员时的 2 次技术犯规。
- 作为队员时的 2 次违反体育运动精神的犯规。
- 作为队员时的 1 次违反体育运动精神的犯规和 1 次技术犯规。
- 作为主教练时的 1 次技术犯规，登记为“C_1”，以及作为队员时的 1 次违反体育运动精神的犯规或技术犯规。
- 作为主教练时的 1 次技术犯规，登记为“B_1”或“B_2”，作为主教练时的 1 次技术犯规，登记为“C_1”，以及作为队员时的 1 次违反体育运动精神的犯规或技术犯规。
- 作为主教练时的 2 次技术犯规，登记为“B_1”或“B_2”，以及作为队员时的 1 次违反体育运动精神的犯规或技术犯规。
- 作为主教练时的 2 次技术犯规，登记为“C_1”。
- 作为主教练时的 1 次技术犯规，登记为“C_1”，以及作为主教练时的 2 次技术犯规，登记为“B_1”或“B_2”。
- 作为主教练时的 3 次技术犯规，登记为“B_1”或“B_2”。

当一名队员兼主教练被自动取消本场比赛资格时，应在记录表上导致其被自动取消比赛资格的那个犯规后登记一个“GD”。被指定为新队长的队员应成为新的队员兼主教练。

36-28 **Example:** In the first quarter, player head coach A1 is charged with a technical foul for faking a foul as a player. In the fourth quarter, A2 dribbles when player head coach A1 is charged with a technical foul for A1's personal unsportsmanlike behaviour as a head coach, entered as a 'C_1'.

Interpretation: Player head coach A1 shall be game disqualified automatically. Only A1's second technical foul is to be penalised and no additional penalty for A1's disqualification shall be administered. The timer must notify a referee immediately when player head coach A1 is charged with 1 technical foul as a player and then with 1 personal technical foul as a head coach and that A1 should be game disqualified automatically. Any team B player shall attempt 1 free throw with no line-up. The game shall be resumed with a team A throw-in from the place nearest to where the ball was located when A1's technical foul occurred. Team A shall have the time remaining on the shot clock.

36-29 **Example:** In the second quarter, player head coach A1 is charged with an unsportsmanlike foul against B1 as a player. In the third quarter, player head coach A1 is charged with a technical foul for an unsportsmanlike behaviour of the team's physiotherapist, entered as a 'B_1'. In the fourth quarter, A2 dribbles when A6 is charged with a technical foul. A6's technical foul shall be entered on player head coach A1 as a 'B_1'.

Interpretation: Player head coach A1 shall be game disqualified automatically. Only A1's second technical foul (for A6's technical foul) is to be penalised and no additional penalty for A1's disqualification shall be administered. The timer must notify a referee immediately when player head coach A1 is charged with 1 unsportsmanlike foul as a player and then charged with 2 technical fouls as head coach as a result of the behaviour of the team bench personnel. A1 shall be game disqualified automatically. Any team B player shall attempt 1 free throw with no line-up. The game shall be resumed with a team A throw-in from the place nearest to where the ball was located when A6's technical foul occurred. Team A shall have the time remaining on the shot clock.

36-28 **举例** 队员兼主教练 A1 在第 1 节作为队员时因骗取犯规被判一起技术犯规。第 4 节，A2 正在运球时，队员兼主教练 A1 作为主教练时因其自身违反体育运动精神的行为被判一起技术犯规，登记为“C_1”。

解释 队员兼主教练 A1 应被自动取消本场比赛资格。应只处罚其第 2 起技术犯规，不再额外执行该取消比赛资格的罚则。当队员兼主教练 A1 作为队员时被判 1 次技术犯规和之后作为主教练时被判 1 次自身的技术犯规而应被自动取消本场比赛资格时，计时员必须立即通知裁判员。应由 B 队任一队员执行 1 次不占位的罚球。应由 A 队在最靠近 A1 发生技术犯规时球所在位置的地点执行掷球入界继续比赛。A 队应拥有剩余的进攻时间。

36-29 **举例** 队员兼主教练 A1 在第 2 节作为队员时被判一起对 B1 的违反体育运动精神的犯规。第 3 节，队员兼主教练 A1 作为主教练时因该队理疗师违反体育运动精神的行为被判一起技术犯规，登记为“B_1”。第 4 节，A2 正在运球时，A6 被判一起技术犯规，A6 的技术犯规应被登记在队员兼主教练 A1 的名下，登记为“B_1”。

解释 队员兼主教练 A1 应被自动取消本场比赛资格。应只处罚其第 2 起技术犯规（因为 A6 的技术犯规），不再额外执行该取消比赛资格的罚则。当队员兼主教练 A1 作为队员时被判 1 次违反体育运动精神的犯规和之后作为主教练因其球队席人员的行为导致被登记 2 次技术犯规时，计时员必须立即通知裁判员。A1 应被自动取消本场比赛资格。应由 B 队任一队员执行 1 次不占位的罚球。应由 A 队在最靠近 A6 发生技术犯规时球所在位置的地点执行掷球入界继续比赛。A 队拥有剩余的进攻时间。

36-30 **Example:** In the second quarter, player head coach A1 is charged with a technical foul for A1's personal unsportsmanlike behaviour as a head coach, entered as a 'C_1'. In the fourth quarter, player head coach A1 is charged with an unsportsmanlike foul against B1 as a player.

Interpretation: Player head coach A1 shall be game disqualified automatically. Only A1's unsportsmanlike foul is to be penalised and no additional penalty for A1's disqualification shall be administered. The timer must notify a referee immediately when player head coach A1 is charged with 1 personal technical foul as a head coach and then with 1 unsportsmanlike foul as a player and that A1 should be game disqualified automatically. B1 shall attempt 2 free throws with no line-up. The game shall be resumed with a team B throw-in from the throw-in line in its frontcourt. Team B shall have 14 seconds on the shot clock.

36-31 **Example:** Player head coach A1 is a player when substitute A6 is charged with a technical foul.

Interpretation: The technical foul as a result of the unsportsmanlike behaviour of the persons permitted to sit on the team bench shall be charged against the player head coach, even if there is a first assistant coach entered on the scoresheet.

36-32 **Example:** During an interval of play

(a) substitute A6

(b) player head coach A1

(c) team A doctor

is charged with a technical foul.

Interpretation: The technical foul is charged against

(a) A6 as a player,

(b) A1 as a player,

(c) A1 as a player head coach,

even if there is a first assistant coach entered on the scoresheet.

36-30 **举例** 队员兼主教练 A1 在第 2 节作为主教练时因其自身违反体育运动精神的行为被登记了一起技术犯规，登记为“C_1”。第 4 节，队员兼主教练 A1 作为队员时被判一起对 B1 的违反体育运动精神的犯规。

解释 队员兼主教练 A1 应被自动取消本场比赛资格。应只处罚其违反体育运动精神的犯规，不再额外执行该取消比赛资格的罚则。当队员兼主教练 A1 作为主教练时被判 1 次自身的技术犯规和之后作为队员时被判 1 次违反体育运动精神的犯规而应被自动取消本场比赛资格时，计时员必须立即通知裁判员。应由 B1 执行 2 次不占位的罚球。应由 B 队在其前场的掷球入界线处执行掷球入界继续比赛。B 队应拥有 14 秒进攻时间。

36-31 **举例** 队员兼主教练 A1 作为队员时，替补队员 A6 被判一起技术犯规。

解释 该技术犯规是被允许坐在球队席上的人员违反体育运动精神的行为所致，即使记录表上填入了第一助理教练，也应将这起技术犯规登记在队员兼主教练的名下。

36-32 **举例** 在一次比赛休息期间：

（a）替补队员 A6

（b）队员兼主教练 A1

（c）A 队队医

被判一起技术犯规。

解释 即使记录表上填入了第一助理教练，也应将这起技术犯规登记在：

（a）作为队员的 A6 名下。

（b）作为队员的 A1 名下。

（c）作为队员兼主教练的 A1 名下。

36-33 **Example:** Player head coach A1 has committed 4 fouls as a player and 1 technical foul as a head coach.

Interpretation: Player head coach A1 shall not continue as a player as A1 has committed a total of 5 fouls as a player and as a head coach. A1 may continue as a head coach.

36-34 **Example:** Player head coach A1 has committed 1 technical foul as a player and 1 technical foul as a head coach.

Interpretation: Player head coach shall be game disqualified automatically (GD) for committing 2 personal technical fouls ('C').

36-35 **Statement:** With the game clock shows 2:00 or less in the fourth quarter and in each overtime, when the referee is required to place the ball at the disposal of the thrower-in and with a player defending the thrower-in, the following procedure shall apply:

- The referee shall use an 'illegal boundary line crossing' signal as a warning to the defensive player before the ball is at the disposal of the thrower-in.
- If the defensive player then moves any part of the body over the boundary line to interfere with the throw-in, a technical foul shall be called without further warning.

36-36 **Example:** With 1:08 on the game clock in the fourth quarter, A1 has the ball in the hands for a throw-in from behind the sideline in its

(a) frontcourt.

(b) backcourt.

The referee shows to B1 the 'illegal boundary line crossing' warning signal. B1 moves the hands over the boundary line to block A1's throw-in.

Interpretation: As the referee showed a warning signal to B1 before handing the ball to A1, B1 shall be charged with a technical foul for interfering with the throw-in. Any team A player shall attempt 1 free throw with no line-up. The game shall be resumed with a team A throw-in from the place nearest to where the ball was located when B1's technical foul occurred. Team A shall have on the shot clock

36-33 **举例** 队员兼主教练 A1 作为队员时发生了 4 次犯规，作为主教练时发生了 1 次技术犯规。

解释 队员兼主教练 A1 不应作为队员继续比赛，因为 A1 作为队员以及作为主教练时一共发生了 5 次犯规。A1 可以继续作为主教练比赛。

36-34 **举例** 队员兼主教练 A1 作为队员时发生了 1 次技术犯规，作为主教练时发生了 1 次技术犯规。

解释 因发生了 2 次自身的技术犯规（“C”），队员兼主教练应被自动取消本场比赛资格（GD）。

36-35 **陈述** 当第 4 节和每一决胜期比赛计时钟显示 2:00 或更少时，要求裁判员在将球置于掷球入界队员可处理，并且有一名队员正防守着该掷球入界队员的情况下，应执行下述程序。

- 在掷球入界队员可处理球之前，裁判员应对防守队员做出“非法越过界线”的手势作为警告。
- 在此之后，如果防守队员将其身体的任何部分移动越过界线以干扰掷球入界，应判一起技术犯规，不作进一步警告。

36-36 **举例** 第 4 节，比赛计时钟显示 1:08 时，A1 双手持球，在其:

（a）前场的边线后执行掷球入界。

（b）后场的边线后执行掷球入界。

裁判员对 B1 做出了“非法越过界线”的警告手势。B1 伸手越过界线去阻挡 A1 的掷球入界。

解释 由于裁判员在向 A1 递交球之前已经给予了 B1 警告，应对 B1 的干扰掷球入界宣判一起技术犯规。应由 A 队任一队员执行 1 次不占位的罚球。应由 A 队在最靠近 B1 发生技术犯规时球所在位置的地点执行掷球入界继续比赛。

(a) 14 seconds, if 13 seconds or less are shown on the shot clock and the time remaining if 14 seconds or more are shown on the shot clock.

(b) 24 seconds.

36-37 **Statement:** During the first 3 quarters and when the game clock shows more than 2:00 in the fourth quarter and in each overtime, a throw-in situation occurs. If a defensive player moves any part of the body over the boundary line to interfere with the throw-in, the following procedure shall apply:

- The referee shall interrupt the game immediately and use a verbal warning to the defensive player and that team's head coach. This warning shall apply to all players of that team for the remainder of the game.
- If a defensive player then again moves any part of the body over the boundary line to interfere with the throw-in, a technical foul shall be called without further warning.

36-38 **Example:** With 4:27 on the game clock in the second quarter, after B1's goal A1 has the ball in the hands for a throw-in from behind the endline. B1 moves the hands over the endline to block A1's throw-in.

Interpretation:

(a) If a team B player has interfered with a throw-in for the first time in the game, the referees shall interrupt the game immediately and shall use a verbal warning to B1 and the team B head coach. This warning shall apply to all team B players for the remainder of the game.

(b) If the referee has already given a verbal warning to any team B player for interfering with a throw-in, B1 shall be charged with a technical foul. Any team A player shall attempt 1 free throw with no line-up. The game shall be resumed with a team A throw-in from behind its endline. Team A shall have 24 seconds on the shot clock.

（a）如果进攻计时钟显示 13 秒或更少，则 A 队应拥有 14 秒进攻时间；如果进攻计时钟显示 14 秒或更多，则 A 队应拥有剩余的进攻时间。

（b）A 队应拥有 24 秒进攻时间。

36-37 **陈述** 在前 3 节比赛期间以及第 4 节和每一决胜期中的比赛计时钟显示多于 2:00 期间，发生了一起掷球入界的情况。如果一名防守队员将其身体的任何部分移动越过界线以干扰掷球入界，应执行下述程序。

- 裁判员应立即停止比赛，并对该防守队员和该队的主教练给予口头警告。该警告应适用于在剩余比赛中的所有该队队员。
- 如果一名防守队员再次将其身体的任何部分移动越过界线以干扰掷球入界，应判一起技术犯规，不作进一步警告。

36-38 **举例** 第 2 节，比赛计时钟显示 4:27 时，B1 中篮后，A1 在端线后双手持球执行掷球入界。B1 伸手越过端线去阻挡 A1 的掷球入界。

解释

（a）如果这是 B 队队员在本场比赛中第一次干扰掷球入界，裁判员应立即停止比赛，并对 B1 和 B 队的主教练给予口头警告。该警告应适用于在剩余比赛中的所有 B 队队员。

（b）如果裁判员在本场比赛中已经对任一 B 队队员因干扰掷球入界给予口头警告，应判 B1 一起技术犯规。应由 A 队任一队员执行 1 次不占位的罚球。应由 A 队在其端线后执行掷球入界继续比赛。A 队应拥有 24 秒进攻时间。

36-39 **Statement:** When a technical foul is called, the 1 free-throw penalty with no line-up shall be administered immediately. After the free throw the game shall be resumed from the place nearest to where the ball was located when the technical foul occurred.

36-40 **Example:** With 21 seconds on the shot clock, A1 dribbles in the backcourt when B1 is charged with a technical foul.

Interpretation: Any team A player shall attempt 1 free throw with no line-up. The game shall be resumed with a team A throw-in from the place nearest to where the ball was located when B1's technical foul occurred. Team A shall have a new 8-second period and 24 seconds on the shot clock.

36-41 **Example:** With 21 seconds on the shot clock, A1 dribbles in the backcourt when A2 is charged with a technical foul.

Interpretation: Any team B player shall attempt 1 free throw with no line-up. The game shall be resumed with a team A throw-in from the place nearest to where the ball was located when A2's technical foul occurred. Team A shall have 5 seconds to move the ball to the frontcourt. Team A shall have 21 seconds on the shot clock.

36-42 **Example:** B1 fouls A1 on an attempt for a 2-point goal. The ball does not enter the basket.

(a) Before A1's first of 2 free throws, A2 is charged with a technical foul.

(b) After A1's first of 2 free throws, A2 is charged with a technical foul.

Interpretation:

(a) Any team B player or substitute shall attempt 1 free throw with no line-up. A1 shall then attempt 2 free throws.

(b) Any team B player shall attempt 1 free throw with no line-up. A1 shall then attempt the second free throw.

In both cases, the game shall be resumed as after any last free throw.

36-39 陈述 宣判了一起技术犯规后，应立即执行其不占位的 1 次罚球罚则。罚球后，应在最靠近发生技术犯规时球所在位置的地点执行掷球入界继续比赛。

36-40 举例 进攻计时钟显示 21 秒，A1 在其后场运球时，B1 被判一起技术犯规。

解释 应由 A 队任一队员执行 1 次不占位的罚球。应由 A 队在最靠近 B1 发生技术犯规时球所在位置的地点执行掷球入界继续比赛。A 队应拥有一个新的 8 秒周期及 24 秒进攻时间。

36-41 举例 进攻计时钟显示 21 秒，A1 在其后场运球时，A2 被判一起技术犯规。

解释 应由 B 队任一队员执行 1 次不占位的罚球。应由 A 队在最靠近 A2 发生技术犯规时球所在位置的地点执行掷球入界继续比赛。A 队还有 5 秒使球进入其前场。A 队应拥有 21 秒进攻时间。

36-42 举例 B1 对 2 分试投的 A1 犯规。球未中篮。

（a）在 A1 执行其 2 次罚球中的第一次之前，A2 被判了一起技术犯规。

（b）在 A1 执行其 2 次罚球中的第一次之后，A2 被判了一起技术犯规。

解释

（a）应由 B 队任一队员或替补队员执行 1 次不占位的罚球。然后，应由 A1 执行 2 次罚球。

（b）应由 B 队任一队员执行 1 次不占位的罚球。然后，应由 A1 执行其第 2 次罚球。

在这两种情况下，应如同任何最后一次罚球后那样继续比赛。

36-43 **Example:** During a time-out, A2 is charged with a technical foul.

Interpretation: The time-out shall be completed. After the time-out, any team B player or substitute shall attempt 1 free throw with no line-up. The game shall be resumed from the place nearest to where the game was stopped before the time-out.

36-44 **Example:** A1's shot for a goal is in the air when a technical foul is called against

(a) B1 or team B doctor.

(b) A2 or team A doctor.

Interpretation:

(a) Any team A player shall attempt 1 free throw.

(b) Any team B player shall attempt 1 free throw.

If A1's shot had entered the basket, the goal shall count. The game shall be resumed with a team B throw-in from any place behind the endline.

If A1's shot did not enter the basket, the game shall be resumed with an alternating possession throw-in from the place nearest to where the ball was located when the technical foul occurred.

36-45 **Example:** A1 has the ball in the hands during an act of shooting when a technical foul is called against

(a) B1 or team B doctor.

(b) A2 or team A doctor.

Interpretation:

(a) Any team A player shall attempt 1 free throw. If A1's shot had entered the basket, the goal shall count. The game shall be resumed with a team B throw-in from any place behind the endline.

36-43 举例 一次暂停期间，A2 被判一起技术犯规。

解释 应等暂停结束。暂停结束后，应由 B 队任一队员或替补队员执行 1 次不占位的罚球。应在最靠近暂停前比赛被停止的地点继续比赛。

36-44 举例 A1 投篮离手的球在空中时，一起技术犯规判给了：

（a）B1 或 B 队队医。

（b）A2 或 A 队队医。

解释

（a）应由 A 队任一队员执行 1 次罚球。

（b）应由 B 队任一队员执行 1 次罚球。

如果 A1 投球中篮，应计得分。应由 B 队在其端线后任意地点执行掷球入界继续比赛。

如果 A1 投球未中篮，应在最靠近发生技术犯规时球所在位置的地点按照交替拥有掷球入界继续比赛。

36-45 举例 A1 双手持球做投篮动作的过程中，一起技术犯规判给了：

（a）B1 或 B 队队医。

（b）A2 或 A 队队医。

解释

（a）应由 A 队任一队员执行 1 次罚球。如果 A1 投球中篮，应计得分。应由 B 队在其端线后的任意地点执行掷球入界继续比赛。

(b) Any team B player shall attempt 1 free throw. If A1's shot had entered the basket, the goal shall not count. The game shall be resumed with a team A throw-in from the free-throw line extended.

In both cases, if A1's shot did not enter the basket, the game shall be resumed with a team A throw-in from the place nearest to where the ball was located when the technical foul occurred.

(b) 应由 B 队任一队员执行 1 次罚球。如果 A1 投球中篮，不应计得分。应由 A 队在罚球线延长线处执行掷球入界继续比赛。

在这两种情况下，如果 A1 投球未中篮，应由 A 队在最靠近发生技术犯规时球所在位置的地点执行掷球入界继续比赛。

Article 37 Unsportsmanlike foul

37-1 **Statement:** Any illegal contact by the player from behind or laterally against an opponent, who is progressing towards the opponents' basket and with no opponent players between the progressing player and the basket, shall be called as an unsportsmanlike foul until the offensive player starts the act of shooting. However, any contact not legitimately attempting to directly play the ball or an excessive, hard contact meeting the criteria of an unsportsmanlike foul may be called as an unsportsmanlike foul at any time of the game.

37-2 **Example:** A1 dribbles towards the basket on a fast break and there is no opponent player between A1 and the opponents' basket. B1 contacts A1 illegally from behind and a foul against B1 is called.

Interpretation: This is an unsportsmanlike foul by B1.

37-3 **Example:** Finishing a fast break and before A1 has the ball in the hands to start an act of shooting, B1 contacts A1's arm from behind

(a) trying to steal the ball.

(b) with a contact meeting the criteria of an unsportsmanlike foul.

Interpretation: In both cases, this is an unsportsmanlike foul by B1.

37-4 **Example:** Finishing a fast break, A1 has the ball in the hands in an act of shooting when B1 contacts A1's arm from behind

(a) trying to block the ball.

(b) with a contact meeting the criteria of an unsportsmanlike foul.

Interpretation:

(a) This is a personal foul by B1.

(b) This is an unsportsmanlike foul by B1.

37-5 **Example:** A1 passes the ball from the backcourt to A2 who is in the frontcourt progressing towards the opponents' basket with no team B player between A2 and the basket. A2 jumps in the air and before catching the ball, B1 fouls A2 from behind. A foul against B1 is called.

第 37 条　违反体育运动精神的犯规

37-1　**陈述**　当一名正朝向对方球篮行进的队员被对方队员从后面或侧面造成任何非法身体接触，且该行进队员和对方球篮之间没有对方队员，应判对方队员一起违反体育运动精神的犯规，该原则在进攻队员开始其投篮动作之前均适用。然而，在比赛的任何时间，任何不是合理篮球动作的接触，或达到违反体育运动精神的犯规标准的过分的、严重的身体接触，都可以被判为一起违反体育运动精神的犯规。

37-2　**举例**　A1 向球篮运球快攻，并且在 A1 和对方球篮之间没有对方队员。B1 从 A1 后面造成非法接触，B1 被判犯规。

解释　这是 B1 的一起违反体育运动精神的犯规。

37-3　**举例**　在即将完成快攻的 A1 双手持球开始做投篮动作之前，B1 从后面触及了 A1 的手臂：

（a）试图去断球。

（b）该接触已达到一起违反体育运动精神的犯规的标准。

解释　这两种情况都是一起 B1 的违反体育运动精神的犯规。

37-4　**举例**　在即将完成快攻的 A1 双手持球并做投篮动作时，B1 从 A1 后面触及了 A1 的手臂：

（a）试图去封盖球。

（b）该接触已达到一起违反体育运动精神的犯规的标准。

解释

（a）这是 B1 的一起侵人犯规。

（b）这是 B1 的一起违反体育运动精神的犯规。

37-5　**举例**　A1 在其后场将球传向位于其前场并正朝向对方球篮行进的 A2，此时 A2 和对方球篮之间没有 B 队队员。A2 跳起在空中，在接到传球之前，B1 从 A2 后面对其犯规。B1 被判犯规。

Interpretation: This is an unsportsmanlike foul by B1 for an illegal contact on a progressing player from behind with no team B player between A2 and the basket after the ball has been released on a pass to A2.

37-6 **Example:** A1 has the ball in the hands in the backcourt. A2 in the frontcourt is progressing towards the opponents' basket with no team B player between A2 and the basket. Before A1 releases the ball for a pass to A2, B1 fouls A2 from behind.

Interpretation: This is not an unsportsmanlike foul by B1 as A1 had not yet released the pass to A2.

37-7 **Example:** B1 in the backcourt taps the ball away from dribbler A1. B1 then attempts to gain control of the ball. With no team A player between B1 and the basket, A2 contacts B1 from behind or laterally.

Interpretation: This is an unsportsmanlike foul by A2 when B1 attempted to gain control of the ball, with no team A player between B1 and the basket.

37-8 **Statement:** After a player is charged with a fifth personal foul, that player becomes an excluded player. Any further technical foul or disqualifying foul or an unsportsmanlike behaviour foul by this player shall be charged and entered on the scoresheet against the head coach as a 'B' and penalised accordingly.

37-9 **Example:** B1 fouls dribbler A1. This is B1's fifth foul and the second team B foul in the quarter. While going to the team bench, B1 pushes A2.

Interpretation: With the fifth foul, B1 becomes an excluded player. B1's unsportsmanlike behaviour shall be charged as a technical foul against the team B head coach, entered as a 'B_1'. Any team A player shall attempt 1 free throw with no line-up. The game shall be resumed with a team A throw-in from the place nearest to where B1's unsportsmanlike behaviour occurred.

37-10 **Example:** Dribbler A1 fouls B1. This is A1's fifth foul in the quarter. While going to the team bench, A1 is assessed a technical foul for verbally abusing a referee.

解释 这是B1的一起违反体育运动精神的犯规。因为在传向行进队员A2的球离手后，A2被B1从后面造成了非法接触，且当时在A2和B队球篮之间没有B队队员。

37-6 **举例** 位于后场的A1双手持球，位于前场并正朝向对方球篮行进的A2和对方球篮之间没有B队队员。A1传向A2的球离手之前，B1从A2后面对其犯规。

解释 这不是B1的一起违反体育运动精神的犯规，因为A1将要传向A2的球尚未离手。

37-7 **举例** 位于后场的B1将运球队员A1手中的球拍离。然后，B1试图去控制球。A2从B1后面或侧面触及了B1，并且在B1和对方球篮之间没有A队队员。

解释 这是A2的一起违反体育运动精神的犯规。因为当B1试图去控制球时，B1和对方球篮之间没有A队队员。

37-8 **陈述** 一名队员在被登记了其个人的第5次犯规后，就成为一名出局的队员。之后该队员出现的任何技术犯规或取消比赛资格的犯规或违反体育运动精神行为的犯规，都应在记录表上的主教练名下登记“B”，并按相关规定处罚。

37-9 **举例** B1对运球队员A1犯规。这是B1的第5次犯规，也是该节B队的第2次全队犯规。B1在回其球队席的途中推了A2。

解释 B1在其第5次犯规时，成为一名出局的队员。B1违反体育运动精神的行为应作为一起技术犯规登记在B队主教练名下，登记为“B_1”。应由A队任一队员执行1次不占位的罚球。应由A队在最靠近B1发生违反体育运动精神的行为的地点执行掷球入界继续比赛。

37-10 **举例** 运球队员A1对B1犯规。这是该节A1的第5次犯规。A1在回其球队席的途中因辱骂裁判员被判一起技术犯规。

Interpretation: With the fifth foul, A1 becomes an excluded player. A1's technical foul shall be charged against the team A head coach, entered as a 'B_1'. Any team B player shall attempt 1 free throw with no line-up. The game shall be resumed with a team B throw-in from the place nearest to where A1's team control foul occurred.

37-11 **Example:** A1 fouls B1. This is A1's fifth foul and the second team A foul in the quarter. While going to the team bench, A1 pushes B1. B1 now pushes A1. B1 is charged with an unsportsmanlike foul.

Interpretation: With the fifth foul, A1 becomes an excluded player. A1's unsportsmanlike behaviour shall be charged as a technical foul against the team A head coach, entered as a 'B_1'. B1's unsportsmanlike foul shall be charged against B1, entered as an 'U_2'. Any team B player shall attempt 1 free throw with no line-up. The substitute for A1 shall attempt 2 free throws with no line-up. The game shall be resumed with a team A throw-in from the throw-in line in its frontcourt. Team A shall have 14 seconds on the shot clock.

解释 A1 在其第 5 次犯规时，成为一名出局的队员。A1 的技术犯规应登记在 A 队主教练名下，登记为“B_1”。应由 B 队任一队员执行 1 次不占位的罚球。应由 B 队在最靠近 A1 发生控制球队犯规的地点执行掷球入界继续比赛。

37-11 举例 A1 对 B1 犯规。这是 A1 的第 5 次犯规，也是该节 A 队的第 2 次全队犯规。A1 在回其球队席的途中推了 B1。B1 即刻回推了 A1。B1 被判一起违反体育运动精神的犯规。

解释 A1 在其第 5 次犯规时，成为一名出局的队员。A1 违反体育运动精神的行为应作为一起技术犯规登记在 A 队主教练名下，登记为“B_1”。B1 的违反体育运动精神的犯规则应登记在其本人名下，登记为“U_2”。应由 B 队任一队员执行 1 次不占位的罚球。应由替换 A1 的队员执行 2 次不占位的罚球。应由 A 队在其前场的掷球入界线处执行掷球入界继续比赛。A 队应拥有 14 秒进攻时间。

Article 38 Disqualifying foul

38-1 **Statement:** Any disqualified person is no longer a person permitted to sit on the team bench. Therefore, that person may no longer be penalised for any unsportsmanlike behaviour.

38-2 **Example:** A1 is disqualified for a flagrant unsportsmanlike behaviour. A1 leaves the court and verbally abuses a referee.

Interpretation: A1 is already disqualified and may no longer be penalised for the verbal abuses. The crew chief or the commissioner, if present, shall send a report describing the incident to the organising body of the competition.

38-3 **Statement:** When a player is disqualified for a flagrant unsportsmanlike behaviour, the penalty shall be the same as for any other disqualifying non-contact foull.

38-4 **Example:** A1 commits a travelling violation. Frustrated, A1 verbally abuses a referee. A1 is charged with a disqualifying foul.

Interpretation: A1 becomes a disqualified player. A1's disqualifying foul is charged against A1, entered as a 'D_2'. Any team B player shall attempt 2 free throws with no line-up. The game shall be resumed with a team B throw-in from the throw-in line in its frontcourt. Team B shall have 14 seconds on the shot clock.

38-5 **Statement:** When the head coach is charged with a disqualifying foul, it shall be entered as a 'D_2'.

When any other person permitted to sit on the team bench is disqualified, the head coach shall be charged with a technical foul, entered as a 'B_2'. The penalty shall be the same as for any other disqualifying non-contact foul.

38-6 **Example:** A1 is charged with a fifth personal foul. This is the second team A foul in the quarter. While going to the team bench,

(a) A1 verbally abuses a referee.

(b) A1 punches B2 in the face.

In both cases, A1 is assessed a disqualifying foul.

第 38 条　取消比赛资格的犯规

38-1　陈述　任何被取消比赛资格的人员不再被允许坐在其球队席上。因此，不能再对该人员的任何违反体育运动精神的行为进行处罚。

38-2　举例　A1 因为严重违反体育运动精神的行为被取消比赛资格。A1 在离开比赛场地时辱骂了裁判员。

解释　A1 已被取消比赛资格，不能再因其辱骂的行为进行处罚。主裁判员或到场的临场代表，应出具描述该事件的报告，送交竞赛的组织部门。

38-3　陈述　当一名队员因非身体接触的严重违反体育运动精神的行为被取消比赛资格，其罚则应与任何其他的取消比赛资格的犯规的罚则相同。

38-4　举例　A1 发生了带球走违例。由于不满情绪，A1 辱骂了裁判员。A1 被判取消比赛资格的犯规。

解释　A1 成为一名被取消比赛资格的队员。A1 的取消比赛资格的犯规，应在其名下登记“D_2”。应由 B 队任一队员执行 2 次不占位的罚球。应由 B 队在其前场的掷球入界线处执行掷球入界继续比赛。B 队应拥有 14 秒进攻时间。

38-5　陈述　当一名主教练被判取消比赛资格的犯规，应登记“D_2”。

当任何其他被允许坐在其球队席上的人员被取消比赛资格，应登记该队主教练一起技术犯规，登记为“B_2”。其罚则应与任何其他非身体接触的取消比赛资格的犯规的罚则相同。

38-6　举例　A1 被判了其个人的第 5 次犯规。这是该节 A 队的第 2 次全队犯规。A1 在回其球队席的途中：

（a）辱骂了裁判员。

（b）用拳打了 B2 的脸。

在这两种情况下，A1 被判了一起取消比赛资格的犯规。

Interpretation: With the fifth personal foul, A1 becomes an excluded player. A1 becomes a disqualified excluded player for verbally abusing a referee or for punching B2. A1's disqualifying foul shall be entered on the scoresheet against A1 as a 'D' and against the team A head coach, as a 'B_2'. In

(a) any team B player shall attempt 2 free throws with no line-up.

(b) B2 shall attempt 2 free throws with no line-up.

In both cases, the game shall be resumed with a team B throw-in from the throw-in line in its frontcourt. Team B shall have 14 seconds on the shot clock.

38-7 **Statement:** Any flagrant unsportsmanlike action by a player or a person permitted to sit on the team bench is a disqualifying foul. The disqualifying foul can be a result of their actions

- directed towards a person from the opposing team, referees, table officials, commissioner or spectators.
- directed against any member of the own team.
- for intentionally damaging game equipment.

38-8 **Example:** The following flagrant unsportsmanlike actions may occur:

(a) A1 punches team-mate A2.

(b) A1 leaves the court and punches a spectator.

(c) A6 in the team bench area punches team-mate A7.

(d) A6 hits the scorer's table and damages the shot clock.

Interpretation:

(a) and (b) A1 shall be disqualified. A1's disqualifying foul shall be charged against A1, entered as a 'D_2' .

(c) and (d) A6 shall be disqualified. A6's disqualifying foul shall be assessed against A6 entered as a 'D' and charged against A6's head coach, entered as a 'B_2' .

解释 A1 在其个人的第 5 次犯规时，成为一名出局的队员。A1 因辱骂裁判员或拳击 B2，又成为一名被取消比赛资格的出局的队员。A1 的取消比赛资格的犯规，应在记录表上 A1 的名下登记“D”，并在其主教练名下登记“B_2”。

在（a）中，应由 B 队任一队员执行 2 次不占位的罚球。

在（b）中，应由 B2 执行 2 次不占位的罚球。

在这两种情况下，应由 B 队在其前场的掷球入界线处执行掷球入界继续比赛。B 队应拥有 14 秒进攻时间。

38-7 **陈述** 一名队员或一名被允许坐在球队席上的人员，所做出任何严重违反体育运动精神的行为，是一起取消比赛资格的犯规。他们如出现下述行为便会导致一起取消比赛资格的犯规。

- 针对对方队的人员、裁判员、记录台人员、临场代表或观众（犯规）。
- 针对本队的任何成员（犯规）。
- 故意损坏比赛器材。

38-8 **举例** 可能发生下述严重违反体育运动精神的行为：

（a）A1 拳击了同队队员 A2。

（b）A1 离开比赛场地并拳击了一名观众。

（c）A6 在其球队席区域内拳击了同队队员 A7。

（d）A6 碰撞记录台并损坏进攻计时钟。

解释

（a）和（b） A1 应被取消比赛资格。A1 取消比赛资格的犯规应登记在其本人名下并登记为“D_2”。

（c）和（d） A6 应被取消比赛资格。A6 取消比赛资格的犯规应登记在其本人名下并登记为“D”，同时在其主教练名下登记“B_2”。

Any team B player shall attempt 2 free throws with no line-up. The game shall be resumed with a team B throw-in from the throw-in line in its frontcourt. Team B shall have 14 seconds on the shot clock.

38-9 **Statement:** If a player is disqualified and on the way to the dressing room acts in a manner that is consistent with an unsportsmanlike foul or a disqualifying foul, these additional actions shall not be penalised and shall only be reported to the governing body of the competition.

38-10 **Example:** A1 is charged with a disqualifying foul for verbally abusing a referee. On the way to the dressing room

(a) A1 pushes B1 in a manner that is consistent with an unsportsmanlike foul.

(b) A1 punches B1 in a manner that is consistent with a disqualifying foul.

Interpretation: After A1 is disqualified, A1's additional foul cannot be charged and penalised. A1's action shall be reported by the crew chief or commissioner, if present, to the governing body of the competition.

In both cases, team B shall be awarded 2 free throws with no line-up for A1's disqualifying foul. The game shall be resumed with a team B throw-in from the throw-in line in its frontcourt. Team B shall have 14 seconds on the shot clock.

应由B队任一队员执行2次不占位的罚球。应由B队在其前场的掷球入界线处执行掷球入界继续比赛。B队应拥有14秒进攻时间。

38-9 陈述 如果一名队员被取消比赛资格，并且在去球队更衣室的途中，出现了与违反体育运动精神的犯规或取消比赛资格的犯规标准相符合的行为，这些额外的行为不应受到处罚，只应向竞赛的组织部门报告。

38-10 举例 A1因辱骂裁判员，被判取消比赛资格的犯规。A1在前往球队更衣室的途中：

（a）推了B1，该行为符合一起违反体育运动精神的犯规的标准。

（b）拳击了B1，该行为符合一起取消比赛资格的犯规的标准。

解释 在A1被取消比赛资格后，A1额外的犯规不能被登记和处罚。A1的行为应由主裁判员或到场的临场代表向竞赛的组织部门报告。

在这两种情况下，对A1的取消比赛资格的犯规，应由B队执行2次不占位的罚球。应由B队在其前场的掷球入界线处执行掷球入界继续比赛。B队应拥有14秒进攻时间。

Article 39 Fighting

39-1 Statement: If after a fight all penalties have cancelled each other, the team which was in the control of the ball or was entitled to the ball when the fight started shall be awarded a throw-in from the place nearest to where the ball was located when the fight started. The team shall have the time remaining on the shot clock when the game was stopped.

39-2 Example: Team A has possession of the ball for

(a) 20 seconds

(b) 5 seconds

when a situation which may lead to a fight on the court occurs. The referees disqualify 2 substitutes of each team for leaving their team bench areas.

Interpretation: The game shall be resumed with a team A throw-in, which controlled the ball before the fight situation started, from the place nearest to where the ball was located when the fight situation started with

(a) 4 seconds

(b) 19 seconds

on the shot clock.

39-3 Statement: A team's head coach shall be charged with a single technical foul for a disqualification of the head coach, the first assistant coach (if one or both do not assist the referees to maintain or to restore order), any substitute, any excluded player or any accompanying delegation member for leaving the team bench area during a fight. If the technical foul includes the disqualification of the head coach, it shall be entered on the scoresheet against that head coach as a 'D_2'. If the technical foul includes only the disqualification(s) of other persons permitted to sit on the team bench, it shall be entered against the head coach as a 'B_2'. The penalty shall be 2 free throws with no line-up and possession of the ball for the opponents.

第 39 条　打架

39-1　陈述　如果打架后所有的罚则都已相互抵消，应判给在打架开始时控制球的队或拥有球权的队，在最靠近打架开始时球所在位置的地点执行掷球入界。该队应拥有进攻计时钟在比赛停止时显示的剩余时间。

39-2　举例　A 队控制球已达：

（a）20 秒时，

（b）5 秒时，

比赛场地上发生了一起可能导致打架的情况。裁判员取消了每队 2 名离开他们球队席区域的替补队员的比赛资格。

解释　应由打架开始前控制球的 A 队在最靠近打架开始时球所在位置的地点执行掷球入界继续比赛，并在进攻计时钟上显示：

（a）4 秒。

（b）19 秒。

39-3　陈述　在打架中，主教练、第一助理教练（如果他们中的一人或两人都不去协助裁判员维持或恢复秩序）、任一替补队员、任一出局的队员或任一随队人员因离开球队席区域而被取消比赛资格，应在主教练名下登记一起单一的技术犯规。如果该技术犯规包含了取消该主教练的比赛资格的情况，则应在记录表上该主教练的名下登记“D_2”。如果该技术犯规只包含了取消被允许坐在球队席上的其他人员的比赛资格的情况，则应在该主教练的名下登记“B_2”。罚则应是对方队执行 2 次不占位的罚球及拥有随后的球权。

For each additional disqualifying foul, the penalty shall be 2 free throws with no line-up and possession of the ball for the opponents.

All penalties shall be administered unless there are equal penalties against both teams to be cancelled. In this case, the game shall be resumed from the throw-in line in the team's frontcourt as for any other disqualifying foul. The opposing team shall have 14 seconds on the shot clock.

39-4 **Example:** During a fight A6 enters the court. A6 shall be disqualified.

Interpretation: A6's disqualification shall be entered against A6 as a 'D' and the remaining foul spaces shall be entered as an 'F'. The team A head coach shall be charged with a technical foul, entered against that head coach as a 'B_2'. Any team B player shall attempt 2 free throws with no line-up. The game shall be resumed with a team B throw-in from the throw-in line in its frontcourt. Team B shall have 14 seconds on shot clock.

39-5 **Example:** A1 and B1 start a fight on the court. A6 and B6 enter the court but do not get involved in the fight. A7 also enters the court and punches B1 in the face.

Interpretation: A1 and B1 shall be disqualified, entered against them as a 'D_C'. A7 shall be disqualified, entered against A7 as a 'D_2'. A7's remaining foul spaces on the scoresheet shall be entered as an 'F'. A6 and B6 shall be disqualified for entering the court during a fight, entered against them as a 'D'. A6's and B6's remaining foul spaces on the scoresheet shall be entered as an 'F'. The team A head coach and the team B head coach shall be charged with technical fouls, entered against them as a 'B_C'. The penalties for both disqualifying fouls (A1, B1) and both technical fouls (A6, B6) shall cancel each other. A7's disqualifying foul penalty for an active involvement in the fight, entered against A7 as a 'D_2', shall be administered. The substitute for B1 shall attempt 2 free throws with no line-up. The game shall be resumed with a team B throw-in from the throw-in line in its frontcourt. Team B shall have 14 seconds on the shot clock.

> 对于额外出现的每一起取消比赛资格的犯规，罚则应是对方队执行 2 次不占位的罚球及拥有随后的球权。
>
> 所有罚则都应被执行，除非双方球队有相同的罚则可以抵消。这种情况下，应如同任何取消比赛资格的犯规一样在对方队前场的掷球入界线处执行掷球入界继续比赛。该队应拥有 14 秒进攻时间。

39-4 举例 A6 在一起打架中进入比赛场地。A6 应被取消比赛资格。

解释 A6 的取消比赛资格的犯规应被登记“D”，并且，在 A6 留有的犯规空格内应都登记“F”。A 队主教练应被登记 1 次技术犯规，在其名下登记为“B_2”。应由 B 队任一队员执行 2 次不占位的罚球。应由 B 队在其前场的掷球入界线处执行掷球入界继续比赛。B 队应拥有 14 秒进攻时间。

39-5 举例 A1 和 B1 在比赛场地上开始打架。此时 A6 和 B6 进入比赛场地，但是他们没有参与打架。A7 也进入了比赛场地并用拳打了 B1 的脸。

解释 A1 和 B1 应被取消比赛资格，在他们的名下登记“D_c”。A7 应被取消比赛资格，在 A7 的名下登记“D_2”。记录表上，在 A7 的剩余犯规空格内都登记“F”。A6 和 B6 因为在打架中进入比赛场地应被取消比赛资格，在他们的名下登记“D”。记录表上，在 A6 和 B6 的剩余犯规空格内都登记“F”。A 队主教练和 B 队主教练应被判技术犯规，在他们的名下登记“B_c”。（A1，B1）两个取消比赛资格的犯规的罚则和（A6，B6）两个技术犯规的罚则应相互抵消。因为 A7 积极参与了打架，登记在 A7 名下“D_2”的取消比赛资格的罚则应被执行。应由替换 B1 的队员执行 2 次不占位的罚球。应由 B 队在其前场的掷球入界线处执行掷球入界继续比赛。B 队应拥有 14 秒进攻时间。

39-6 **Example:** A1 and B1 start a fight on the court. A6 and the team A manager enter the court and get actively involved in the fight.

Interpretation: A1 and B1 shall be disqualified, entered against them as a 'D_C'. The penalties for both disqualifying fouls (A1, B1) shall cancel each other. The team A head coach shall be charged with a technical foul, entered against that head coach as a 'B_2' for A6 and the team A manager leaving the team bench area. A6 shall be disqualified for an active involvement in the fight, entered against A6 as a 'D_2'. A6's remaining foul spaces shall be entered on the scoresheet as an 'F'. The team A manager's disqualifying foul for an active involvement in the fight shall be charged and entered against the team head coach, entered against the team head coach as a circled 'B_2' and shall not count towards the head coach's possible automatic disqualification.

Any team B player(s) shall attempt 6 free throws with no line-up (2 free throws for the team A head coach technical foul for A6 and the team A manager leaving their team bench area; 2 free throws for A6's disqualification for an active involvement in the fight; and 2 free throws for the team A head coach's technical foul for the team A manager's disqualification for an active involvement in the fight).

The game shall be resumed with a team B throw-in from the throw-in line in its frontcourt. Team B shall have 14 seconds on the shot clock.

39-7 **Example:** The team A head coach leaves the team bench area and gets actively involved in a fight on the court by strongly pushing B1.

Interpretation: The team A head coach shall be charged with a disqualifying foul for leaving the team bench area and not assisting the referees to restore order, entered on the scoresheet against the team A head coach as a 'D_2'. The team A head coach shall not be charged with another disqualifying foul for an active involvement in the fight. The team A head coach's remaining foul spaces shall be entered on the scoresheet as an 'F'. Any team B player shall attempt 2 free throws with no line-up. The game shall be resumed with a team B throw-in from the throw-in line in its frontcourt. Team B shall have 14 seconds on the shot clock.

39-6 **举例** A1 和 B1 在比赛场地上开始打架。A6 和 A 队管理人员进入了比赛场地并积极参与打架。

解释 A1 和 B1 应被取消比赛资格，在他们的名下登记“D_C”。（A1，B1）两个取消比赛资格的犯规的罚则应相互抵消。因为 A6 和 A 队管理人员离开球队席区域，应登记 A 队主教练 1 次技术犯规，在其名下登记“B_2”。A6 因积极参与打架，应被取消比赛资格，在 A6 的名下登记“D_2”。记录表上，在 A6 的剩余犯规空格内都登记“F”。A 队管理人员因积极参与打架被判的取消比赛资格的犯规，应登记在其主教练名下并在“B_2”上套一个圆圈，该犯规不应被计入主教练在比赛中可能要被自动取消比赛资格的犯规次数中。

应由 B 队任一队员执行 6 次不占位的罚球（2 次罚球是 A 队主教练因为 A6 和 A 队管理人员离开他们的球队席区域而登记的技术犯规的罚则；2 次罚球是因为 A6 积极参与打架被判取消比赛资格的犯规的罚则；另外 2 次罚球是 A 队主教练因为 A 队管理人员积极参与打架而登记的技术犯规的罚则）。

应由 B 队在其前场的掷球入界线处执行掷球入界继续比赛。B 队应拥有 14 秒进攻时间。

39-7 **举例** A 队主教练离开球队席区域并大力推开 B1，积极参与了比赛场地上的打架。

解释 A 队主教练因为离开球队席区域，并且不协助裁判员维持秩序，应被判取消比赛资格的犯规，在记录表上该主教练的名下登记“D_2”。不应登记 A 队主教练因其积极参与打架的另一个取消比赛资格的犯规。记录表上，在 A 队主教练的剩余犯规空格内都登记“F”。应由 B 队任一队员执行 2 次不占位的罚球。应由 B 队在其前场的掷球入界线处执行掷球入界继续比赛。B 队应拥有 14 秒进攻时间。

39-8 **Example:** During a time-out some substitutes or accompanying delegation members of either team enter the court and remain within the vicinity of their team bench area. At that time a situation which may lead to the fight occurs on the court and

(a) all persons already on the court because of the time-out remain in their positions within the vicinity of their team bench area.

(b) some of the persons already on the court because of the time-out leave their positions within the vicinity of their team bench area and some players get actively involved in the situation which may lead to a fight.

Interpretation:

(a) No person already on the court because of the time-out shall be disqualified.

(b) All persons already on the court because of the time-out leaving their positions within the vicinity of their team bench area and all players getting actively involved in the situation which may lead to a fight shall be disqualified.

39-8 **举例** 一次暂停期间，任一球队的一些替补队员或随队人员进入了比赛场地，并滞留在靠近其球队席区域的位置。此时，比赛场地上发生了一起可能导致打架的情况，然后：

（a）因暂停而已经在比赛场地上的人员均停留在了靠近其球队席区域的位置。

（b）因暂停而已经在比赛场地上的人员中，一些人员离开了靠近其球队席区域的位置，还有一些人员积极参与到了这起可能导致打架的情况下。

解释

（a）所有这些因暂停而已经在比赛场地上的人员都不应被取消比赛资格。

（b）因暂停而已经在比赛场地上的人员中，离开了靠近其球队席区域的人员和积极参与到了这起可能导致打架的情况下的人员应被取消比赛资格。

Article 42 Special situations

42-1 **Statement:** In special game situations with a number of potential penalties to be administered during the same game clock stopped period, referees must pay particular attention to the order in which the violation or fouls occurred in determining which penalties shall be administered and which penalties shall be cancelled.

42-2 **Example:** B1 is charged with an unsportsmanlike foul against shooter A1. The ball is in the air when the shot clock signal sounds. The ball

(a) misses the ring.

(b) touches the ring but does not enter the basket.

(c) enters the basket.

Interpretation: In all cases, B1's unsportsmanlike foul shall not be disregarded.

(a) The team A shot clock violation (the ball missed the ring) shall be disregarded as it occurred after B1's unsportsmanlike foul. A1 shall attempt 2 or 3 free throws with no line-up.

(b) This is not a shot clock violation by team A. A1 shall attempt 2 or 3 free throws with no line-up.

(c) A1 shall be awarded 2 or 3 points and 1 additional free throw with no line-up.

In all cases, the game shall be resumed with a team A throw-in from the throw-in line in its frontcourt. Team A shall have 14 seconds on the shot clock.

42-3 **Example:** B1 fouls A1 in the act of shooting for a goal. After the foul, with A1 still in the act of shooting, B2 fouls A1.

Interpretation: B2's foul shall be disregarded unless it is an unsportsmanlike foul or a disqualifying foul.

42-4 **Example:** B1 is charged with an unsportsmanlike foul against dribbler A1. After the foul, the team A head coach and the team B head coach are charged with technical fouls.

第 42 条　特殊情况

42-1　陈述　在同一个停止比赛计时钟的时段内有多个罚则要被执行的特殊比赛情况下，裁判员必须对所发生的违例或犯规的顺序给予特别的注意，从而决定哪些罚则应被执行，哪些罚则应被抵消。

42-2　举例　B1 被判对投篮队员 A1 的违反体育运动精神的犯规。球在空中时，进攻计时钟信号响。该球：

（a）未触及篮圈。

（b）触及篮圈，但未进入球篮。

（c）进入球篮。

解释　上述所有情况下，B1 的违反体育运动精神的犯规不能被忽略。

（a）A 队的进攻时间违例（球未触及篮圈）应被忽略，因为它发生在 B1 的违反体育运动精神的犯规之后。A1 应执行 2 次或 3 次不占位的罚球。

（b）这不是 A 队的进攻时间违例。A1 应执行 2 次或 3 次不占位的罚球。

（c）应判给 A1 得 2 分或 3 分，追加 1 次不占位的罚球。

上述所有情况下，应由 A 队在其前场的掷球入界线处执行掷球入界继续比赛。A 队应拥有 14 秒进攻时间。

42-3　举例　B1 对正在做投篮动作的 A1 犯规。该犯规之后，A1 仍在做投篮动作时又被 B2 犯规。

解释　B2 的犯规应被忽略，除非它是一起违反体育运动精神的犯规或取消比赛资格的犯规。

42-4　举例　B1 被判对运球队员 A1 发生一起违反体育运动精神的犯规。该犯规之后，A 队主教练和 B 队主教练分别被判一起技术犯规。

Interpretation: The equal penalties for the 2 head coaches' technical fouls shall be cancelled. A1 shall attempt 2 free throws with no line-up. The game shall be resumed with a team A throw-in from the throw-in line in its frontcourt. Team A shall have 14 seconds on the shot clock.

42-5 **Example:** B1 fouls A1 on a shot for a successful goal. A1 is then charged with a technical foul.

Interpretation: A1's goal shall count. The penalties for both fouls are equal and shall cancel each other. The game shall be resumed as after any successful goal.

42-6 **Example:** B1 fouls A1 on a shot for a successful goal. A1 is then charged with a technical foul, followed by a team B head coach technical foul.

Interpretation: A1's goal shall count. The penalties for all fouls are equal and shall be cancelled in the order in which they occurred. The penalties for B1's personal foul and A1's technical foul shall cancel each other. For the team B head coach technical foul, any team A player shall attempt 1 free throw with no line-up. The game shall be resumed as after any successful goal.

42-7 **Example:** B1 is charged with an unsportsmanlike foul against A1 on a shot for a successful goal. A1 is then charged with a technical foul.

Interpretation: A1's goal shall count. The penalties for both fouls are not equal and shall not cancel each other. Any team B player shall attempt 1 free throw with no line-up. A1 shall attempt 1 free throw with no line-up. The game shall be resumed with a team A throw-in from the throw-in line in its frontcourt. Team A shall have 14 seconds on the shot clock.

42-8 **Example:** B1 fouls dribbler A1 in the frontcourt.

(a) This is the third team B foul in the quarter.

(b) This is the fifth team B foul in the quarter.

A1 then throws the ball against B1's body (hands, legs, torso etc).

解释 两队主教练的技术犯规的相同罚则应被抵消。应由A1执行2次不占位的罚球。应由A队在其前场的掷球入界线处执行掷球入界继续比赛。A队应拥有14秒进攻时间。

42-5 **举例** B1对正在投篮的A1犯规，球中篮。随后A1被判一起技术犯规。

解释 A1的中篮应计得分。两起犯规的相同罚则应相互抵消。应如同任何中篮后那样继续比赛。

42-6 **举例** B1对正在投篮的A1犯规，球中篮。随后A1被判一起技术犯规，B队主教练也被判一起技术犯规。

解释 A1的中篮应计得分。所有犯规的罚则相同，应按它们发生的顺序依次抵消。B1侵人犯规的罚则和A1技术犯规的罚则应相互抵消。对于B队主教练的技术犯规，应由A队任一队员执行1次不占位的罚球。应如同任何中篮后那样继续比赛。

42-7 **举例** B1对正在投篮的A1发生一起违反体育运动精神的犯规，球中篮。随后，A1被判一起技术犯规。

解释 A1的中篮应计得分。双方的犯规罚则不同，不能相互抵消。应由B队任一队员执行1次不占位的罚球。再由A1执行1次不占位的罚球。应由A队在其前场的掷球入界线处执行掷球入界继续比赛。A队应拥有14秒进攻时间。

42-8 **举例** 运球队员A1在其前场被B1犯规。

（a）这是该节B队的第3次全队犯规。

（b）这是该节B队的第5次全队犯规。

随后，A1将球抛中B1的身体（手、腿、躯干等）。

Interpretation: B1 shall be charged with a personal foul. A1 shall be charged with a technical foul. Any team B player shall attempt 1 free throw with no line-up.

(a) The game shall be resumed with a team A throw-in from its frontcourt nearest to the place where B1's foul occurred. Team A shall have the time remaining on the shot clock, if 14 seconds or more are shown on the shot clock. Team A shall have 14 seconds on the shot clock, if 13 seconds or less are shown on the shot clock.

(b) A1 shall attempt 2 free throws. The game shall be resumed as after any last free throw.

42-9 **Example:** B1 fouls dribbler A1.

(a) This is the third team B foul in the quarter.

(b) This is the fifth team B foul in the quarter.

A1 then throws the ball from a short distance directly to B1's face (head).

Interpretation: B1 shall be charged with a personal foul. A1 shall be charged with a disqualifying non-contact foul.

(a) The team A possession of the ball shall be cancelled as there is a further penalty to be administered.

(b) The substitute for A1 shall attempt 2 free throws with no line-up.

In both cases, any team B player shall attempt 2 free throws with no line-up. The game shall be resumed with a team B throw-in from the throw-in line in its frontcourt. Team B shall have 14 seconds on the shot clock.

42-10 **Example:** With 8 seconds on the shot clock, B1 in the backcourt fouls A1. B2 is then charged with a technical foul.

(a) B1's foul is the fourth team B foul and B2's technical foul is the fifth team B foul in the quarter.

(b) B1's foul is the fifth team B foul and B2's technical foul is the sixth team B foul in the quarter.

解释 应判 B1 的侵人犯规和 A1 的技术犯规。应由 B 队任一队员执行 1 次不占位的罚球。

（a）应由 A 队在其前场最靠近 B1 发生犯规的地点执行掷球入界继续比赛。如果进攻计时钟显示 14 秒或更多，则 A 队应拥有剩余的进攻时间；如果进攻计时钟显示 13 秒或更少，则 A 队应拥有 14 秒进攻时间。

（b）应由 A1 执行 2 次罚球，应如同任何最后一次罚球后那样继续比赛。

42-9 **举例** B1 对运球队员 A1 犯规。

（a）这是该节 B 队的第 3 次全队犯规。

（b）这是该节 B 队的第 5 次全队犯规。

随后，A1 拿球近距离直接掷向 B1 的脸（头部）。

解释 应判 B1 的侵人犯规和 A1 的非身体接触的取消比赛资格的犯规。

（a）因为还有进一步的罚则要执行，应取消 A 队的球权。

（b）替换 A1 的队员应执行 2 次不占位的罚球。

在这两种情况下，应由 B 队任一队员执行 2 次不占位的罚球。应由 B 队在其前场的掷球入界线处执行掷球入界继续比赛。B 队应拥有 14 秒进攻时间。

42-10 **举例** 进攻计时钟显示 8 秒时，B1 在其后场被判对 A1 犯规。然后，B2 被判一起技术犯规。

（a）B1 的犯规是该节 B 队的第 4 次全队犯规，B2 的技术犯规是该节 B 队的第 5 次全队犯规。

（b）B1 的犯规是该节 B 队的第 5 次全队犯规，B2 的技术犯规是该节 B 队的第 6 次全队犯规。

(c) A1 was fouled in the act of shooting and the ball does not enter the basket.

(d) A1 was fouled in the act of shooting and the ball enters the basket.

Interpretation: In all cases, for B2's technical foul any team A player shall attempt 1 free throw with no line-up. After the free throw

(a) the game shall be resumed with a team A throw-in in its frontcourt from the place nearest to where the foul against A1 occurred. Team A shall have 14 seconds on the shot clock.

(b) A1 shall attempt 2 free throws. The game shall be resumed as after any last free throw.

(c) A1 shall attempt 2 or 3 free throws. The game shall be resumed as after any last free throw.

(d) A1's goal shall count. A1 shall attempt 1 free throw. The game shall continue as after any last free throw.

42-11 **Example:** With 8 seconds on the shot clock, B1 is charged with an unsportsmanlike foul against A1.

(a) A2

(b) B2

is then charged with a technical foul.

Interpretation:

(a) Any team B player shall attempt 1 free throw with no line-up.

(b) Any team A player shall attempt 1 free throw with no line-up.

In both cases, after the free throw for the technical foul A1 shall attempt 2 free throws with no line-up. The game shall be resumed with a team A throw-in from the throw-in line in its frontcourt. Team A shall have 14 seconds on the shot clock.

42-12 **Statement:** If double fouls or fouls with equal penalties are charged during free-throw activity, the fouls shall be entered on the scoresheet, however the penalties shall not be administered.

（c）A1 被犯规时正在做投篮动作，球未中篮。

（d）A1 被犯规时正在做投篮动作，球中篮。

解释 上述所有情况下，对于 B2 的技术犯规，应由 A 队任一队员执行 1 次不占位的罚球。罚球后：

（a）应由 A 队在其前场最靠近 A1 被犯规的地点执行掷球入界继续比赛。A 队应拥有 14 秒进攻时间。

（b）应由 A1 执行 2 次罚球，应如同任何最后一次罚球后那样继续比赛。

（c）应由 A1 执行 2 次或 3 次罚球，应如同任何最后一次罚球后那样继续比赛。

（d）A1 的中篮应计得分。应由 A1 执行 1 次罚球，应如同任何最后一次罚球后那样继续比赛。

42-11 举例 进攻计时钟显示 8 秒时，判了 B1 对 A1 的一起违反体育运动精神的犯规，然后：

（a）A2 被判了一起技术犯规。

（b）B2 被判了一起技术犯规。

解释

（a）应由 B 队任一队员执行 1 次不占位的罚球。

（b）应由 A 队任一队员执行 1 次不占位的罚球。

在这两种情况下，在执行完技术犯规的罚球后，应由 A1 执行 2 次不占位的罚球。应由 A 队在其前场的掷球入界线处执行掷球入界继续比赛，A 队应拥有 14 秒进攻时间。

42-12 陈述 如果在罚球期间发生了一起双方犯规或是相同罚则的犯规，这些犯规应被登记在记录表上，但不应执行这些罚则。

42-13 **Example:** A1 is awarded 2 free throws.

(a) After the first free throw,

(b) After the successful second free throw, but before team B has the ball as its disposal for the throw-in from behind its endline,

(c) After the unsuccessful second free throw, but before either team gains control of the ball,

(d) After the unsuccessful second free throw, but after either team gains control of the ball,

A2 and B2 are charged with a double foul or with technical fouls.

Interpretation: A2's and B2's foul penalties shall be cancelled.

(a) A1 shall attempt the second free throw and the game shall continue as after any last free throw.

(b) Team B shall have a throw-in from its endline.

(c) This is a jump ball situation.

(d) The team which has gained control of the ball shall be awarded a throw-in.

42-14 **Statement:** If a technical foul is called, the free throw penalty shall be administered immediately with no line-up. This is not valid for a technical foul charged against the head coach for the disqualification of any other person permitted to sit on the team bench. The penalty for such a technical foul (2 free throws and a throw-in from the throw-in line in the team's frontcourt) shall be administered in the order in which all violations and fouls have occurred unless they were cancelled.

42-15 **Example:** B1 fouls A1. This is the fifth team B foul in the quarter. A situation which may lead to a fight then occurs on the court. A6 enters the court but does not get actively involved in the fight.

42-13 举例 判给 A1 执行 2 次罚球。

（a）在第 1 次罚球后，

（b）在成功的第 2 次罚球后，但在 B 队从其端线后执行掷球入界可处理球之前，

（c）在不成功的第 2 次罚球后，但在任一队获得控制球之前，

（d）在不成功的第 2 次罚球后，但在任一队获得控制球之后，

判了 A2 和 B2 一起双方犯规或各一起技术犯规。

解释 A2 和 B2 犯规的罚则应相互抵消。

（a）A1 应执行其第 2 次罚球且应如同任何最后一次罚球后那样继续比赛。

（b）应判给 B 队在其端线后执行掷球入界。

（c）这是一次跳球情况。

（d）应判给已经获得控制球的球队执行掷球入界。

42-14 陈述 如果宣判了一起技术犯规，应立即执行该不占位的罚球罚则。但这一条不适用于被允许坐在球队席上的任何其他人员，因被取消比赛资格而登记在主教练名下的技术犯规。这样的技术犯规罚则（2 次罚球和在球队前场的掷球入界线处执行掷球入界）应依照所有违例和犯规发生的顺序执行，除非它们被抵消。

42-15 举例 B1 对 A1 犯规。这是该节 B 队的第 5 次全队犯规。随后，比赛场地上发生了一起可能导致打架的情况。A6 进入比赛场地，但没有积极参与打架。

Interpretation: A6 shall be disqualified for entering the court during a fight. The team A head coach shall be charged with a technical foul, entered against the team A head coach as a 'B_2'. A1 shall attempt 2 free throws with no line-up. Any team B player shall attempt 2 free throws with no line-up for the team A head coach technical foul. The game shall be resumed with a team B throw-in from the throw-in line in its frontcourt. Team B shall have 14 seconds on the shot clock.

42-16 **Statement:** In the case of double fouls and after cancellation of equal penalties against both teams, if there are no other penalties remaining for administration, the game shall be resumed with a throw-in by the team that had control of the ball or was entitled to the ball before the first infraction.

In the case neither team had control of the ball nor was entitled to the ball before the first infraction, this is a jump ball situation. The game shall be resumed with an alternating possession throw-in.

42-17 **Example:** During the interval of play between the first and second quarter, A1 and B1 are charged with disqualifying fouls or the team A head coach and the team B head coach are charged with technical fouls.

The alternating possession arrow favours

(a) team A.

(b) team B.

Interpretation: The equal penalties against both teams shall be cancelled.

In both cases, the game shall be resumed with a throw-in from the centre line extended by the team entitled to the next alternating possession. When the ball touches or is legally touched by a player on the court, the direction of the arrow shall be reversed in favour of the opponent's team.

42-18 **Example:** A team control foul or a double dribble violation is called against dribbler A1. When the game is resumed with a team B throw-in, B2 fouls A2

解释 A6 在一起打架中进入比赛场地，A6 应被取消比赛资格。应在 A 队主教练名下登记 1 次技术犯规，登记为"B_2"。应由 A1 执行 2 次不占位的罚球。应由 B 队任一队员执行 A 队主教练技术犯规的 2 次不占位的罚球。应由 B 队在其前场的掷球入界线处执行掷球入界继续比赛。B 队应拥有 14 秒进攻时间。

42-16 陈述 如果把双方球队犯规和双方球队相同的罚则抵消后，没有其他剩余要执行的罚则，应由在第一起规则违犯前已控制球或拥有球权的队执行掷球入界继续比赛。

如果在第一起规则违犯前，既没有球队控制球，也没有球队拥有球权，这是一次跳球情况。应由交替拥有掷球入界继续比赛。

42-17 举例 在第 1 节和第 2 节之间的比赛休息期间，A1 和 B1 均被判取消比赛资格的犯规，或 A 队主教练和 B 队主教练均被判技术犯规。

交替拥有箭头指向：

（a）A 队的进攻方向。

（b）B 队的进攻方向。

解释 这两个相同的罚则应被相互抵消。

在这两种情况下，应由拥有下一次交替拥有掷球入界权的球队在中线延长线处执行掷球入界继续比赛。当球触及一名场上队员或被一名场上队员合法触及时，交替拥有箭头的方向应反转并指向对方队的进攻方向。

42-18 举例 运球队员 A1 被判一起控制球队犯规或两次运球违例。在 B 队掷球入界期间，B2 对 A2 犯规，该犯规发生在：

(a) before

(b) after

the ball is at team B disposal for the throw-in. This is the third team B foul in the quarter.

Interpretation:

Both infractions occurred in the same game clock stopped period and

(a) before the ball became live for team B's throw-in. Therefore, the equal penalties shall be cancelled.

As team A was in control of the ball before the first infraction, the game shall be resumed with a team A throw-in from the place nearest to where A1's foul or violation occurred. Team A shall have the time remaining on the shot clock.

(b) after the ball became live for team B's throw-in. The penalty for the first infraction can no longer be used for cancelling.

The throw-in penalty for B2's foul cancels the prior right to possession of the ball for A1's infraction. The game shall be resumed with a team A throw-in from the place nearest to where B2's foul occurred. If from the backcourt, team A shall have 24 seconds. If from the frontcourt, team A shall have 14 seconds on the shot clock.

（a）B 队掷球入界可处理球之前。

（b）B 队掷球入界可处理球之后。

这是该节 B 队的第 3 次全队犯规。

解释 两起规则违犯发生在同一个比赛计时钟停止的时段中，且

（a）在 B 队掷球入界的球成活球之前，因此，这两个相同的罚则应被相互抵消。

因为在第一起规则违犯之前 A 队控制球，应由 A 队在最靠近 A1 犯规或违例的地点执行掷球入界继续比赛。A 队应拥有进攻计时钟显示的剩余时间。

（b）在 B 队掷球入界的球成活球之后，第一起规则违犯的罚则不再能被用作抵消。

应取消先前 A1 的规则违犯所产生的球权，执行 B2 犯规的掷球入界罚则。应由 A 队在最靠近 B2 发生犯规的地点执行掷球入界继续比赛。如果在其后场执行掷球入界，A 队应拥有 24 秒进攻时间；如果在其前场执行掷球入界，A 队应拥有 14 秒进攻时间。

Article 43 Free throws

43-1 Statement: The players in the free-throw rebound places shall be entitled to occupy alternating positions in these spaces. The players not in the free-throw rebound places shall remain behind the free-throw line extended and behind the 3-point goal line until the free throw ends.

43-2 Example: A1 attempts a last free throw. None of the team B players occupy the free-throw rebound places to which they are entitled to.

Interpretation: During the free-throws the players may occupy only the rebound places to which they are entitled to. If they decide not to occupy their rebound places, they shall remain behind the free-throw line extended and behind the 3-point line until the free throw ends.

43-3 Statement: It is a jump ball situation, if during the last free throw players of both teams commit a free throw violation.

43-4 Example: B2 enters the restricted area before the ball has left A1's hands on a last free throw. A1's free throw misses the ring.

Interpretation: This is a free throw violation by B2 and A1. A jump ball situation occurs.

第 43 条 罚球

43-1 陈述 在罚球抢篮板球分位区内的队员们应有权在这些空间交错占位。不在罚球抢篮板球分位区内的队员们应留在罚球线延长线和 3 分中篮线后面，直到罚球结束。

43-2 举例 A1 执行最后一次罚球。没有任何 B 队队员在他们有权占据的罚球抢篮板球分位区占位。

解释 罚球期间，队员们可以在只属于他们有权占据的抢篮板球分位区占位。如果这些队员决定不在这些抢篮板球分位区占位，他们就应留在罚球线延长线和 3 分线后面，直到罚球结束。

43-3 陈述 如果双方球队在最后一次罚球中都发生违例，这是一次跳球情况。

43-4 举例 B2 在 A1 最后一次罚球球离手前进入限制区。A1 的罚球未触及篮圈。

解释 这是 B2 和 A1 的罚球违例。一次跳球情况发生。

Article 44 Correctable errors

44-1 **Statement:** Referees may correct category 1 errors only if a rule is incorrectly applied in the following situations:

- Awarding an unmerited free throw(s).
- Failing to award a merited free throw(s).
- Permitting the wrong player to attempt a free throw(s).
- Directing the wrong player to attempt a free throw(s).
- Erroneously awarding or cancelling of a point(s).
- Reporting a foul on the wrong player, coach or team.
- Scorekeeping errors, including:
  - — failing to record or erroneously recording points.
  - — failing to record or recording a foul on the wrong player, coach or team.
  - — failing to record or recording a time-out on the wrong team.
- Game clock errors, including malfunctions, or errors in starting or stopping the game clock correetly or in setting the correct time on the game clock.

Referees may correct category 2 errors only if a rule is incorrectly applied in the following situations:

- Shot clock errors, including malfunctions, or errors in starting or stopping the shot clock or in setting the correct time on the shot clock.

44-2 **Statement:** To be correctable, category 1 errors must be recognised and corrected by the referees, commissioner, if present, or table officials as follows:

- If the error occurs before the game clock shows 2:00 minutes or less in the fourth quarter, the error must be recognised and corrected before 2:00 minutes or less are remaining on the game clock.

第 44 条　可纠正的失误

44-1 陈述　仅当某条规则在下列第一类失误情况中被错误地应用时，裁判员才可以纠正。

- 判给不应得的罚球。
- 没有判给应得的罚球。
- 允许错误的队员执行罚球。
- 指定错误的队员执行罚球。
- 错误地判给得分或取消得分。
- 将一起犯规报告在错误的队员、主教练或球队名下。
- 记录表登记的失误，包括：

  ——未记录或错误地记录得分。

  ——未登记一起犯规或将一起犯规登记在错误的队员、主教练或球队名下。

  ——未登记一次暂停或将一次暂停登记在错误的球队名下。
- 比赛计时的失误，包括设备故障、错误地开动或停止了比赛计时钟，或是在比赛计时钟上设置了错误的时间。

仅当某条规则在下列第二类失误情况中被错误地应用时，裁判员才可以纠正。

- 进攻计时的失误，包括设备故障、错误地开动或停止了进攻计时钟，或是在进攻计时钟上设置了错误的时间。

44-2 陈述　要纠正这些第一类失误，它们就必须被裁判员、到场的临场代表或记录台人员按如下原则确认和纠正。

- 如果失误发生在第 4 节比赛计时钟显示 2:00 分钟或更少之前，该失误必须在比赛计时钟剩余 2:00 分钟或更少之前被确认和纠正。

- If the error occurs before the game clock shows 2:00 minutes or less in the fourth quarter, but the referees stop the game for the first time with 2:00 minutes or less remaining on the game clock, the error must be recognised and corrected before the ball becomes live again.
- If the error occurs after the game clock shows 2:00 minutes or less in the fourth quarter or in an overtime, the error must be recognised and corrected before the ball becomes live after the first time the referees have stopped the game for any reason following the error.

44-3 **Example:** With 3:37 on the game clock in the second quarter, B1 fouls A1. This is the fourth team B foul in the quarter. A1 is erroneously awarded 2 free throws. The error is recognised

(a) with 4:48 on the game clock in the fourth quarter.

(b) with 0:39 on the game clock in the fourth quarter.

Interpretation:

In (a), the error is correctable.

In (b), the opportunity to correct the error expired. The error is no longer correctable and shall be disregarded.

44-4 **Example:** With 2:13 on the game clock in the fourth quarter, B1 fouls A1. This is the sixth team B foul in the fourth quarter. A1 is awarded 2 free throws. Instead of A1, the referee directs A2 to attempt the free throws. The error is recognised

(a) when the game is stopped with 1:49 on the game clock in the fourth quarter (this being the first game stoppage after the free throws).

(b) when the game is stopped with 1:23 on the game clock in the fourth quarter (this being the third game stoppage after the free throws).

Interpretation:

In (a), the error is correctable.

- 如果失误发生在第 4 节比赛计时钟显示 2:00 分钟或更少之前，但裁判员在第 4 节比赛计时钟显示 2:00 分钟或更少时首次停止比赛，该失误必须在球再次成为活球之前被确认和纠正。
- 如果失误发生在第 4 节比赛计时钟显示 2:00 分钟或更少之后或发生在决胜期中，裁判员在失误发生后因任何原因首次停止比赛之后，且球成活球之前，该失误必须被确认和纠正。

44-3 举例 第 2 节，比赛计时钟显示 3:37 时，B1 对 A1 犯规。这是该节 B 队的第 4 次全队犯规。错误地判给 A1 执行 2 次罚球。该失误被确认在：

（a）第 4 节比赛计时钟显示 4:48 时。

（b）第 4 节比赛计时钟显示 0:39 时。

解释

在（a）中，该失误可纠正。

在（b）中，可纠正该失误的时机已过。该失误不再可纠正并应被忽略。

44-4 举例 第 4 节，比赛计时钟显示 2:13 时，B1 对 A1 犯规，这是第 4 节 B 队的第 6 次全队犯规。判给 A1 执行 2 次罚球。裁判员指定 A2 执行了这 2 次罚球，而不是 A1。该失误被确认在：

（a）第 4 节比赛计时钟显示 1:49 时，比赛被停止（这是罚球后的首次比赛中断）。

（b）第 4 节比赛计时钟显示 1:23 时，比赛被停止（这是罚球后的第三次比赛中断）。

解释

在（a）中，该失误可纠正。

In (b), the opportunity to correct the error has expired. The error is no longer correctable and shall be disregarded.

44-5 **Example:** With 1:14 on the game clock in the fourth quarter, B1 fouls A1 in the act of shooting for a 2-point goal. The ball does not enter the basket. The referee erroneously awards A1 2 points and 1 additional free throw. The error is recognised

(a) before the game is resumed after the free throw.

(b) the first time the game is stopped after the game continues following the free throw with 0:59 on the game clock in the fourth quarter.

(c) during the interval of play between the fourth quarter and the first overtime.

(d) with 3:59 on the game clock in the overtime.

Interpretation:

In (a), and (b), the error is correctable.

In (c) and (d), the opportunity to correct the error has expired. The error is no longer correctable and shall be disregarded.

44-6 **Statement:** If the error constitutes the referee erroneously awarding an unmerited free throw(s), and the error is recognised within the time limits in the rules, the error shall be corrected as follows:

The free throw(s) attempted because of the error shall be cancelled and the game shall be resumed as follows:

- If the game clock has not started after the error, the ball shall be awarded for a throw-in from the free-throw line extended to the team whose free throws had been cancelled.
- If the game clock has already started after the error, the game shall be resumed from the place nearest to where it was stopped to correct the error.

44-7 **Example:** With 3:37 on the game clock in the second quarter, B1 fouls A1. This is the fourth team B foul in the quarter. The referee erroneously awards A1 2 free throws. The error is recognised

在（b）中，可纠正该失误的时机已过。该失误不再可纠正并应被忽略。

44-5 举例 第 4 节，比赛计时钟显示 1:14 时，B1 对正在做 2 分试投的 A1 犯规。球未进入球篮。裁判员错误地判给 A1 得 2 分并执行 1 次额外的罚球。该失误被确认在：

（a）罚球后，继续比赛前。

（b）罚球后，继续比赛，然后首次停止比赛，此时第 4 节比赛计时钟显示 0:59。

（c）第 4 节和第一个决胜期之间的比赛休息期间。

（d）决胜期比赛计时钟显示 3:59 时。

解释

在（a）和（b）中，该失误可纠正。

在（c）和（d）中，可纠正该失误的时机已过。该失误不再可纠正并应被忽略。

44-6 陈述 如果是由裁判员错误地判给不应得的罚球而造成的失误，并且该失误在规则规定的时限内被确认，应按如下原则纠正失误。

因失误而执行的罚球应被取消，应按如下方式继续比赛：

- 如果在失误发生后比赛计时钟尚未开动，应将球判给被取消罚球的球队在罚球线延长线处执行掷球入界。
- 如果在失误发生后比赛计时钟已经开动，应在最靠近因纠正失误而停止比赛的地点继续比赛。

44-7 举例 第 2 节，比赛计时钟显示 3:37 时，B1 对 A1 犯规。这是该节 B 队的第 4 次全队犯规。裁判员错误地判给 A1 执行 2 次罚球。该失误被确认在：

(a) after the ball is at A1's disposal for the first free throw.

(b) after A1 completes both free throws, but before the game clock starts following the second free throw.

(c) with 4:48 on the game clock in the fourth quarter.

Interpretation:

In all cases, the error is correctable. The free throws, whether made or missed, shall be cancelled.

In (a), and (b), the game shall be resumed with a team A throw-in at the free-throw line extended, opposite the scorer's table, with 14 seconds on the shot clock.

In (c), after the correction of the error the game shall be resumed from the place nearest to where it was stopped to correct the error.

44-8 **Statement:** If the error constitutes the referee erroneously failing to award a merited free throw(s), and the error is recognised within the time limits in the rules, the error shall be corrected as follows:

- If there has been no change in possession of the ball after the error occurred, the game shall be resumed after the correction of the error as after any last free throw.
- If the same team scores a goal after having been erroneously awarded possession of the ball for a throw-in, the error shall be disregarded.
- If the game clock has already started, and there has been a change of possession after the correction of the error, the game shall be resumed from the place nearest to where it was stopped to correct the error.

44-9 **Example:** B1 fouls A1 in the second quarter. This is the fifth team B foul in the quarter. Team A is erroneously awarded a throw-in. Immediately after A2 dribbles

(a) in the frontcourt

(b) in the frontcourt when B2 taps the ball out-of-bounds

(c) and scores

（a）A1 的第 1 次罚球可处理球后。

（b）A1 完成这两次罚球后，但在第 2 次罚球后比赛计时钟开动之前。

（c）第 4 节比赛计时钟显示 4:48 时。

解释

上述所有情况下，失误可纠正。无论这些罚球中篮与否，都应被取消。

在（a）和（b）中，应由 A 队在记录台对侧的罚球线延长线处执行掷球入界继续比赛，A 队应拥有 14 秒进攻时间。

在（c）中，在纠正失误后，应在最靠近因纠正失误而停止比赛的地点继续比赛。

44-8 陈述 如果是由裁判员错误地没有判给应得的罚球而造成的失误，并且该失误在规则规定的时限内被确认，应按如下原则纠正失误。

- 如果在该失误发生后球权没有改变，在该失误被纠正后，应如同任何最后一次罚球后那样继续比赛。
- 如果在错误地判给了掷球入界权之后，该队得分了，则应忽略该失误。
- 如果比赛计时钟已开动，并且球权已发生改变，在该失误被纠正后，应在最靠近因纠正失误而停止比赛的地点继续比赛。

44-9 举例 第 2 节中，B1 对 A1 犯规，这是该节 B 队的第 5 次全队犯规。错误地判给了 A 队执行掷球入界。

（a）A2 在其前场运球后，

（b）A2 在其前场运球，球被 B2 拍出界后，

（c）A2 运球并得分后，

when the error of not awarding A1 2 free throws is recognised.

Interpretation:

In (a) and (b), the error is correctable. A1 shall attempt 2 free throws and the game shall continue after the second free throw as after any last free throw.

In (c), team A has scored a goal following the error. The error is no longer correctable and shall be disregarded.

44-10 **Example:** B1 fouls A1 in the second quarter. This is the fifth team B foul in the quarter. Team A is erroneously awarded a throw-in. A2 scores a goal after having been erroneously awarded a throw-in. The error is recognised

(a) when the ball is at the disposal of B1 for an endline throw-in after A2's goal.

(b) when the referees stop the game after an additional 3 minutes of play.

(c) during the half-time.

(d) with 2:54 on the game clock in the fourth quarter.

Interpretation:

In all cases, the error shall be disregarded as team A scored a goal after having been erroneously awarded a throw-in.

44-11 **Example:** B1 fouls A1 in the act of shooting in the second quarter. After that, the team B head coach is charged with a technical foul. Team A is erroneously awarded only 2 free throws for the B1 foul. A1 attempts 2 free throws, the second free throw is successful.

The error is recognised

(a) when the ball is at the disposal of B2 for an endline throw-in after A1's second free throw.

(b) when the referees stop the game after 3 minutes playing time.

(c) during the half-time.

(d) with 1:54 on the game clock in the fourth quarter.

没有判给 A1 2 次罚球的失误立即被确认。

解释

在（a）和（b）中，失误可纠正。A1 应执行 2 次罚球，在第 2 次罚球后，应如同任何最后一次罚球后那样继续比赛。

在（c）中，A 队在发生失误后已中篮得分。该失误不再可纠正并应被忽略。

44-10 举例 第 2 节中，B1 对 A1 犯规，这是该节 B 队的第 5 次全队犯规。错误地判给了 A 队执行掷球入界。A2 在被错误地判给掷球入界后中篮得分。该失误被确认在：

（a）A2 中篮后，B1 从其端线后的掷球入界可处理球时。

（b）比赛又进行了 3 分钟后，裁判员停止比赛时。

（c）半时比赛休息期间。

（d）第 4 节比赛计时钟显示 2:54 时。

解释

上述所有情况下，该失误应被忽略，因为 A 队在被错误地判给掷球入界后已中篮得分。

44-11 举例 第 2 节，B1 对正在做投篮动作的 A1 犯规。随后，B 队主教练被判一起技术犯规。A 队被错误地仅判给了 B1 犯规的 2 次罚球。A1 执行了 2 次罚球，且第 2 次罚球成功。

该失误被确认在：

（a）A1 的第 2 次罚球后，B2 从其端线后的掷球入界可处理球时。

（b）比赛又进行了 3 分钟后，裁判员停止比赛时。

（c）半时比赛休息期间。

（d）第 4 节比赛计时钟显示 1:54 时。

Interpretation:

In (a), (b) and (c), the error is correctable.

A1 shall attempt the free throw with no line-up. The game shall be resumed from the place nearest to where it was stopped to correct the error.

In (d), the opportunity to correct the error has expired. The error is no longer correctable and shall be disregarded.

44-12 **Example:** B1 fouls dribbler A1 in the third quarter. This is the fifth team B foul in the quarter. A1 is awarded 2 free throws. After the first unsuccessful free throw, B1 rebounds the ball and the game erroneously continues. The error is recognised

(a) when B2 dribbles on the court.

(b) with 2:54 on the game clock in the fourth quarter.

(c) with 0:39 on the game clock in the fourth quarter.

(d) with 4:32 on the game clock in the overtime.

Interpretation:

In (a) and (b), the error is correctable. A1 shall attempt the second merited free throw. If A1 is on the team bench eligible to play, A1 must re-enter the game to attempt the free throw. If A1 has been excluded or disqualified, the team A head coach shall designate the free-throw shooter.

The free throw shall be attempted with no line-up. The game shall be resumed from the place nearest to where it was stopped to correct the error.

In (c) and (d), the opportunity to correct the error has expired. The error is no longer correctable and shall be disregarded.

44-13 **Statement:** If the error constitutes permitting the wrong player attempting a free throw(s), the free throw(s), whether made or missed, shall be cancelled. If the game has not yet been resumed, the ball shall be awarded to the opponents for a throw-in from the free-throw line extended opposite the scorer's table.

解释

在（a）（b）和（c）中，失误可纠正。

A1 应执行 1 次不占位的罚球。应在最靠近因纠正失误而停止比赛的地点继续比赛。

在（d）中，可纠正该失误的时机已过。该失误不再可纠正并应被忽略。

44-12 举例 第 3 节，B1 对运球队员 A1 犯规，这是该节 B 队的第 5 次全队犯规。判给 A1 执行 2 次罚球。在第 1 次不成功的罚球后，B1 获得篮板球并且比赛错误地继续进行。该失误被确认在：

（a）B2 在比赛场地上运球时。

（b）第 4 节比赛计时钟显示 2:54 时。

（c）第 4 节比赛计时钟显示 0:39 时。

（d）决胜期比赛计时钟显示 4:32 时。

解释

在（a）和（b）中，失误可被纠正。A1 应执行第 2 次应得的罚球。如果 A1 正坐在球队席上且有参赛资格，A1 必须重新进入比赛场地执行罚球。如果 A1 已出局或被取消比赛资格，A 队主教练应指定该罚球队员。

该罚球应不占位执行。应在最靠近因纠正失误而停止比赛的地点继续比赛。

在（c）和（d）中，可纠正该失误的时机已过。该失误不再可纠正并应被忽略。

44-13 陈述 如果是由错误的队员执行罚球而造成的失误，无论该罚球中篮与否，都应被取消。如果尚未继续比赛，应将球判给对方在记录台对侧的罚球线延长线处执行掷球入界。

If the game has been resumed, it shall be stopped to correct the error. After the correction of the error the game shall be resumed from the place nearest to where it was stopped.

If the referees recognise, before the ball has left the hands of the free-throw shooter for the first free throw, that a wrong player has the intention to attempt the next free throw(s), the wrong player shall be immediately replaced by the correct free-throw shooter without any penalty.

44-14 **Example:** B1 fouls dribbler A1 when the game clock signal sounds for the end of the third quarter. This is the sixth team B foul in the quarter. The referees decide that B1's foul occurred with 0.3 of a second on the game clock. A1 is awarded 2 free throws. Instead of A1, it is A2 who attempts 2 free throws. The error is recognised after the ball has left A2's hands for the first free throw.

Interpretation: A2's 2 free throws shall be cancelled. The game shall be resumed with a team B throw-in from the free-throw line extended opposite the scorer's table in its backcourt, with 0.3 of a second on the game clock.

44-15 **Example:** With 3 seconds on the game clock in the third quarter, B1 fouls A1 in the act of shooting. A1 is awarded 2 free throws. Instead of A1, it is A2 who attempts 2 free throws. The third quarter ends. The error is recognised

(a) during the interval of play between the third and fourth quarter.

(b) after the ball is live to start the fourth quarter, with more than 2:00 minutes on the game clock in the fourth quarter.

(c) with 2:00 minutes or less on the game clock in the fourth quarter.

Interpretation:

In (a) and (b), the error is correctable. A2's 2 free throws shall be cancelled.

In (a), the fourth quarter shall start with an alternating possession throw-in from the centre line extended.

> 如果已经继续比赛，则应停止比赛去纠正失误。在该失误被纠正后，应在最靠近停止比赛的地点继续比赛。
>
> 如果一名错误的队员有意执行罚球，且在该队员的第 1 次罚球球离手前被裁判员确认了，该错误的队员应立即被正确的罚球队员替换，不作任何处罚。

44-14 **举例** B1 对运球队员 A1 犯规时，结束第 3 节的比赛计时钟信号响。这是该节 B 队的第 6 次全队犯规。裁判员决定 B1 的犯规发生时，比赛计时钟应显示 0.3 秒。判给 A1 执行 2 次罚球。A2 执行了这 2 次罚球，而不是 A1。在 A2 的第 1 次罚球球离手后，裁判员确认了该失误。

解释 A2 的 2 次罚球应被取消。应由 B 队在其后场记录台对侧的罚球线延长线处执行掷球入界继续比赛，比赛计时钟应显示 0.3 秒。

44-15 **举例** 第 3 节，比赛计时钟显示 3 秒时，B1 对正在做投篮动作的 A1 犯规。判给 A1 执行 2 次罚球。A2 执行了这 2 次罚球，而不是 A1。第 3 节比赛结束，该失误被确认在：

（a）第 3 节和第 4 节之间的比赛休息期间。

（b）第 4 节开始球成活球之后，且第 4 节比赛计时钟显示多于 2:00 分钟时。

（c）第 4 节比赛计时钟显示 2:00 分钟或更少时。

解释

在（a）和（b）中，该失误可纠正。A2 的 2 次罚球应被取消。

在（a）中，应在中线延长线处执行交替拥有掷球入界开始第 4 节比赛。

In (b), the game shall be resumed from the place nearest to where it was stopped to correct the error.

In (c), the opportunity to correct the error has expired. The error is no longer correctable and shall be disregarded. The game shall continue.

44-16 **Statement:** If the error constitutes the referee directing the wrong player to attempt a free throw(s), the free throws, whether made or missed, shall be cancelled and the correct player shall attempt a replacement free throw(s).

The game shall continue as after any last free throw, unless the game has continued and was stopped for the correction of the error, in which case the game shall be resumed from the place it was stopped to correct the error.

44-17 **Statement:** B1 fouls dribbler A1 when the game clock signal sounds for the end of the third quarter. This is the sixth team B foul in the quarter. The referees decide that B1's foul occurred with 0.3 of a second on the game clock. A1 is awarded 2 free throws. Instead of A1, the referees direct A2 to attempt the 2 free throws. The error is recognised after the ball has left A2's hands for the first free throw.

Interpretation: A2's free throw shall be cancelled. A1 shall attempt 2 free throws. The game shall continue as after any last free throw.

44-18 **Example:** B1 fouls A1 in the act of shooting. A1 is awarded 2 free throws. Instead of A1, the referee directs A2 to attempt 2 free throws. During the second free throw the ball touches the ring, A3 rebounds it and scores 2 points. The error is recognised before the ball is at the disposal of team B for the throw-in from behind its endline.

Interpretation: The 2 free throws attempted by A2, whether made or missed, shall be cancelled. A3's goal shall remain valid. A1 shall attempt 2 free throws with no line-up. The game shall be resumed with a team B throw-in from the place nearest to where the game was stopped to correct the error, in this case from behind its endline.

44-19 **Statement:** If the error constitutes the referee erroneously awarding or cancelling points, and the error is recognised within the time limits in the rules, the error shall be corrected on the scoresheet as follows:

在（b）中，应在最靠近因纠正失误而停止比赛的地点继续比赛。

在（c）中，可纠正该失误的时机已过。该失误不再可纠正并应被忽略。应继续比赛。

44-16 陈述 如果是由裁判员指定错误的队员执行罚球而造成的失误，无论该罚球中篮与否，都应被取消，并应由正确的队员重新执行该罚球。

应如同任何最后一次罚球后那样继续比赛，除非比赛已经继续进行并且为了纠正失误而被停止，在这样的情况下，应在因纠正失误而停止比赛的地点继续比赛。

44-17 举例 B1 对运球队员 A1 犯规时，结束第 3 节的比赛计时钟信号响。这是该节 B 队的第 6 次全队犯规。裁判员决定 B1 的犯规发生时，比赛计时钟应显示 0.3 秒。判给 A1 执行 2 次罚球。裁判员指定 A2 执行了这 2 次罚球，而不是 A1。A2 的第 1 次罚球球离手后，该失误被确认。

解释 A2 的罚球应被取消。应由 A1 执行 2 次罚球。应如同任何最后一次罚球后那样继续比赛。

44-18 举例 B1 对正在做投篮动作的 A1 犯规。判给 A1 执行 2 次罚球。裁判员指定 A2 执行了这 2 次罚球，而不是 A1。在第 2 次罚球离手的球触及篮圈后，A3 获得篮板球并得到 2 分。B 队从其端线后的掷球入界可处理球前，该失误被确认。

解释 无论这 2 次罚球中篮与否，都应被取消。A3 的中篮应保留有效。应由 A1 执行 2 次不占位的罚球。应由 B 队在最靠近因纠正失误而停止比赛的地点执行掷球入界继续比赛。在该情况下，该掷球入界的地点是在 B 队的端线后。

44-19 陈述 如果是由裁判员错误地判给得分或取消得分而造成的失误，并且该失误在规则规定的时限内被确认，应按如下原则在记录表上纠正失误。

- The points shall be cancelled or awarded as applicable.
- If a free throw(s) was erroneously awarded, the free throw(s) attempted, if made, shall be cancelled as a result of an error correction.
- If a free throw(s) was erroneously not awarded, the free throws shall be attempted by the player entitled to these free throws as a result of an error correction.

44-20 **Example:** With 0:57 on the game clock in the fourth quarter, A1 has released the ball on a shot for a goal when A2 commits a foul away from the ball. The ball legally enters the basket, but the referees erroneously cancel the goal. The error is recognised

(a) with 0:43 seconds on the game clock in the fourth quarter, when the game is stopped by the referees for the first time following the error.

(b) after the ball is live after the game was stopped with 0:43 on the game clock in the fourth quarter.

Interpretation:

In (a), the error is correctable. The scoresheet shall be corrected by adding 2 points to the team A. The game shall be resumed from the place it was stopped to correct the error.

In (b), the opportunity to correct the error has expired. The error is no longer correctable and shall be disregarded.

44-21 **Example:** With 3:32 on the game clock in the second quarter, B1 fouls A1 in the act of shooting for a 2-point goal. The ball does not enter the basket. The referee erroneously awards A1 2 points and 1 additional free throw. The error is recognised when the game is stopped with

(a) 5:21 on the game clock in the third quarter.

(b) 1:02 in the fourth quarter or any time in the overtime.

Interpretation: The error of erroneously awarding a 2-point goal in the second quarter is correctable at any time before 2:00 minutes or less are on the game clock in the fourth quarter.

- 应取消或判给所适用情况中的该得分。
- 如果错误地判给了罚球，作为纠正失误的结果，该罚球如中篮，应被取消。
- 如果错误地没有判给罚球，作为纠正失误的结果，应由有该罚球权的队员执行该罚球。

44-20 举例 第 4 节，比赛计时钟显示 0:57 时，当 A1 投篮的球已离手时，A2 发生了一起投篮情况之外的犯规。球合法进入球篮，但裁判员错误地取消了中篮。该失误被确认在：

（a）第 4 节比赛计时钟显示 0:43，裁判员在发生失误后首次停止比赛时。

（b）第 4 节比赛计时钟显示 0:43 时比赛被停止后，球成活球后。

解释

在（a）中，该失误可纠正。应给 A 队加上 2 分以纠正记录表。应在因纠正失误而停止比赛的地点继续比赛。

在（b）中，可纠正该失误的时机已过。该失误不再可纠正并应被忽略。

44-21 举例 第 2 节，比赛计时钟显示 3:32 时，B1 对正在做 2 分试投的 A1 犯规。球未进入球篮。裁判员错误地判给 A1 得 2 分并执行 1 次额外的罚球。

（a）第 3 节比赛计时钟显示 5:21 时，

（b）第 4 节剩余 1:02，或决胜期进行到任何时间时，

比赛停止，该失误被确认。

解释 如在第 4 节比赛计时钟显示 2:00 分钟或更少之前的任何时间，该错误地判给 2 分中篮的失误可纠正。

In (a), the error is correctable. The scorer, after consulting the crew chief, shall cancel the erroneously awarded goal. A1 shall attempt 1 free throw regardless of whether the first free throw in the second quarter was made or missed.

A1 must enter the game to attempt 1 free throw unless A1 has been excluded or disqualified. If A1 has been excluded or disqualified, any team A player or substitute designated by the team A head coach shall attempt the free throw.

The game shall be resumed from the place nearest to where it was stopped to correct the error.

In (b), the opportunity to correct the error has expired. The error is no longer correctable and shall be disregarded.

44-22 **Statement:** If the error constitutes the referee reporting a foul on the wrong player, coach or team, and the error is recognised within the time limits in the rules, the error shall be corrected as follows:

The scoresheet shall be corrected, and any player or coach inadvertently excluded or disqualified as a result of the wrongly reported foul shall be reinstated, and any player or coach who become excluded or disqualified due to the correction shall be excluded or disqualified. No penalty shall be applied.

44-23 **Example:** With 5:47 on the game clock in the first quarter, B1 fouls A1. The referee reports the foul on B2. The error is recognised

(a) during the half-time.

(b) when the game is stopped with 2:21 on the game clock in the fourth quarter.

(c) when the game is stopped with 2:00 on the game clock in the fourth quarter or any time in the overtime.

Interpretation: The error of reporting the foul on the wrong player is correctable at any time before 2:00 minutes or less are on the game clock in the fourth quarter.

在（a）中，该失误可纠正。记录员应在与主裁判员商议之后取消错误判给的中篮。无论第 2 节中的那第 1 次罚球中篮与否，A1 应执行 1 次罚球。

A1 必须重新回到比赛场地执行 1 次罚球，除非 A1 已出局或被取消比赛资格。如果 A1 已出局或被取消比赛资格，A 队主教练指定的任一 A 队队员或替补队员应执行该罚球。

应在最靠近因纠正失误而停止比赛的地点继续比赛。

在（b）中，可纠正该失误的时机已过。该失误不再可纠正并应被忽略。

44-22 陈述 如果是由裁判员将一起犯规报告在错误的队员、主教练或球队名下而造成的失误，并且该失误在规则规定的时限内被确认，应按如下原则纠正失误。

应纠正记录表，由于犯规被错误地报告而被无意判出局或取消比赛资格的任何队员或主教练应恢复参赛权，并且任何因纠正失误而成为出局或被取消比赛资格的队员或主教练应被判出局或取消比赛资格。不应执行任何罚则。

44-23 举例 第 1 节，比赛计时钟显示 5:47 时，B1 对 A1 犯规。裁判员将犯规报告在 B2 名下，该失误被确认在：

（a）半时比赛休息期间。

（b）第 4 节比赛计时钟显示 2:21，比赛被停止时。

（c）第 4 节比赛计时钟显示 2:00 或决胜期进行到任何时间，比赛被停止时。

解释 在第 4 节比赛计时钟显示 2:00 分钟或更少之前的任何时间，这起将犯规报告在错误的队员名下的失误可纠正。

In (a) and (b), the error is correctable. The scorer, after consulting the crew chief, shall correct the scoresheet by removing the foul charged on B2 in error and correctly adding a foul to B1. If B2 had been excluded in error, B2 shall be reinstated. If B1 should have been excluded earlier, B1 shall now be excluded. No additional penalty shall be applied.

In (c), the opportunity to correct the error has expired. The error is no longer correctable and shall be disregarded.

44-24 **Statement:** If a scorekeeping error, including failing to record or

- erroneously recording points or
- recording a foul on the wrong player, coach or team or
- recording a time-out on the wrong team

is recognised within the time limits in the rules, then the scoresheet shall be corrected. Any player or coach inadvertently excluded or disqualified as a result of the wrongly reported foul shall be reinstated and any player or coach who become excluded or disqualified due to the correction shall be excluded or disqualified. No penalty shall be applied.

44-25 **Example:** With 3:45 on the game clock in the fourth quarter, team A requests a second time-out in the second half. The scorer erroneously records the time-out as the second team B time-out in the second half. The ball goes out-of-bounds and the referees stop the game

(a) with 2:02 on the game clock in the fourth quarter, and team B is awarded a time-out.

(b) with 1:45 on the game clock in the fourth quarter, and team B is awarded a time-out.

Team B is told this is the third time-out in the second half, therefore team B has no more time-outs remaining. The team B head coach insists that an error has occurred. The scorer consults the crew chief and the error is recognised.

在（a）和（b）中，该失误可纠正。记录员应在与主裁判员商议之后删除因该失误而登记在 B2 名下的犯规，并在 B1 名下增加一次犯规以纠正记录表。如果 B2 因该失误而被判出局，B2 应恢复参赛权。如果 B1 先前应当已经被判出局，则此时 B1 应被判出局。不应执行任何额外罚则。

在（c）中，可纠正该失误的时机已过。该失误不再可纠正并应被忽略。

44-24 陈述 如果发生记录表登记的失误，包括：

- 未记录或错误地记录得分，或
- 未登记一起犯规或将一起犯规登记在错误的队员、主教练或球队名下，或
- 未登记一次暂停或将一次暂停登记在错误的球队名下，

并且该失误在规则规定的时限内被确认，则应纠正记录表。由于犯规被错误地报告而被无意判出局或取消比赛资格的任何队员或主教练应恢复参赛权，并且任何因纠正失误而成为出局或被取消比赛资格的队员或主教练应被判出局或取消比赛资格。不应执行任何罚则。

44-25 举例 第 4 节，比赛计时钟显示 3:45 时，A 队请求了下半时的第 2 次暂停。记录员将该下半时的第 2 次暂停错误地登记在了 B 队名下。球出界了，并且裁判员停止比赛时：

（a）第 4 节比赛计时钟显示 2:02，B 队被准予一次暂停。

（b）第 4 节比赛计时钟显示 1:45，B 队被准予一次暂停。

B 队被告知这是该队下半时的第 3 次暂停，因此 B 队已没有剩余的暂停。B 队主教练坚信发生了一起失误。记录员在与主裁判员商议之后确认了该失误。

Interpretation:

In (a), the error is correctable. The scorer, after consulting the crew chief, shall correct the scoresheet by removing the time-out recorded against the team B and recording the time-out against team A.

In (b), the error of recording the time-out on the wrong team is no longer correctable as the error must be recognised before 2:00 minutes or less are on the game clock in the fourth quarter.

If the time-out has started, team B is using its last time-out entitled to in the second half. If the time-out has not started, the team B head coach may withdraw the time-out request.

44-26 **Example:** With 3:34 on the game clock in the first quarter, the team A head coach is charged with a technical foul. The scorer erroneously records the technical foul against the team B head coach. The error is recognised

(a) during the half-time.

(b) when the game is stopped with 3:31 on the game clock in the fourth quarter.

(c) when the game is stopped with 1:02 on the game clock in the fourth quarter or any time in the overtime.

Interpretation: The error of recording the technical foul on the wrong team is correctable before 2:00 minutes or less are on the game clock in the fourth quarter.

In (a) and (b), the error is correctable. The scorer, after consulting the crew chief, shall correct the scoresheet by removing the technical foul recorded against the team B head coach and correctly recording it against the team A head coach. No penalty shall be applied.

In (c), the opportunity to correct the error has expired. The error is no longer correctable and shall be disregarded.

The game shall be resumed from the place it was stopped to correct the error.

解释

在（a）中，记录员应在与主裁判员商议之后删除登记在 B 队名下的那次暂停，并在 A 队名下登记那次暂停以纠正记录表。

在（b）中，该暂停登记在错误的球队名下的失误不再可纠正，因为该失误必须在第 4 节比赛计时钟显示 2:00 分钟或更少之前被确认。

如果暂停已开始，B 队正在使用的是其下半场有权被准予的最后一次暂停。如果暂停尚未开始，B 队主教练可以取消该暂停请求。

44-26 举例 第 1 节，比赛计时钟显示 3:34 时，A 队主教练被判 1 次技术犯规。记录员将该技术犯规错误地登记在了 B 队主教练名下。该失误被确认在：

（a）半时比赛休息期间。

（b）第 4 节比赛计时钟显示 3:31，比赛被停止时。

（c）第 4 节比赛计时钟显示 1:02 或决胜期进行到任何时间，比赛被停止时。

解释 在第 4 节比赛计时钟显示 2:00 分钟或更少之前，这起将技术犯规报告在错误的球队名下的失误可纠正。

在（a）和（b）中，该失误可纠正。记录员应在与主裁判员商议之后删除登记在 B 队主教练名下的技术犯规，并在 A 队主教练名下登记该技术犯规以纠正记录表。不应执行任何罚则。

在（c）中，可纠正该失误的时机已过。该失误不再可纠正并应被忽略。

应在因纠正失误而停止比赛的地点继续比赛。

44-27 Statement: If the error constitutes game clock errors, including malfunctions, or errors in starting or stopping the game clock correctly or in setting the correct time on the game clock, the error shall be corrected as follows:

If the error is recognised within the time limits in the rules, the game clock shall be corrected, with time added or subtracted as necessary to correct the error.

44-28 Example: With 2:44 on the game clock in the first quarter, the game clock is stopped for an out-of-bounds violation. After the throw-in, with 24 seconds on the shot clock, due to a game clock malfunction, it has no visible display. The referees stop the game, with 15 seconds on the shot clock.

Interpretation: The error of the game clock failing to run is correctable. The game shall be resumed from the place it was stopped with 2:35 on the game clock, with 15 seconds on the shot clock.

44-29 Example: With 2:43 on the game clock in the first quarter, the game clock is stopped for an out-of-bounds violation. Before the throw-in, the visible display on the game clock disappears. The timer resets the system. When the system is again working, the game clock is erroneously set to 1:43. The error is recognised

(a) when the game is stopped with 0:27 on the game clock in the first quarter.

(b) during the half-time.

(c) during the interval between the third and fourth quarters.

(d) when the game is stopped with 2:21 on the game clock in the fourth quarter.

(e) when the game is stopped with 1:15 on the game clock in the fourth quarter or any time in the overtime.

Interpretation: In (a), (b), (c) and (d), the error of the game clock being set incorrectly is correctable.

In (a), 1 minute shall be added to the game clock. The game shall be resumed from the place it was stopped, with 1:27 on the game clock.

44-27 陈述 如果是由比赛计时的失误，包括设备故障、错误地开动或停止了比赛计时钟，或是在比赛计时钟上设置了错误的时间而造成的失误，应按如下原则纠正失误。

如果该失误在规则规定的时限内被确认，比赛计时钟应被纠正，应通过必要地加上或减去时间来纠正失误。

44-28 举例 第 1 节，比赛计时钟显示 2:44 时，比赛计时钟因出界违例而停止。在执行掷球入界后，进攻计时钟显示 24 秒，比赛计时钟因出现故障而造成其显示不可见。裁判员停止比赛，进攻计时钟显示 15 秒。

解释 比赛计时钟未运行的失误可纠正。应从比赛被停止的位置继续比赛，比赛计时钟应显示 2:35，进攻计时钟应显示 15 秒。

44-29 举例 第 1 节，比赛计时钟显示 2:43 时，比赛计时钟因出界违例而停止。在执行掷球入界前，比赛计时钟上可见的显示消失。计时员重置了系统。当系统再次运作时，比赛计时钟被错误地设置到 1:43。该失误被确认在：

（a）第 1 节比赛计时钟显示 0:27，比赛被停止时。

（b）半时比赛休息期间。

（c）第 3 节和第 4 节之间的比赛休息期间。

（d）第 4 节比赛计时钟显示 2:21，比赛被停止时。

（e）第 4 节比赛计时钟显示 1:15 或决胜期进行到任何时间，比赛被停止时。

解释 在（a）（b）（c）和（d）中，错误地设置了比赛计时钟的失误可纠正。

在（a）中，比赛计时钟应被加上 1 分钟。应从比赛被停止的位置继续比赛，比赛计时钟应显示 1:27。

In (b) after the half-time interval, the teams shall play 1 minute in the same direction they played the first half, with team fouls and time-outs continuing from the time when the game was stopped for half-time. The 1:00 shall start with an alternating possession throw-in for the team entitled to the alternating possession throw-in. After the 1:00 of play, the third quarter shall start with an alternating possession throw-in for the team entitled to the next alternating possession throw-in.

In (c), the fourth quarter shall be played with 11 minutes duration.

In (d), 1 minute shall be added to the game clock. The game shall be resumed from the place it was stopped, with 3:21 on the game clock.

In (e), the opportunity to correct the error has expired. The error is no longer correctable.

44-30 **Statement:** To be correctable, the shot clock category 2 error must be recognised by the referees, commissioner, if present, or table officials and corrected

- when the ball is live immediately following the error and the referees stop the game to correct the error, or
- when for the first time the referees stop the game for any reason, the team in control of the ball at the time of the error remains the team in control or the team entitled to possession of the ball when the game is stopped.

The shot clock shall be corrected to the correct time.

Shot clock errors are no longer correctable after

- a change of possession of a live ball after the error.
- the team in control of the ball scores a valid goal.
- the ball becomes dead when the game clock sounds for the end of the game.

44-31 **Example:** With 20 seconds on the shot clock, A1 dribbles in the frontcourt when the shot clock is suddenly reset to 24 seconds. The error is recognised 4 seconds later

(a) when the referees stop the game.

在（b）中，在半时比赛休息期间结束后，双方球队应朝他们上半时进攻的相同方向进行 1 分钟的比赛，其全队犯规和暂停次数应从半时比赛休息期间的比赛停止处延续。该 1 分钟的比赛应由拥有交替拥有掷球入界权的球队以交替拥有掷球入界开始。在该 1 分钟的比赛后，第 3 节应由拥有下一次交替拥有掷球入界权的球队以交替拥有掷球入界开始。

在（c）中，第 4 节应进行时长 11 分钟的比赛。

在（d）中，比赛计时钟应被加上 1 分钟。应从比赛被停止的位置继续比赛，比赛计时钟应显示 3:21。

在（e）中，可纠正该失误的时机已过。该失误不再可纠正。

44-30 陈述 要纠正进攻计时钟的第二类失误，它们就必须被裁判员、到场的临场代表或记录台人员在下列时间确认和纠正。

- 在发生失误后球立即成活球，然后裁判员因纠正失误而停止比赛时，或
- 在裁判员因任何原因首次停止比赛时，该失误发生时控制球或拥有球权的队应仍然控制球或仍然拥有球权。

进攻计时钟应被纠正到正确的时间。

下列情况后，进攻计时钟不再是可纠正的。

- 发生失误后，在活球期间发生球权转换。
- 控制球队有效的中篮得分。
- 在结束比赛计时钟信号响且球成死球时。

44-31 举例 进攻计时钟显示 20 秒，A1 在其前场运球，突然进攻计时钟复位到 24 秒。4 秒后，

（a）当裁判员停止比赛时，

(b) when the game is stopped as a result of B3 tapping the ball out-of-bounds.

Interpretation: In both cases, team A shall be awarded a throw-in from the place nearest to where the game was stopped. The shot clock shall be reset to 16 seconds.

44-32 **Example:** Team A is awarded a frontcourt throw-in. The shot clock should be set to 14 seconds but it is incorrectly set to 24 seconds. A1 catches the ball on the court and dribbles in the frontcourt for 10 seconds. The error is recognised

(a) when the referees stop the game.

(b) when the game is stopped as a result of B3 tapping the ball out-of-bounds.

Interpretation: In both cases, team A shall be awarded a throw-in from the place nearest to where the game was stopped. The shot clock shall be reset to 4 seconds.

44-33 **Example:** Team A is awarded a backcourt throw-in. The shot clock should be set to 24 seconds but it is incorrectly set to 14 seconds. A1 catches the ball on the court and dribbles into the frontcourt. The error is recognised 8 seconds later

(a) when the referees stop the game.

(b) when the game is stopped as a result of B1 tapping the ball out-of-bounds.

Interpretation: In both cases, team A shall be awarded a throw-in from the place nearest to where the game was stopped. The shot clock shall be reset to 16 seconds.

44-34 **Example:** Team A is awarded a backcourt throw-in. The shot clock should be set to 24 seconds but it is incorrectly set to 14 seconds. A1 catches the ball on the court, dribbles into the frontcourt and attempts a shot for a goal. The shot clock signal sounds while the ball is in the air. The ball

(a) misses the ring and is immediately rebounded by A2. The referees stop the game for a shot clock violation.

（b）当 B3 将球拍出界导致比赛停止时，

该失误被确认。

解释　在这两种情况下，应判给 A 队在最靠近比赛被停止的地点执行掷球入界。进攻计时钟应复位到 16 秒。

44-32　举例　判给 A 队在其前场执行掷球入界。进攻计时钟应当复位到 14 秒，但却错误地复位到了 24 秒。A1 在比赛场地上接球并在其前场运球 10 秒。该失误被确认在：

（a）裁判员停止比赛时。

（b）B3 将球拍出界导致比赛停止时。

解释　在这两种情况下，应判给 A 队在最靠近比赛被停止的地点执行掷球入界。进攻计时钟应复位到 4 秒。

44-33　举例　判给 A 队在其后场执行掷球入界。进攻计时钟应当复位到 24 秒，但却错误地复位到了 14 秒。A1 在比赛场地上接球并运球进入其前场。8 秒后，

（a）当裁判员停止比赛时，

（b）当 B1 将球拍出界导致比赛停止时，

该失误被确认。

解释　在这两种情况下，应判给 A 队在最靠近比赛被停止的地点执行掷球入界。进攻计时钟应复位到 16 秒。

44-34　举例　判给 A 队在其后场执行掷球入界。进攻计时钟应当复位到 24 秒，但却错误地复位到了 14 秒。A1 在比赛场地上接球，运球进入其前场并尝试一次投篮。当球在空中时，进攻计时钟信号响。球：

（a）未触及篮圈，A2 立即获得篮板球。裁判员因进攻时间违例而停止比赛。

(b) misses the ring and is immediately rebounded by B2. The referees stop the game for a shot clock violation.

The table officials recognise the error of incorrectly setting the shot clock.

Interpretation:

In both cases, the shot clock violation shall be disregarded.

In (a), team A shall be awarded a throw-in from the place nearest to where the game was stopped, with 10 seconds on the shot clock.

In (b), as team B gained the new possession of the ball, team B shall be awarded a throw-in from the place nearest to where the game was stopped, with 24 seconds on the shot clock.

44-35 **Example:** Team A is awarded a backcourt throw-in. The shot clock should be set to 24 seconds but it is incorrectly set to 14 seconds. A1 catches the ball on the court, dribbles into the frontcourt and attempts a shot for a goal.

(a) A1's shot is unsuccessful after which B2 gains control of the ball and starts a dribbling.

(b) A1's shot is successful.

The referees recognise the error and stop the game to correct the shot clock.

Interpretation: In both cases, the error is no longer correctable, because after the error

(a) there has been a change of possession.

(b) the same team scored a goal.

（b）未触及篮圈，B2 立即获得篮板球。裁判员因进攻时间违例而停止比赛。

记录台人员确认了该错误地设置了进攻计时钟的失误。

解释 在这两种情况下，进攻时间违例应被忽略。

在（a）中，应判给 A 队在最靠近比赛被停止的地点执行掷球入界，A 队应拥有 10 秒进攻时间。

在（b）中，因 B 队获得了新的球权，应判给 B 队在最靠近比赛被停止的地点执行掷球入界，B 队应拥有 24 秒进攻时间。

44-35 举例 判给 A 队在其后场执行掷球入界。进攻计时钟应当复位到 24 秒，但却错误地复位到了 14 秒。A1 在比赛场地上接球，运球进入其前场并尝试一次投篮。

（a）A1 的投篮未成功，随后 B2 获得控制球并开始一次运球。

（b）A1 的投篮成功。

裁判员确认了该失误并停止比赛以纠正进攻计时钟。

解释 在这两种情况下，该失误不再可纠正，因为在发生失误后：

（a）发生了球权转换。

（b）同一球队中篮得分了。

Appendix B The scoresheet – Disqualifying fouls

B-1 Examples for disqualifying fouls of various persons:

1. Only the **head coach** is disqualified.

For leaving the team bench area and not assisting or attempting to assist the referees

Head coach	D_2	F	F
First assistant coach			
Penalty: 2 free throws+possession			

For the active involvement in the fight

Head coach	D_2	F	F
First assistant coach			
Penalty: 2 free throws+possession			

2. Only the **first assistant coach** is disqualified.

For leaving the team bench area and not assisting or attempting to assist the referees

Head coach	B_2		
First assistant coach	D	F	F
Penalty: 2 free throws+possession			

For the active involvement in the fight

Head coach	B_2		
First assistant coach	D_2	F	F
Penalty: 4 free throws+possession			

3. Both the **head coach** and the **first assistant coach** are disqualified.

For leaving the team bench area and not assisting or attempting to assist the referees

Head coach	D_2	F	F
First assistant coach	D	F	F
Penalty: 2 free throws+possession			

For the active involvement in the fight

Head coach	D_2	F	F
First assistant coach	D_2	F	F
Penalty: 4 free throws+possession			

4. A **substitute** is disqualified.

For leaving the team bench area and not assisting or attempting to assist the referees

Head coach	B_2				
First assistant coach					
Player 7	P_2	P_2	D	F	F
Penalty: 2 free throws+possession					

For the active involvement in the fight

Head coach	B_2				
First assistant coach					
Player 7	P_2	P_2	D_2	F	F
Penalty: 4 free throws+possession					

附录 B　记录表——取消比赛资格的犯规

B-1　相关人员取消比赛资格的犯规举例

1. 只有**主教练**被取消比赛资格。

因离开球队席区域且不协助或不试图去协助裁判员：

主教练	D_2	F	F
第一助理教练			
罚则：2 次罚球 + 球权			

因积极参与打架：

主教练	D_2	F	F
第一助理教练			
罚则：2 次罚球 + 球权			

2. 只有**第一助理教练**被取消比赛资格。

因离开球队席区域且不协助或不试图去协助裁判员：

主教练	B_2		
第一助理教练	D	F	F
罚则：2 次罚球 + 球权			

因积极参与打架：

主教练	B_2		
第一助理教练	D_2	F	F
罚则：4 次罚球 + 球权			

3. 主教练和**第一助理教练**都被取消比赛资格。

因离开球队席区域且不协助或不试图去协助裁判员：

主教练	D_2	F	F
第一助理教练	D	F	F
罚则：2 次罚球 + 球权			

因积极参与打架：

主教练	D_2	F	F
第一助理教练	D_2	F	F
罚则：4 次罚球 + 球权			

4. 1 名**替补队员**被取消比赛资格。

因离开球队席区域且不协助或不试图去协助裁判员：

主教练	B_2				
第一助理教练					
队员 7	P_2	P_2	D	F	F
罚则：2 次罚球 + 球权					

因积极参与打架：

主教练	B_2				
第一助理教练					
队员 7	P_2	P_2	D_2	F	F
罚则：4 次罚球 + 球权					

5. Two **substitutes** and an **excluded player** are disqualified.

Head coach	B_2					
First assistant coach						
Player 7	P_2	P_2	D	F	F	
Player 10	P_2	T_1	P	P	D	F
Player 11	P_3	T_1	P	P	P	DF
Penalty: 2 free throws+possession						

Head coach	B_2					
First assistant coach						
Player 7	P_2	P_2	D_2	F	F	
Player 10	P_2	T_1	P	P	D_2	F
Player 11	P_3	T_1	P	P	P	D_2F
Penalty: 8 free throws+possession						

6. An **accompanying delegation member** is disqualified.

Head coach	B_2	B	
First assistant coach			
Penalty: 2 free throws+possession			

Head coach	B_2	B_2	
First assistant coach			
Penalty: 4 free throws+possession			

7. **Two accompanying delegation members** are disqualified.

Head coach	B_2	B	B
First assistant coach			
Penalty: 2 free throws+possession			

Head coach	B_2	B_2	B_2
First assistant coach			
Penalty: 6 free throws+possession			

5. 2 名**替补队员**和 1 名**出局的队员**被取消比赛资格。

主教练	B_2					
第一助理教练						
队员 7	P_2	P_2	D	F	F	
队员 10	P_2	T_1	P	P	D	F
队员 11	P_3	T_1	P	P	P	DF
罚则：2 次罚球 + 球权						

主教练	B_2					
第一助理教练						
队员 7	P_2	P_2	D_2	F	F	
队员 10	P_2	T_1	P	P	D_2	F
队员 11	P_3	T_1	P	P	P	D_2F
罚则：8 次罚球 + 球权						

6. 1 名**随队人员**被取消比赛资格。

主教练	B_2	B	
第一助理教练			
罚则：2 次罚球 + 球权			

主教练	B_2	B_2	
第一助理教练			
罚则：4 次罚球 + 球权			

7. 2 **名随队人员**被取消比赛资格。

主教练	B_2	B	B
第一助理教练			
罚则：2 次罚球 + 球权			

主教练	B_2	B_2	B_2
第一助理教练			
罚则：6 次罚球 + 球权			

B-2 Examples of the technical fouls against the head coach for the personal unsportsmanlike behaviour or for any other reason, combined with the disqualification of an accompanying delegation member for leaving the team bench area during a fight:

1. In the first quarter there is a fight situation with a disqualification of an **accompanying delegation member**. In the third quarter, a technical foul is called against the **head coach** for the personal unsportsmanlike behaviour.

Head coach	B_2	(B)	C_1
First assistant coach			
Penalty:1 free throw			

Head coach is not disqualified

2. In the first quarter there is a fight situation with a disqualification of an **accompanying delegation member**. In the third quarter, a technical foul is called against the **head coach** for any other reason.

Head coach	B_2	(B)	B_1
First assistant coach			
Penalty:1 free throw			

Head coach is not disqualified

3. In the first quarter there is a fight situation with a disqualification of an **accompanying delegation member**. In the third quarter, a technical foul is called against the **head coach** for the personal unsportsmanlike behaviour. In the fourth quarter, another technical foul is called against the **head coach** for the personal unsportsmanlike behaviour.

Head coach	B_2	(B)	C_1
First assistant coach			
Penalty:1 free throw			

C_1 GD

Head coach is disqualified automatically for 2 C-fouls

4. In the first quarter there is a fight situation with a disqualification of an **accompanying delegation member**. In the third quarter, a technical foul is called against the **head coach** for any other reason. In the fourth quarter, another technical foul is called against the **head coach** for any other reason.

Head coach	B_2	(B)	B_1
First assistant coach			
Penalty:1 free throw			

B_1 GD

Head coach is disqualified automatically for 3 B-fouls

B-2 因主教练自身违反体育运动精神的行为或因任何其他的原因，加上在打架中随队人员因离开球队席区域被取消比赛资格而登记在其名下的技术犯规的举例

1. 第 1 节有一起打架情况，1 名**随队人员**被取消比赛资格。
   第 3 节，该**主教练**因其自身违反体育运动精神的行为被判了一次技术犯规。

主教练	B_2	(B)	C_1
第一助理教练			
罚则：1 次罚球			

该主教练**不被取消比赛资格**

2. 第 1 节有一起打架情况，1 名**随队人员**被取消比赛资格。
   第 3 节，该**主教练**因任何其他原因被判了一次技术犯规。

主教练	B_2	(B)	B_1
第一助理教练			
罚则：1 次罚球			

该主教练**不被取消比赛资格**

3. 第 1 节有一起打架情况，1 名**随队人员**被取消比赛资格。
   第 3 节，该**主教练**因其自身违反体育运动精神的行为被判了一次技术犯规。
   第 4 节，该**主教练**因其自身违反体育运动精神的行为被判了另一次技术犯规。

主教练	B_2	(B)	C_1	C_1 GD
第一助理教练				
罚则：1 次罚球				

该主教练因被**登记 2 次技术犯规 (C) 被自动取消比赛资格**

4. 第 1 节有一起打架情况，1 名**随队人员**被取消比赛资格。
   第 3 节，该**主教练**因任何其他原因被判了一次技术犯规。
   第 4 节，该**主教练**因任何其他原因被判了另一次技术犯规。

主教练	B_2	(B)	B_1	B_1 GD
第一助理教练				
罚则：1 次罚球				

该主教练因被**登记 3 次技术犯规 (B) 被自动取消比赛资格**

B-3 Examples of the player head coach fouls committed as a player and as a coach:

1. A player head coach has committed 4 fouls as a player and 1 technical foul as a head coach.

Player 22 (CAP)	P	P_2	P_1	P_2	B
Head coach (CAP)	B_1				
First assistant coach					
Penalty: 1 free throw					

Player head coach is an excluded player

2. A player head coach who has committed 1 technical foul as a player and 1 technical foul as a head coach.

Player 22 (CAP)	P	T_1	P_2	C	GD
Head coach (CAP)	C_1				
First assistant coach					
Penalty: 1 free throw					

Player head coach is disqualified automatically

B-3 队员兼主教练作为一名队员和作为一名主教练时发生犯规的举例

1. 一名队员兼主教练作为队员时发生 4 次犯规，作为主教练时发生 1 次技术犯规。

队员 22 (CAP)	P	P_2	P_1	P_2	B

主教练 (CAP)	B_1		
第一助理教练			
罚则：1 次罚球			

该队员兼主教练**成为一名出局的队员**

2. 一名队员兼主教练作为队员时发生 1 次技术犯规，作为主教练时发生 1 次技术犯规。

队员 22 (CAP)	P	T_1	P_2	C	GD

主教练 (CAP)	C_1		
第一助理教练			
罚则：1 次罚球			

该队员兼主教练**被自动取消比赛资格**

Appendix F Instant Replay System (IRS)

F-1 Definition

F-1.1 Statement: Before the game the crew chief shall approve the IRS equipment and inform both head coaches of its availability. Only the IRS equipment approved by the crew chief can be used for an IRS review.

F-1.2 Example: A1 attempts a successful shot for a goal when the game clock signal sounds for the end of the game. There is no approved IRS equipment available. The team B manager states that they recorded the game with the team video camera from an elevated position and presents the video material to the referees for a review.

Interpretation: The team B manager's request to use the team's video for a review shall be denied.

F-2 General principles

F-2.1 Statement: In the case of an Instant Replay System (IRS) review at the end of a quarter or overtime, the referees shall keep both teams on the court. The interval of play between the quarters or before the overtime shall start only after the referee communicates the final decision.

F-2.2 Example: A1 attempts a successful shot for a goal. At approximately the same time the game clock signal sounds for the end of the quarter. The referees become uncertain whether the shot was released during playing time and decide to use the IRS review. The teams are moving to their benches.

Interpretation: The referees shall keep both teams on the court. The interval of play shall start after the referee communicates the final decision.

F-2.3 Statement: The IRS review shall be conducted by the referees at the first opportunity following the situation to be reviewed. This opportunity occurs when the game clock is stopped and the ball is dead. However, if after a successful goal the referees do not stop the game, the review shall be conducted at the first opportunity when the referees stop the game without placing either team at a disadvantage.

附录 F　即时回放系统（IRS）

F-1　定义

F-1.1　陈述　在比赛前，主裁判员应批准 IRS 设备，并将该设备的可用性通知双方主教练。只有经主裁判员批准的 IRS 设备，才可以用于 IRS 复审。

F-1.2　举例　A1 尝试投篮并中篮，此时结束比赛的计时钟信号响起。该比赛没有经批准的 IRS 设备可用。B 队的管理人员提出该队使用球队摄像机在高处对比赛进行了录像，并将该录像资料提供给裁判员供复审。

解释　应拒绝 B 队管理人员关于使用其球队录像进行复审的要求。

F-2　一般原则

F-2.1　陈述　如果在某节或某决胜期的结束时使用即时回放系统（IRS）复审，裁判员应将双方球队留在比赛场地上。在裁判员宣布最终决定后，节与节之间或决胜期开始之前的比赛休息期间才开始。

F-2.2　举例　A1 尝试投篮并中篮。几乎同时，结束该节的比赛计时钟信号响。裁判员不确定该投篮是否在比赛时间内球离手，并决定使用 IRS 复审。双方球队正在回到他们球队席的途中。

解释　裁判员应将双方球队留在比赛场地上。在裁判员宣布最终决定后，比赛休息期间才开始。

F-2.3　陈述　裁判员应在有待复审的情况发生之后出现首次机会时执行 IRS 复审。该机会出现在当比赛计时钟被停止且球成死球时。然而，如果在一次中篮后裁判员没有停止比赛，该复审应在裁判员不将任一队置于不利的情况下首次停止比赛时执行。

F-2.4 **Example:** A1 attempts a successful shot for a 3-point goal. The game is resumed with an immediate B1 throw-in and team B starts a fast break. The referees become uncertain whether A1's shot was released from the 3-point goal area and decide to use the IRS review.

Interpretation: The first opportunity to stop the game for the review is when the ball becomes dead after the goal. It may happen that during the game there might not be enough time for the referees to react for the review. In this case, the referees shall stop the game without placing team B at a disadvantage as soon as the fast break is finished or when the game is stopped for the first time after the goal.

F-2.5 **Statement:** A time-out or substitution request may be cancelled after the IRS review ends and the referee communicates the final decision.

F-2.6 **Example:** A1 attempts a successful shot for a goal. The team B head coach requests a time-out. The referees become uncertain whether A1's shot was released from the 3-point goal area and decide to use the IRS review. During the review the team B head coach wants to cancel the request for a time-out.

Interpretation: The team B request for a time-out shall not be administered until after the referee communicates the final IRS decision. The time-out request may be withdrawn at any time during the review until after the referee communicates the final IRS decision and is ready to administer the time-out.

F-2.7 **Example:** B1 is charged with an unsportsmanlike foul. The team B head coach requests a time-out. The referees become uncertain whether B1's foul was an unsportsmanlike foul. B6 requests a substitution for B1. During the review B6 returns to the team bench.

Interpretation: B6's request for a substitution and the team B head coach request for a time-out shall not be administered until after the referee communicates the final IRS decision. The substitution request may be withdrawn at any time during the review until after the referee communicates the final IRS decision and is ready to administer the time-out.

F-2.4 **举例** A1 尝试 3 分投篮并中篮。B1 迅速执行掷球入界继续比赛，并使 B 队开始一次快攻。裁判员不确定 A1 的投篮是否在 3 分中篮区域球离手，并决定执行 IRS 复审。

解释 该首次停止比赛并执行复审的机会是当球中篮并成死球时。在比赛期间，裁判员可能来不及对是否执行复审做出反应。在该情况下，裁判员应在不置 B 队于不利的情况下，在快攻结束时，或者在球中篮后比赛首次被停止时即刻停止比赛。

F-2.5 **陈述** 在 IRS 复审结束，并且裁判员宣布最终决定后，暂停或替换请求可以被取消。

F-2.6 **举例** A1 尝试投篮并中篮。B 队主教练请求一次暂停。裁判员不确定 A1 的投篮是否在 3 分中篮区域球离手，并决定执行 IRS 复审。在复审期间，B 队主教练希望取消其暂停请求。

解释 在裁判员宣布 IRS 的最终决定后，才能执行 B 队暂停的请求。该暂停请求可以在复审期间的任何时间被取消，直到裁判员宣布 IRS 的最终决定后并准备执行暂停为止。

F-2.7 **举例** B1 被判一起违反体育运动精神的犯规。B 队主教练请求一次暂停。裁判员不确定 B1 的犯规是否是一起违反体育运动精神的犯规。B6 请求替换 B1。在复审期间，B6 回到其球队席。

解释 在裁判员宣布 IRS 的最终决定后，才能执行 B6 的替换和 B 队主教练的暂停请求。该替换请求可以在复审期间的任何时间被取消，直到裁判员宣布 IRS 的最终决定后并准备执行暂停为止。

F-3.1 At the end of the quarter or each overtime

F-3.1.1 **Example:** A1 attempts a successful shot for a goal when the game clock signal sounds for the end of the quarter. The referees become uncertain whether A1's shot was released before the end of playing time.

Interpretation: The IRS review can be used to decide, at the end of the quarter, whether A1's successful shot was released before the game clock signal sounded for the end of the quarter.

If the review provides the ball was released before the end of playing time for the quarter, the crew chief shall confirm A1's goal as successful.

If the review provides the ball was released after the end of playing time for the quarter, A1's goal shall be cancelled.

F-3.1.2 **Example:** Team B is leading by 2 points. B1 fouls A1 when the game clock signal sounds for the end of the first overtime. This is the fifth team B foul in the fourth quarter. The referees become uncertain whether B1's foul occurred before the end of the first overtime.

Interpretation: The IRS review can be used to decide, at the end of each overtime, whether B1's foul occurred before the game clock signal sounded for the end of the first overtime.

If the review provides that B1's foul occurred before the game clock signal sounded, A1 shall attempt 2 free throws. The game shall be resumed as after any last free throw with the time remaining on the game clock when the foul occurred.

If the review provides that B1's foul occurred after the game clock signal sounded, B1's foul shall be disregarded. Any unsportsmanlike action shall only be reported to the governing body of the competition.

F-3.1.3 **Example:** B1 fouls A1 on an unsuccessful shot for a 2-point goal when the game clock signal sounds for the end of the second overtime.

Interpretation: The IRS review can be used to decide, at the end of the second overtime, whether B1's foul occurred before the game clock signal sounded for the end of the second overtime.

F-3.1 在一节或每一决胜期结束时

F-3.1.1 **举例** A1 尝试投篮并中篮，此时结束该节的比赛计时钟信号响。裁判员不确定 A1 的投篮是否在比赛时间结束前球离手。

解释 在一节比赛结束时，IRS 复审可用于确定 A1 投篮是否在结束该节的比赛计时钟信号响之前球离手。

如果复审证实该球是在该节的比赛时间结束之前已离手，主裁判员应确认 A1 中篮成功。

如果复审证实该球是在该节的比赛时间结束之后才离手，A1 的中篮应被取消。

F-3.1.2 **举例** B 队领先 2 分。结束第 1 个决胜期的比赛计时钟信号响时，B1 对 A1 犯规。这是 B 队在第 4 节的第 5 次全队犯规。裁判员不确定 B1 的犯规是否发生在第 1 个决胜期结束之前。

解释 在每一决胜期结束时，IRS 复审可用于确定 B1 的犯规是否发生在结束第 1 个决胜期的比赛计时钟信号响之前。

如果复审证实 B1 的犯规发生在比赛计时钟信号响之前，A1 应执行 2 次罚球。应如同任何最后一次罚球后那样继续比赛，比赛计时钟应显示发生犯规时的剩余时间。

如果复审证实 B1 的犯规发生在比赛计时钟信号响之后，则应忽略 B1 的犯规。只应向竞赛的组织部门报告任何违反体育运动精神的行为。

F-3.1.3 **举例** A1 在做 2 分试投时被 B1 犯规，球未中篮，此时结束第 2 个决胜期的比赛计时钟信号响。

解释 在第 2 个决胜期结束时，IRS 复审可用于确定 B1 的犯规是否发生在结束第 2 个决胜期的比赛计时钟信号响之前。

If the review provides that B1's foul occurred before the game clock signal sounded, A1 shall attempt 2 free throws. The game shall be resumed as after any last free throw with the remaining time on the game clock.

If the review provides that B1's foul occurred after the game clock signal sounded, B1's foul shall be disregarded unless the foul meets the criteria of an unsportsmanlike foul or a disqualifying foul and there is a third overtime to follow.

F-3.1.4 **Example:** A1 attempts a successful shot for a 3-point goal when the game clock signal sounds for the end of the quarter. The referees become uncertain whether A1 touched the boundary line on the shot.

Interpretation: The IRS review can be used to decide, at the end of the quarter, whether A1's successful shot for a goal was released before the game clock signal sounded for the end of the quarter. If so, the review can furthermore be used to decide whether an out-of-bounds violation of the shooter occurred and if so, how much time shall be shown on the game clock.

F-3.1.5 **Example:** A1 attempts a successful shot for a 2-point goal when the game clock signal sounds for the end of the quarter. The referees become uncertain whether a shot clock violation by team A occurred.

Interpretation: The IRS review can be used to decide, at the end of the quarter, whether A1's successful shot for a goal was released before the game clock signal sounded for the end of the quarter. If so, the review can furthermore be used to decide whether a shot clock violation by team A occurred.

If the review provides A1's successful shot was released 0.4 of a second before the game clock signal sounded for the end of the quarter and, if the review furthermore provides the ball was still in A1's hands when the shot clock signal sounded 0.2 of a second prior to A1's successful shot for goal was released, A1's goal shall not count. The game shall be resumed with a team B throw-in from the place nearest to where the shot clock violation occurred. Team B shall have 0.6 of a second on the game clock. The shot clock shall be switched off.

如果复审证实 B1 的犯规发生在比赛计时钟信号响之前，则应由 A1 执行 2 次罚球。应如同任何最后一次罚球后那样继续比赛，比赛计时钟应显示剩余时间。

如果复审证实 B1 的犯规发生在比赛计时钟信号响之后，则应忽略 B1 的犯规，除非该犯规达到了违反体育运动精神的犯规或是取消比赛资格的犯规的标准，并且之后仍须进行第 3 个决胜期。

F-3.1.4 **举例** A1 尝试 3 分投篮并中篮，此时结束该节的比赛计时钟信号响。裁判员不确定 A1 投篮时是否触及了界线。

解释 在一节比赛结束时，IRS 复审可用于确定 A1 成功的投篮是否在结束该节的比赛计时钟信号响之前球离手。如果是，该复审还可以进一步用来确定该投篮队员是否发生了出界违例。以及如果发生了出界违例，比赛计时钟应显示多少时间。

F-3.1.5 **举例** A1 尝试 2 分投篮并中篮，此时结束该节的比赛计时钟信号响。裁判员不确定 A 队是否发生了进攻时间违例。

解释 在一节比赛结束时，IRS 复审可用于确定 A1 成功的投篮是否在结束该节的比赛计时钟信号响之前球离手。如果是，该复审还可以进一步确定 A 队是否发生了进攻时间违例。

如果复审证实 A1 成功的投篮是在结束该节的比赛计时钟信号响之前 0.4 秒时球离手，并且如果该复审进一步证实在 A1 投篮球离手前 0.2 秒，球仍在 A1 的手上时，进攻计时钟信号响，那么 A1 的中篮不应计得分。应由 B 队在最靠近进攻时间违例发生的地点执行掷球入界继续比赛。B 队应拥有比赛计时钟显示的 0.6 秒。应关闭进攻计时钟。

F-3.1.6 **Example:** A1 attempts a successful shot for a goal when the game clock signal sounds for the end of the second quarter. The referees become uncertain whether A1's successful shot for a goal was released before the game clock signal sounded for the end of the quarter and if so, whether team A violated the 8-second rule.

Interpretation: The IRS review can be used to decide, at the end of the quarter, whether A1's successful shot for a goal was released before the game clock signal sounded for the end of the quarter. The review can furthermore be used to decide whether an 8-second violation by team A occurred.

If the review provides A1's successful shot was released before the game clock signal sounded for the end of the quarter and, if the review furthermore provides that prior to the A1's shot for a successful goal team A violated the 8-second rule when the game clock showed 3.4 seconds, A1's goal shall not count. The game shall be resumed with a team B throw in in its frontcourt from the place nearest to where the 8-second violation occurred. Team B shall have 3.4 seconds on the game clock. The shot clock shall be switched off.

If the review provides team A did not violate the 8-second rule, A1's goal shall count. The second quarter has ended. The second half shall be started with an alternating possession throw-in at the centre line extended.

F-3.1.7 **Example:** With 2.5 seconds on the game clock, A1 attempts a shot for a goal. The ball touches the ring, B1 rebounds it and starts a dribble. At this time, the game clock signal sounds for the end of the game. The referees become uncertain whether B1 stepped out-of-bounds when landing with the rebounded ball on the court.

Interpretation: The IRS review cannot be used to decide, whether a non-shooting player was out-of-bounds.

F-3.2 **The game clock shows 2:00 or less in the fourth quarter and in each overtime**

F-3.2.1 **Example:** With 1:41 on the game clock in the fourth quarter, A1 attempts a successful shot for a goal when the shot clock signal sounds. The referees become uncertain whether the ball was released before the shot clock signal sounded and

F-3.1.6 **举例** A1 尝试投篮并中篮，此时结束第 2 节的比赛计时钟信号响。裁判员不确定 A1 成功的投篮是否在结束该节的比赛计时钟信号响之前球离手，并且，如果是，A 队是否发生 8 秒违例。

解释 在一节比赛结束时，IRS 复审可用于确定 A1 成功的投篮是否在结束该节的比赛计时钟信号响之前球离手。该复审还可以进一步确定 A 队是否发生了 8 秒违例。

如果复审证实 A1 成功的投篮是在结束该节的比赛计时钟信号响之前球离手，并且如果该复审还进一步证实在 A1 投篮之前，比赛计时钟显示 3.4 秒时，A 队 8 秒违例了，那么 A1 的中篮不应计得分。应由 B 队在其前场最靠近 8 秒违例发生的地点执行掷球入界继续比赛。B 队应拥有比赛计时钟显示的 3.4 秒。应关闭进攻计时钟。

如果复审证实 A 队没有违反 8 秒规则。A1 的中篮应计得分。第 2 节结束。应在中线延长线处以交替拥有掷球入界开始下半时比赛。

F-3.1.7 **举例** 比赛计时钟显示 2.5 秒时，A1 尝试投篮。球触及了篮圈，B1 获得篮板球并开始运球。此时，结束该节的比赛计时钟信号响。裁判员不确定 B1 持球落回比赛场地时是否踩在界外。

解释 IRS 复审不能用于确定一名非投篮队员是否出界。

F-3.2 在第 4 节和每一决胜期比赛计时钟显示 2:00 或更少时

F-3.2.1 **举例** 第 4 节，比赛计时钟显示 1:41 时，A1 尝试投篮并中篮，此时进攻计时钟信号响。裁判员不确定进攻计时钟信号响之前球是否离手，在：

(a) before the ball is live for the team B throw-in after the goal.

(b) after the ball is live for the team B throw-in when, after the goal the first time the referees stop the game for any reason.

(c) after the ball is live following the first time the referees stop the game.

Interpretation: The IRS review can be used to decide, when the game clock shows 2:00 or less in the fourth quarter, whether A1's shot for a successful goal was released before the shot clock signal sounded.

The referees are authorized to stop the game immediately to review whether a successful goal was released before the shot clock signal sounded before the ball enters the basket and the game clock is stopped. The review can occur at the latest until the ball became live following the first time the referees stopped the game.

In (a) the referees shall stop the game immediately and conduct the review before resuming the game.

In (b) the referees shall conduct the review when they have stopped the game for any reason, after the situation for the review occurred.

In (c) the time limit to use the review ended when the ball became live following the first time the referees stopped the game. The original decision remains valid.

In (a) or (b) if the review provides the ball was still in A1's hands when the shot clock signal sounded, this is a shot clock violation. A1's goal shall not count.

In (a) the game shall be resumed with a team B throw-in from the free-throw line extended.

In (b) the game shall be resumed with a throw-in for the team that had control of the ball or was entitled to the ball from the place nearest to where the ball was located when the game was stopped, or with free throws if applicable.

In (a) or (b) if the review provides the ball had left A1's hands on a shot before the shot clock signal sounded, the shot clock signal shall be disregarded. A1's goal shall count.

（a）球中篮后，B 队掷球入界的球成活球之前。

（b）球中篮后，B 队掷球入界的球成活球之后，裁判员因任何原因首次停止比赛时。

（c）裁判员首次停止比赛，随后球成活球之后。

解释 在第 4 节比赛计时钟显示 2:00 或更少时，IRS 复审可用于确定 A1 投篮是否在进攻计时钟信号响之前球离手。

当球中篮且比赛计时钟停止时，裁判员有权立即停止比赛并对一次投篮是否在进攻计时钟信号响之前球离手执行复审。该复审最迟可以在裁判员首次停止比赛且球成为活球之前执行。

在（a）中，裁判员应立即停止比赛，并在继续比赛之前执行复审。

在（b）中，在有待复审的情况发生之后，裁判员应在因任何原因停止比赛时执行复审。

在（c）中，裁判员首次停止比赛，随后球成活球时，可使用复审的时限已过。应维持最初决定。

在（a）或（b）中，如果复审证实进攻计时钟信号响时球仍在A1 手中,则这是一起进攻时间违例。A1 的中篮不应计得分。

在（a）中，应由 B 队在罚球线延长线处执行掷球入界继续比赛。

在（b）中，应由已控制球的队或拥有球权的队在最靠近停止比赛时球所在位置的地点执行掷球入界继续比赛，或执行已判给的罚球继续比赛。

在（a）或（b）中，如果复审证实进攻计时钟信号响之前 A1 的投篮球已离手，应忽略进攻计时钟信号。A1 的中篮应计得分。

In (a) the game shall be resumed with a team B throw-in from behind its endline as after any successful goal.

In (b) the game shall be resumed with a throw-in for the team that had control of the ball or was entitled to the ball from the place nearest to where the ball was located when the game was stopped, or with free throws if applicable.

F-3.2.2 **Example:** With 1:39 on the game clock in the fourth quarter, A1 is in the act of shooting when a foul occurred away from the shooting situation. The personal foul is called against

(a) B2 for fouling A2. This is the third team foul of the quarter.

(b) B2 for fouling A2. This is the fifth team fouls of the quarter.

(c) A2 for fouling B2.

Interpretation: IRS review can be used to decide, when the game clock shows 2:00 or less in the fourth quarter, whether

(i) the act of shooting had started when the foul was called against an opponent of the shooter; or

(ii) the ball was still in the hands of the shooter when the foul was called against a team-mate of the shooter.

In (a) if the review provides A1 was not in the act of shooting, the ball became dead when B2's foul occurred and the goal, if made, shall not count. If the review provides A1 was in the act of shooting, the goal, if made, shall count. In both cases, the game shall be resumed with a team A throw-in from the place nearest to where the B2's foul occurred.

In (b) if the review provides A1 was not in the act of shooting, the ball became dead when B2's foul occurred and the goal, if made, shall not count. If the review provides A1 was in the act of shooting the goal, if made, shall count. In both cases, A2 shall attempt 2 free throws as a result of the B2's foul. The game shall continue as after any last free throw.

在（a）中，应由B队在其端线后如同任何中篮后执行掷球入界那样继续比赛。

在（b）中，应由已控制球的队或拥有球权的队在最靠近停止比赛时球所在位置的地点执行掷球入界继续比赛，或执行已判给的罚球继续比赛。

F-3.2.2 举例 第4节，比赛计时钟显示1:39，A1正在做投篮动作时，发生了一起投篮情况之外的犯规。裁判员判下述队员侵人犯规。

（a）B2对A2犯规。这是该节B队的第3次全队犯规。

（b）B2对A2犯规。这是该节B队的第5次全队犯规。

（c）A2对B2犯规。

解释 在第4节比赛计时钟显示2:00或更少时，IRS复审可用于确定：

（i）在宣判投篮队员的一名对方队员犯规时，投篮动作是否已经开始；或

（ii）在宣判投篮队员的一名同队队员犯规时，球是否还在投篮队员的手中。

在（a）中，如果复审证实A1没有正在做投篮动作，那么B2发生犯规时球成死球，如中篮不应计得分。如果复审证实A1正在做投篮动作，如中篮，应计得分。在这两种情况下，应由A队在最靠近B2发生犯规的地点执行掷球入界继续比赛。

在（b）中，如果复审证实A1没有正在做投篮动作，那么B2发生犯规时球成死球，如中篮，不应计得分。如果复审证实A1正在做投篮动作，如中篮，应计得分。在这两种情况下，A2应执行B2犯规导致的2次罚球。应如同任何最后一次罚球后那样继续比赛。

In (c) if the review provides the ball has left the hands of the shooter the goal, if made, shall count. The game shall be resumed with a team B throw-in from the place nearest to where the A2's foul occurred. If the review provides the ball was still in the hands of the shooter, the ball became dead when the A2's foul occurred and the goal, if made, shall not count. The game shall be resumed with a team B throw-in from the free-throw line extended.

F-3.2.3 **Example:** With 1:37 on the game clock in the fourth quarter, the shot clock signal sounds. At approximately the same time, A1 scores a goal from the frontcourt and A2 fouls B2 away from the ball in team A's frontcourt. This is the third team A foul in the quarter. The referees become uncertain whether the ball was still in A1's hands when the shot clock signal sounded and when A2's foul occurred.

Interpretation: The IRS review can be used to decide, when the game clock shows 2:00 or less in the fourth quarter, whether the ball was still in the hands of the shooter when the shot clock signal sounded, and when the foul away from the shooting situation occurred.

(a) If the review provides that the ball had left A1's hands before the shot clock signal sounded and before A2's foul occurred, A2's foul shall be charged and A1's goal shall count. The shot clock signal shall be disregarded.

(b) If the review provides A2's foul occurred before the ball had left A1's hands and before the shot clock signal sounded, A2's foul shall be charged and A1's goal shall not count.The shot clock signal shall be disregarded.

(c) If the review provides the shot clock signal sounded before the ball had left A1's hands and before A2's foul occurred, this is a shot clock violation by team A and A2's foul shall be disregarded. A1's goal shall not count.

In (a) the game shall be resumed with a team B throw-in from the place nearest to where A2's foul occurred.

In (b) and (c) the game shall be resumed with a team B throw-in in its backcourt from the free-throw line extended.

在（c）中，如果复审证实球已经离开投篮队员的手，如中篮，应计得分。应由B队在最靠近A2发生犯规的地点执行掷球入界继续比赛。如果复审证实球仍在投篮队员的手中，那么A2发生犯规时球成死球，如中篮，不应计得分。应由B队在罚球线延长线处执行掷球入界继续比赛。

F-3.2.3 **举例** 第4节，比赛计时钟显示1:37时，进攻计时钟信号响。大约同时，A1在其前场中篮得分，并且在A队前场的无球区发生了A2对B2的犯规。这是该节A队的第3次全队犯规。裁判员不确定当进攻计时钟信号响以及当A2发生犯规时，球是否仍在A1的手中。

解释 在第4节比赛计时钟显示2:00或更少时，IRS复审可用于确定当进攻计时钟信号响，并且发生一起投篮情况之外的犯规时，球是否仍在投篮队员的手中。

（a）如果复审证实球离开A1的手是在进攻计时钟信号响以及A2发生犯规之前，应登记A2的犯规，A1的中篮应计得分。应忽略进攻计时钟信号。

（b）如果复审证实A2的犯规发生在球离开A1的手以及进攻计时钟信号响之前，应登记A2的犯规，A1的中篮不应计得分。应忽略进攻计时钟信号。

（c）如果复审证实进攻计时钟信号在球离开A1的手以及A2发生犯规之前响起，这是A队的进攻时间违例，应忽略A2的犯规，A1的中篮不应计得分。

在（a）中，应由B队在最靠近A2发生犯规的地点执行掷球入界继续比赛。

在（b）和（c）中，应由B队在其后场的罚球线延长线处执行掷球入界继续比赛。

F-3.2.4 **Example:** With 1:34 on the game clock in the fourth quarter the shot clock signal sounds. At approximately the same time, A1 scores a goal from the frontcourt and B2 fouls A2 away from the ball in team A's frontcourt. This is the third team B foul in the quarter. The referees become uncertain whether the ball was still in A1's hands when the shot clock signal sounded and when B2's foul occurred.

Interpretation: The IRS review can be used to decide, when the game clock shows 2:00 or less in the fourth quarter, whether the ball was still in the hands of the shooter when the shot clock signal sounded, and when the foul away from the shooting situation occurred.

If the review provides B2's foul occurred before the shot clock signal sounded and B2's foul occurred when A1 was in the act of shooting, B2's foul shall be charged and A1's goal shall count. The shot clock signal shall be disregarded. The game shall be resumed with a team A throw-in in its frontcourt from the place nearest to where B2's foul occurred. Team A shall have 14 seconds on the shot clock.

If the review provides the shot clock signal sounded before the ball had left A1's hands and before B2's foul occurred, this is a shot clock violation by team A. B2's foul shall be disregarded and A1's goal shall not count. The game shall be resumed with a team B throw-in in its backcourt from the free-throw line extended.

F-3.2.5 **Example:** With 1:39 on the game clock in the fourth quarter, B1 fouls A1 in the act of shooting. At approximately the same time, away from the shooting situation B2 fouls A2. This is the third team foul of the quarter.

Interpretation: The IRS review can be used to decide, when the game clock shows 2:00 or less in the fourth quarter, whether the act of shooting has started when B1's foul occurred and when B2's foul away from the shooting situation occurred.

If the review provides B1's foul occurred first and A1 was not in the act of shooting when B2's foul occurred, the ball became dead when B1's foul occurred and the goal, if made, shall not count. The game shall be resumed with a team A throw-in from the place nearest to where B1's foul occurred. B2's foul shall be disregarded, unless the foul meets the criteria for an unsportsmanlike foul or a disqualifying foul, as it occurred after the ball was dead.

F-3.2.4 **举例** 第 4 节，比赛计时钟显示 1:34 时，进攻计时钟信号响。大约同时，A1 在其前场中篮得分，并且在 A 队前场的无球区发生了 B2 对 A2 的犯规。这是该节 B 队的第 3 次全队犯规。裁判员不确定当进攻计时钟信号响以及当 B2 发生犯规时，球是否仍在 A1 的手中。

解释 在第 4 节比赛计时钟显示 2:00 或更少时，IRS 复审可用于确定当进攻计时钟信号响，并且发生一起投篮情况之外的犯规时，球是否仍在投篮队员的手中。

如果复审证实 B2 的犯规发生在进攻计时钟信号响之前，并且 B2 的犯规发生时 A1 正在做投篮动作，应登记 B2 的犯规，并且 A1 的中篮应计得分。应忽略进攻计时钟信号。应由 A 队在其前场最靠近 B2 发生犯规的地点执行掷球入界继续比赛。A 队应拥有 14 秒进攻时间。

如果复审证实进攻计时钟信号在球离开 A1 的手以及 B2 发生犯规之前响起，这是 A 队的进攻时间违例，应忽略 B2 的犯规，A1 的中篮不应计得分。应由 B 队在其后场的罚球线延长线处执行掷球入界继续比赛。

F-3.2.5 **举例** 第 4 节，比赛计时钟显示 1:39 时，B1 对正在做投篮动作的 A1 犯规。大约同时，投篮情况之外发生了 B2 对 A2 的犯规。这是该节 B 队的第 3 次全队犯规。

解释 在第 4 节比赛计时钟显示 2:00 或更少时，IRS 复审可用于确定在 B1 发生犯规时和在投篮情况之外的 B2 发生犯规时，投篮动作是否已经开始。

如果复审证实 B1 的犯规发生在先，且 B2 发生犯规时 A1 没有正在做投篮动作，那么 B1 发生犯规时球成死球，如中篮，不应计得分。应由 A 队在最靠近 B1 发生犯规的地点执行掷球入界继续比赛。由于 B2 的犯规发生在球成死球后，应被忽略，除非该犯规达到了一起违反体育运动精神的犯规或取消比赛资格的犯规的标准。

If the review provides B1's foul occurred first and A1 was in the act of shooting when B1's foul occurred A1's goal, if made, shall count. A1 shall attempt 1 free throw. If the goal was not made, A1 shall attempt 2 or 3 free throws. The game shall continue as after any last free throw. B2's foul shall be disregarded, unless B2's foul meets the criteria for an unsportsmanlike foul or a disqualifying foul, as it occurred after the ball was dead.

If the review provides B2's foul occurred first and A1 was in the act of shooting when B1's foul occurred A1's goal, if made, shall count. If B2's foul is the third team B foul in the quarter the game shall be resumed with a team A throw-in from the place nearest to where B2's foul occurred. If B2's foul is the fifth team B foul in the quarter A2 shall attempt 2 free throws. The game shall continue as after any last free throw. B1's foul shall be disregarded, unless B1's foul meets the criteria of an unsportsmanlike foul or a disqualifying foul, as it occurred after the ball was dead.

F-3.2.6 **Example:** With 7.5 seconds on the game clock in the fourth quarter and just before thrower-in A1 releases the ball from the frontcourt, B1 is charged with a technical foul. At approximately the same time, B2 is charged with an unsportsmanlike foul against A2 by another referee. The referees become uncertain in which order the fouls occurred.

Interpretation: The IRS review cannot be used to decide on the order of the fouls occurred. Both fouls shall remain valid. The penalty for a technical foul shall be administered first. Any team A player shall attempt 1 free throw with no line-up. A2 shall then attempt 2 free throws. The game shall be resumed with a team A throw-in from the throw-in line in its frontcourt.

F-3.2.7 **Statement:** The IRS review can be used to decide, when the game clock shows 2:00 or less in the fourth quarter and in each overtime, whether a goaltending or interference was called correctly. If the review provides a goaltending or an interference was called incorrectly the game shall be resumed as follows, if after the call

- the ball has legally entered the basket, the goal shall count and the new offensive team shall be entitled to a throw-in from behind its endline.

如果复审证实B1的犯规发生在先，且B1发生犯规时A1正在做投篮动作，如中篮，应计得分。应由A1执行1次罚球；如未中篮，应由A1执行2次或3次罚球。应如同任何最后一次罚球后那样继续比赛。由于B2的犯规发生在球成死球后，应被忽略，除非B2的犯规达到了一起违反体育运动精神的犯规或取消比赛资格的犯规的标准。

如果复审证实B2的犯规发生在先，且B1发生犯规时A1正在做投篮动作，如中篮，应计得分。如果B2的犯规是该节B队的第3次全队犯规，应由A队在最靠近B2发生犯规的地点执行掷球入界继续比赛；如果B2的犯规是该节B队的第5次全队犯规，应由A2执行2次罚球。应如同任何最后一次罚球后那样继续比赛。由于B1的犯规发生在球成死球后，应被忽略，除非B1的犯规达到了一起违反体育运动精神的犯规或取消比赛资格的犯规的标准。

F-3.2.6 **举例** 第4节，比赛计时钟显示7.5秒时，在位于前场的A1执行掷球入界球离手之前，B1被判一起技术犯规。大约同时，另一名裁判员判了B2对A2的一起违反体育运动精神的犯规。裁判员不确定这些犯规发生的顺序。

解释 裁判员不可以使用IRS复审来确定犯规发生的顺序。2个犯规应保留有效。应首先执行技术犯规的罚则。应由A队任一队员执行1次不占位的罚球。然后，应由A2执行2次罚球。应由A队在其前场的掷球入界线处执行掷球入界继续比赛。

F-3.2.7 **陈述** 在第4节和每一决胜期比赛计时钟显示2:00或更少时，IRS复审可用于确定是否正确地宣判了一起干涉得分或干扰得分违例。如果复审证实裁判员错误地宣判了一起干涉得分或干扰得分，应按如下方式继续比赛，如果宣判后：

- 球合法地进入球篮，中篮应计得分，应判给新的进攻队在其端线后执行掷球入界。

- a player of either team has gained an immediate and clear control of the ball, that team shall be entitled to a throw-in from the place nearest to where the ball was located when the call was made.
- neither team has gained an immediate and clear control of the ball, a jump ball situation occurs.

Immediate and clear control of the ball occurs when, after the call is made, a player directly gains possession of the ball on the court.

The immediate and clear control of the ball must be the first action after the whistle. Any illegal contact to gain possession of the ball or the ball touching or being touched by multiple players is not an immediate and clear control of the ball.

When the ball goes out-of-bounds without a player of either team having gained possession of the ball, the opponent of the team that causes the ball to go out-of-bounds is considered as having gained an immediate and clear control of the ball.

F-3.2.8 **Example:** With 1:33 on the game clock in the fourth quarter, a goaltending violation is called against B1. The referees become uncertain whether the ball was already on its downward flight to the basket. The ball does not enter the basket.

Interpretation: The IRS review can be used to decide, when the game clock shows 2:00 or less in the fourth quarter, whether goaltending was called correctly.

If the review provides that the ball was on its downward flight to the basket, the goaltending violation shall remain valid.

If the review provides that the ball was not yet on its downward flight to the basket, the goaltending decision shall be withdrawn. As the ball did not enter the basket,

- the team which gained an immediate and clear control of the ball shall be entitled to a throw-in from the place nearest to where the ball was located when the call was made.
- if neither team gained an immediate and clear control of the ball, a jump ball situation occurred.

- 某队队员已立即和清晰地获得控制球，应判给该队在最靠近宣判时球所在位置的地点执行掷球入界。
- 没有球队已立即和清晰地获得控制球，一次跳球情况发生。

一次立即和清晰地获得控制球发生在：裁判员作出宣判后，一名队员在比赛场地上直接获得了球权。

一次立即和清晰地获得控制球必须是裁判员鸣哨后发生的第一动作。任何以非法接触而获得球权，或是球触及多名队员或被多名队员触及，都不是立即和清晰地获得控制球。

如果在球出界之前，任一球队的队员都没有获得球权，使球出界方的对方队则被视为是已经立即和清晰地获得控制球。

F-3.2.8 举例 第 4 节，比赛计时钟显示 1:33 时，裁判员宣判了一起 B1 干涉得分违例。裁判员不确定该球在向球篮飞行的途中是否已下落。球未进入球篮。

解释 在第 4 节比赛计时钟显示 2:00 或更少时，IRS 复审可用于确定是否正确地宣判了一起干涉得分。

如果复审证实该球在向球篮飞行的途中是在下落的，该干涉得分违例应保留有效。

如果复审证实该球在向球篮飞行的途中尚未下落，应撤销该干涉得分的决定。由于球未进入球篮，

- 应判给立即和清晰地获得控制球的球队在最靠近宣判时球所在位置的地点执行掷球入界。
- 如果没有球队立即和清晰地获得控制球，一次跳球情况发生。

If the throw-in shall be awarded to team A, the shot clock shall show the time remaining when the call was made.

If the throw-in shall be awarded to team B in its backcourt, team B shall have 24 seconds on the shot clock. If in its frontcourt, team B shall have 14 seconds on the shot clock.

F-3.2.9 Example: With 1:27 on the game clock in the fourth quarter, an interference violation is called against B1. The ball enters the basket.

Interpretation: As the ball has entered the basket there is no need to review the interference violation call. The goal shall count. The game shall be resumed with a team B throw-in from behind its endline, with 24 seconds on the shot clock.

F-3.2.10 Example: With 1:23 on the game clock in the fourth quarter, a goaltending violation is called against B1 or A1. After the call an interference violation is called against

(a) B2.

(b) A2.

The ball enters the basket.

Interpretation: The IRS review provides the goaltending violation by B1 or A1 did not occur. Furthermore, the review provides the interference violation by B2 or by A2 occurred. The penalty for the interference violation shall be administered.

If called against

(a) B2, the goal shall count. The game shall be resumed with a team B throw-in from behind its endline, with 24 seconds on the shot clock.

(b) A2, the goal shall not count. The game shall be resumed with a team B throw-in from the free-throw line extended, with 24 seconds on the shot clock.

如果应由 A 队执行掷球入界，进攻计时钟应显示宣判时的剩余时间。

如果应由 B 队在其后场执行掷球入界，B 队应拥有 24 秒进攻时间；如果在其前场执行掷球入界，应拥有 14 秒进攻时间。

F-3.2.9 **举例** 第 4 节，比赛计时钟显示 1:27 时，裁判员宣判了 B1 干扰得分违例。球进入球篮。

解释 由于球已进入球篮，裁判员没有必要再对该干扰得分违例执行复审。中篮应计得分。应由 B 队在其端线后执行掷球入界继续比赛，B 队应拥有 24 秒进攻时间。

F-3.2.10 **举例** 第 4 节，比赛计时钟显示 1:23 时，裁判员宣判了 B1 或 A1 干涉得分违例。该宣判后，裁判员又宣判了一起：

（a）B2 的干扰得分违例，

（b）A2 的干扰得分违例，

球进入球篮。

解释 IRS 复审证实 B1 或 A1 没有发生干涉得分违例。此外，复审证实 B2 或 A2 发生了干扰得分违例。应执行干扰得分违例的罚则。

如果判的是：

（a）B2 干扰得分违例，中篮应计得分。应由 B 队在其端线后执行掷球入界继续比赛，B 队应拥有 24 秒进攻时间。

（b）A2 干扰得分违例，中篮不应计得分。应由 B 队在罚球线延长线处执行掷球入界继续比赛，B 队应拥有 24 秒进攻时间。

F-3.2.11 **Example:** With 1:19 on the game clock in the fourth quarter, an interference violation is called against

(a) B1.

(b) A1.

The ball does neither enter the basket nor touch the ring and either team gains an immediate and clear control of the ball.

Interpretation: The IRS review provides the interference violation did not occur. In both cases, the team which gained an immediate and clear control of the ball shall be entitled to a throw-in from the place nearest to where the ball was located when the call was made.

If the throw-in is awarded to team A, that team shall have the time remaining on the shot clock. If to team B, that team shall have 24 seconds on the shot clock.

F-3.2.12 **Example:** With 1:15 on the game clock in the fourth quarter, a goaltending violation is called against

(a) B1.

(b) A1.

The ball does not enter the basket but touches the ring and either team gains an immediate and clear control of the ball.

Interpretation: The IRS review provides the goaltending violation did not occur. In both cases, the team which gained an immediate and clear control of the ball shall be entitled to a throw-in from the place nearest to where the ball was located when the call was made.

If the throw-in is awarded to team A, that team shall have 14 seconds on the shot clock. If to team B, that team shall have 24 seconds on the shot clock.

F-3.2.13 **Example:** With 1:11 on the game clock in the fourth quarter, an interference violation is called against

(a) B1.

F-3.2.11 举例 第 4 节，比赛计时钟显示 1:19 时，裁判员宣判了：

（a）B1 干扰得分违例，

（b）A1 干扰得分违例，

球既没有进入球篮，也没有触及篮圈，但有一队立即和清晰地获得了控制球。

解释 IRS 复审证实没有发生干扰得分违例。在这两种情况下，应判给立即和清晰地获得控制球的球队在最靠近宣判时球所在位置的地点执行掷球入界。

如果判给 A 队执行掷球入界，该队应拥有进攻计时钟显示的剩余时间。如果判给 B 队执行掷球入界，该队应拥有 24 秒进攻时间。

F-3.2.12 举例 第 4 节，比赛计时钟显示 1:15 时，裁判员宣判了：

（a）B1 干涉得分违例，

（b）A1 干涉得分违例，

球触及篮圈，但未进入球篮，但有一队立即和清晰地获得了控制球。

解释 IRS 复审证实没有发生干涉得分违例。在这两种情况下，应判给立即和清晰地获得控制球的球队在最靠近宣判时球所在位置的地点执行掷球入界。

如果判给 A 队执行掷球入界，该队应拥有 14 秒进攻时间。如果判给 B 队执行掷球入界，该队应拥有 24 秒进攻时间。

F-3.2.13 举例 第 4 节，比赛计时钟显示 1:11 时，裁判员宣判了：

（a）B1 干扰得分违例，

(b) A1.

The ball does not enter the basket and goes directly out-of-bounds without either team gaining immediate and clear control of the ball on the court.

Interpretation: The IRS review provides the interference violation did not occur. In both cases, the team which did not cause the ball to go out-of-bounds shall be awarded a throw-in.

If the throw-in is awarded to team A, that team shall have the time remaining on the shot clock. If to team B, that team shall have 24 seconds on the shot clock.

F-3.2.14 **Example:** With 1:07 on the game clock in the fourth quarter, a goaltending violation is called against

(a) B1.

(b) A1.

The ball does not enter the basket or touch the ring. After the call the ball is tapped by A2, then tapped by B2 and B3 and finally A4 catches it.

Interpretation: The IRS review provides the goaltending violation did not occur. In both cases, neither team gained an immediate and clear control. This is a jump ball situation.

If the throw-in is awarded to team A, that team shall have the time remaining on the shot clock.

If the throw-in is awarded to team B in its backcourt, team B shall have 24 seconds on the shot clock. If in its frontcourt, team B shall have 14 seconds on the shot clock.

F-3.2.15 **Example:** With 1:03 on the game clock in the fourth quarter, an interference violation is called against

(a) B1.

(b) A1.

（b）A1 干扰得分违例，

球未进入球篮且直接出界，没有球队立即和清晰地获得了控制球。

解释 IRS 复审证实没有发生干扰得分违例。在这两种情况下，应判给未使球出界的球队执行掷球入界。

如果判给 A 队执行掷球入界，该队应拥有进攻计时钟显示的剩余时间。如果判给 B 队执行掷球入界，该队应拥有 24 秒进攻时间。

F-3.2.14 **举例** 第 4 节，比赛计时钟显示 1:07 时，裁判员宣判了：

（a）B1 干涉得分违例，

（b）A1 干涉得分违例，

球既没有进入球篮，也没有触及篮圈。该宣判后，球被 A2 拍击，随后球被 B2 和 B3 拍击，最后球被 A4 拿到。

解释 IRS 复审证实没有发生干涉得分违例。在这两种情况下，没有球队立即和清晰地获得了控制球，这是一次跳球情况。

如果判给 A 队执行掷球入界，该队应拥有进攻计时钟显示的剩余时间。

如果判给 B 队在其后场执行掷球入界，该队应拥有 24 秒进攻时间；如果在其前场执行掷球入界，应拥有 14 秒进攻时间。

F-3.2.15 **举例** 第 4 节，比赛计时钟显示 1:03 时，裁判员宣判了：

（a）B1 干扰得分违例，

（b）A1 干扰得分违例，

The ball does not enter the basket or touch the ring. During the rebound a foul was called against B2 or A2 before an immediate and clear control of the ball is established.

Interpretation: The IRS review provides the interference violation did not occur. In both cases, the foul against B2 or A2 shall be penalised.

F-3.2.16 **Example:** With 1:03 on the game clock in the fourth quarter, a goaltending violation is called against

(a) B1.

(b) A1.

The ball does not enter the basket or touch the ring. During the rebound a foul is called against B2 or A2 before an immediate and clear control of the ball is established.

Interpretation: The IRS review provides the goaltending violation occurred. In both cases, the foul against B2 or A2 shall be disregarded, unless called as an unsportsmanlike foul or a disqualifying foul, as it occurred after the ball was dead.

In (a) the goal shall count. The game shall be resumed with a team B throw-in from behind its endline as after any successful goal.

In (b) the goal shall not count. The game shall be resumed with a team B throw-in from the place nearest to where A1's violation occurred, except from directly behind the backboard.

F-3.2.17 **Example:** With 38 seconds on the game clock in the fourth quarter, A1 attempts a shot for a goal. The ball touches the backboard above the level of the ring and is then touched by B1. The referee decided that B1's touch is legal and therefore did not call a goaltending violation.

Interpretation: The IRS review can be used only if the referees have called a goaltending violation.

F-3.2.18 **Example:** With 36 seconds on the game clock in the fourth quarter, B1 fouls A1 in the act of shooting. The ball touches the backboard above the level of the ring and is then touched by B2. The referee did not call a goaltending violation. The referees become uncertain whether B2 touched the ball legally.

球既没有进入球篮，也没有触及篮圈。在一次立即和清晰的控制球被建立之前，B2 或 A2 在抢篮板球中被判犯规。

解释 IRS 复审证实没有发生干扰得分违例。在这两种情况下，应处罚 B2 或 A2 的犯规。

F-3.2.16 **举例** 第 4 节，比赛计时钟显示 1:03 时，裁判员宣判了：

（a）B1 干涉得分违例，

（b）A1 干涉得分违例，

球既没有进入球篮，也没有触及篮圈。在一次立即和清晰的控制球被建立之前，B2 或 A2 在抢篮板球中被判犯规。

解释 复审证实发生了干涉得分违例。在这两种情况下，由于 B2 或 A2 的犯规发生在球成死球后，应被忽略，除非判的是一起违反体育运动精神的犯规或取消比赛资格的犯规。

在（a）中，中篮应计得分。应由 B 队在其端线后如同任何中篮后执行掷球入界那样继续比赛。

在（b）中，中篮不应计得分。应由 B 队在最靠近 A1 发生违例的地点执行掷球入界继续比赛，篮板正后方除外。

F-3.2.17 **举例** 第 4 节，比赛计时钟显示 38 秒时，A1 尝试投篮。球在篮圈水平面以上触及了篮板后被 B1 触及。裁判员判定 B1 的触球是合法的，因此未宣判干涉得分违例。

解释 IRS 复审只有在裁判员宣判了干涉得分违例后才可以被使用。

F-3.2.18 **举例** 第 4 节，比赛计时钟显示 36 秒时，B1 对正在做投篮动作的 A1 犯规。球在篮圈水平面以上触及了篮板后被 B2 触及。裁判员没有宣判干涉得分违例。此时裁判员不确定 B2 触及球是否合法。

Interpretation: The IRS review can be used only if the referees called a goaltending violation.

F-3.2.19 **Example:** With 28 seconds on the game clock in the fourth quarter, B1 fouls A1 in the act of shooting for a 2-point goal. B2 touches the ball on its way to the basket. The referee calls a goaltending violation. The ball does not enter the basket. The referees become uncertain whether B2 touched the ball illegally.

Interpretation: The IRS review can be used to decide, when the game clock shows 2:00 or less in the fourth quarter, whether B2's goaltending was called correctly.

If the review provides B2 touched the ball on its downward flight, the goaltending violation shall remain valid. A1 shall be awarded 2 points. A1 shall further attempt 1 free throw. The game shall be resumed as after any last free throw.

If the review provides B2 touched the ball on its upward flight, the goaltending decision shall be withdrawn. A1 shall attempt 2 free throws. The game shall be resumed as after any last free throw.

F-3.2.20 **Example:** With 1:37 on the game clock in the fourth quarter the ball goes out-of-bounds. Team A is awarded a throw-in. Team A is granted a time-out. The referees become uncertain of the player who caused the ball to go out-of-bounds.

Interpretation: The IRS review can be used to identify, when the game clock shows 2:00 or less in the fourth quarter, the player who caused the ball to go out-of-bounds. The time-out period shall not start until the review ends and the referee communicates the final decision.

F-3.2.21 **Example:** With 5:53 on the game clock in the first quarter, the ball rolls on the court close to the sideline when A1 and B1 try to gain control of the ball. The ball goes out-of-bounds. Team A is awarded a throw-in. The referees become uncertain of the player who caused the ball to go out-of-bounds.

Interpretation: The IRS review can be used to identify the player who caused the ball to go out-of-bounds only when the game clock shows 2:00 or less in the fourth quarter.

解释 IRS 复审只有在裁判员宣判了干涉得分违例后才可以被使用。

F-3.2.19 **举例** 第 4 节，比赛计时钟显示 28 秒时，B1 对正在做 2 分试投的 A1 犯规。球在飞向球篮的途中被 B2 触及。裁判员宣判了干涉得分违例。球未进入球篮。此时裁判员不确定 B2 触及球是否合法。

解释 在第 4 节比赛计时钟显示 2:00 或更少时，IRS 复审可用于确定是否正确地宣判了 B2 的干涉得分。

如果复审证实 B2 触及了在下落飞行的球，该干涉得分违例应保留有效。应判给 A1 得 2 分，应由 A1 再执行 1 次罚球，应如同任何最后一次罚球后那样继续比赛。

如果复审证实 B2 触及了在上升飞行的球，应撤销该干涉得分的决定。应由 A1 执行 2 次罚球，应如同任何最后一次罚球后那样继续比赛。

F-3.2.20 **举例** 第 4 节，比赛计时钟显示 1:37 时球出界。判给 A 队执行掷球入界。A 队被准予一次暂停。此时裁判员不确定是哪名队员使球出界了。

解释 在第 4 节比赛计时钟显示 2:00 或更少时，IRS 复审可用于确定使球出界的队员。在裁判员完成复审并宣布最终决定后，该暂停时段才开始。

F-3.2.21 **举例** 第 4 节，比赛计时钟显示 5:53 时，球在比赛场地上靠近边线处滚动，A1 和 B1 试图获得该控制球。球出界了。判给 A 队执行掷球入界。此时裁判员不确定是哪名队员使球出界了。

解释 只有在第 4 节比赛计时钟显示 2:00 或更少时，IRS 复审才可用于确定使球出界的队员。

F-3.2.22 **Example:** With 1:45 on the game clock in the overtime A1 close to the sideline passes the ball to A2. During the pass B1 taps the ball out-of-bounds. The referees become uncertain whether A1 was already out-of-bounds when passing the ball to A2.

Interpretation: The IRS review cannot be used to decide, whether a non-shooting player was out-of-bounds.

F-3.3 At any time of the game

F-3.3.1 **Example:** B1 fouls A1 in the act of shooting. The ball enters the basket. The referees become uncertain whether

(a) A1 had started the act of shooting when B1's foul occurred.

(b) B1's foul occurred before A1 has returned with both feet to the floor.

Interpretation: The IRS review cannot be used to decide, at any time of the game, whether B1's foul against A1 shall be considered as a foul against a shooter.

F-3.3.2 **Example:** With 3:47 on the game clock in the second quarter, A1 attempts a successful shot for a 3-point goal. The referees become uncertain whether the ball was released from the 2- or 3-point goal area

(a) before the ball is live for a team B throw-in after the goal.

(b) after the ball is live for a team B throw-in after the goal, when an immediate throw-in does not allow the referees to react for the IRS review.

(c) after the ball is live for a team B throw-in after the goal and the game is stopped for a team B time-out.

Interpretation: The IRS review can be used to decide, at any time of the game, whether A1's successful goal shall count for 2 or 3 points. The review shall be conducted at the first opportunity when the game clock is stopped and the ball is dead. However, the referees are authorised to stop the game for the review immediately. The referee shall in

F-3.2.22 **举例** 决胜期，比赛计时钟显示 1:45 时，靠近边线的 A1 将球传向 A2。传球期间 B1 将球拍出界。此时裁判员不确定 A1 在将球传向 A2 时是否已经在界外了。

解释 IRS 复审不能用于确定一名非投篮队员是否出界。

F-3.3 **在比赛的任何时间**

F-3.3.1 **举例** B1 对正在做投篮动作的 A1 犯规。球进入球篮。裁判员不确定：

（a）B1 的犯规发生时 A1 是否已开始其投篮动作。

（b）B1 的犯规是否发生在 A1 的双脚落回地面之前。

解释 在比赛的任何时间，裁判员都不可以使用 IRS 复审来确定 B1 对 A1 的犯规是否应被视为是一起对一名投篮队员的犯规。

F-3.3.2 **举例** 第 2 节，比赛计时钟显示 3:47 时，A1 尝试 3 分投篮并中篮。

（a）中篮后，且在 B 队掷球入界的球成活球之前，

（b）中篮后，且在 B 队掷球入界的球成活球之后，B 队迅速地执行掷球入界使裁判员没来得及对是否应执行回放复审做出反应，

（c）中篮后，且在 B 队掷球入界的球成活球之后，比赛因 B 队的一次暂停而停止，

此时，裁判员不确定球是从 2 分中篮区域还是 3 分中篮区域离手的。

解释 在比赛的任何时间，IRS 复审可用于确定 A1 的中篮是计 2 分还是 3 分。该复审应在比赛计时钟被首次停止且球成死球时执行。然而，裁判员有权因一次复审而立即停止比赛。裁判员应：

(a) stop the game and conduct the review before the ball is live.

(b) stop the game immediately and conduct the review, without placing either team at a disadvantage. The review must take place after the goal when the referees have stopped the game for the first time for any reason and before the ball is then live again. This is valid also in the last 2 minutes of the fourth quarter or any overtime.

(c) conduct the review before the time-out is administered. After the final decision of the review is communicated, the time-out shall start, unless the head coach withdraws the request for the time-out.

In all cases, after the final decision is communicated, and in (c) after the time-out, the game shall be resumed with a team B throw-in from behind its endline as after any successful goal.

F-3.3.3 **Example:** With 3:44 on the game clock in the second quarter, A1 attempts a successful shot for a 3-point goal. The referees become uncertain whether the ball was released from the 2- or 3-point goal area after the ball is live for a team B throw-in after the goal, when the referees stop the game when B2 is fouled in the act of shooting by A2.

Interpretation: The IRS review can be used to decide, at any time of the game, whether A1's successful goal shall count for 2 or 3 points. The review shall be conducted at the first opportunity when the game clock is stopped and the ball is dead. However, the referees are authorized to stop the game for the review immediately.

The referees shall conduct the review when they have stopped the game for A2's foul as the game is stopped for the first time after the goal. After the final decision is communicated, the game shall be resumed with B2's free throw(s).

F-3.3.4 **Example:** With 3:43 on the game clock in the second quarter, A1 attempts a successful shot for a 3-point goal. The referees become uncertain whether the ball was released from the 2- or 3-point goal area after the ball is live for the team B throw-in after the goal, when B2 is fouled in the act of shooting by A2 and after the ball is live for B2's first or only free throw.

(a) 在球成活球之前停止比赛并执行复审。

(b) 在不将任一队置于不利的情况下立即停止比赛并执行复审。该复审必须在裁判员因任何原因首次停止比赛时以及球再次成为活球之前执行。这在第 4 节或任一决胜期的最后 2 分钟期间也适用。

(c) 在准予暂停之前执行复审。在裁判员宣判复审的最终决定后，该暂停时段才开始，除非该主教练取消了这次暂停请求。

上述所有情况下，在裁判员宣判最终决定后，以及在（c）情况的暂停结束后，应由 B 队在其端线后如同任何中篮后执行掷球入界那样继续比赛。

F-3.3.3 **举例** 第 2 节，比赛计时钟显示 3:44 时，A1 尝试 3 分投篮并中篮。中篮后，且在 B 队掷球入界的球成活球之后，裁判员因 A2 对正在做投篮动作的 B2 犯规而停止比赛，裁判员不确定球是从 2 分中篮区域还是 3 分中篮区域离手的。

解释 在比赛的任何时间，IRS 复审可用于确定 A1 的中篮是计 2 分还是 3 分。该复审应在比赛计时钟被首次停止且球成死球时执行。然而，裁判员有权因一次复审而立即停止比赛。

裁判员应在因 A2 的犯规而停止比赛时执行复审，因为这是中篮后比赛首次被停止。在裁判员宣判最终决定后，应由 B 队执行罚球继续比赛。

F-3.3.4 **举例** 第 2 节，比赛计时钟显示 3:43 时，A1 尝试 3 分投篮并中篮。中篮后，且在 B 队掷球入界的球成活球之后，A2 被判对正在做投篮动作的 B2 犯规，接着在 B2 执行第一次或仅有的一次罚球且球成活球后，裁判员不确定球是从 2 分中篮区域还是 3 分中篮区域离手的。

Interpretation: The time limit to use the IRS review ends when the ball becomes live for B2's first or only free throw. The original decision remains valid.

F-3.3.5 **Example:** B1 fouls A1 in the act of shooting. The ball does not enter the basket. A1 is awarded 3 free throws. The referees become uncertain whether A1's shot for a goal was released from the 3-point goal area.

Interpretation: The IRS review can be used to decide, at any time of the game, whether a player fouled while attempting a shot for goal shall be awarded 2 or 3 free throws. The review shall be conducted before the ball becomes live for the first free throw.

F-3.3.6 **Example:** With 40 seconds on the game clock in the fourth quarter, thrower-in A1 has the ball in the hands or at the disposal when an unsportsmanlike foul is called against B2 on the court. The referees become uncertain whether B2's contact has met the criteria of an unsportsmanlike foul.

Interpretation: The IRS review can be used to decide, at any time of the game, whether B2's unsportsmanlike foul shall be downgraded to a personal foul.

If the review provides the foul met the criteria of an unsportsmanlike foul, B2's foul shall remain an unsportsmanlike foul.

If the review provides the foul did not meet the criteria of an unsportsmanlike foul, B2's foul shall be downgraded to a personal foul. This is a throw-in foul.

F-3.3.7 **Example:** B1 is charged with an unsportsmanlike foul for hitting A1 with an elbow. The referees become uncertain whether B1 hit A1 with an elbow.

Interpretation: The IRS review can be used to decide, at any time of the game, whether a personal foul, an unsportsmanlike foul or a disqualifying foul shall be considered as a technical foul.

If the review provides no contact against A1 by B1 swinging an elbow occurred, B1's foul shall be changed to a technical foul.

解释 在 B2 执行第一次或仅有的一次罚球且球成活球时，可使用 IRS 复审的时限已过。应维持最初决定。

F-3.3.5 **举例** B1 对正在做投篮动作的 A1 犯规。球未进入球篮。判给 A1 执行 3 次罚球。裁判员不确定 A1 的投篮是否从 3 分中篮区域球离手。

解释 在比赛的任何时间，IRS 复审可用于确定一名尝试投篮的队员在被犯规后应被判给 2 次还是 3 次罚球。该复审应在第 1 次罚球且球成活球之前执行。

F-3.3.6 **举例** 第 4 节，比赛计时钟显示 40 秒。掷球入界队员 A1 已双手持球或可处理球时，宣判了比赛场地上 B2 的一起违反体育运动精神的犯规，此时裁判员不确定 B2 的接触是否达到一起违反体育运动精神的犯规的标准。

解释 在比赛的任何时间，IRS 复审可用于确定 B2 的违反体育运动精神的犯规是否应被降级为侵人犯规。

如果复审证实该犯规已达到一起违反体育运动精神的犯规的标准，B2 的犯规应保留为违反体育运动精神的犯规。

如果复审证实该犯规未达到一起违反体育运动精神的犯规的标准，B2 的犯规应被降级为侵人犯规。这是一起掷球入界时的犯规。

F-3.3.7 **举例** B1 因肘击 A1 被判一起违反体育运动精神的犯规。裁判员不确定 B1 是否肘击到了 A1。

解释 在比赛的任何时间，IRS 复审可用于确定一起侵人犯规、违反体育运动精神的犯规或取消比赛资格的犯规，是否应被判定为一起技术犯规。

如果复审证实 B1 的挥肘没有触及到 A1。B1 的犯规应被改判为一起技术犯规。

F-3.3.8 **Example:** B1 is charged with a personal foul. The referees become uncertain whether the foul shall be upgraded to an unsportsmanlike foul or whether a contact occurred at all.

Interpretation: The IRS review can be used to decide, at any time of the game, whether a personal foul shall be upgraded to an unsportsmanlike foul. However, if the review provides there was no contact at all, the personal foul cannot be cancelled.

F-3.3.9 **Example:** A1 dribbles towards the basket on a fast break with no defensive player between A1 and the opponents' basket. B1 reaches for the ball with the arm and contacts A1 from the side. B1 is charged with an unsportsmanlike foul. The referees become uncertain whether B1's foul was called correctly as an unsportsmanlike foul.

Interpretation: The IRS review can be used to decide, at any time of the game, whether an unsportsmanlike foul shall be downgraded to a personal foul or upgraded to a disqualifying foul. However, if the review provides A1 was responsible for the contact by hitting B1's arm, B1's defensive unsportsmanlike foul can be downgraded to a personal foul but cannot be cancelled or exchanged for A1's team control foul.

F-3.3.10 **Example:** B1 fouls dribbler A1. The referees become uncertain whether B1's foul shall be upgraded to an unsportsmanlike foul.

Interpretation: The IRS review can be used to decide, at any time of the game, whether a personal foul shall be upgraded to an unsportsmanlike foul. However, if the review provides A1 was responsible for the contact by charging into B1, B1's defensive foul cannot be cancelled or exchanged for A1's team control foul.

F-3.3.11 **Example:** Dribbler A1 commits a travelling violation followed by B1's unsportsmanlike foul against A1. The referees become uncertain whether B1's foul was called correctly as an unsportsmanlike foul.

Interpretation: The IRS review can be used to decide, at any time of the game, whether an unsportsmanlike foul shall be downgraded to a personal foul or upgraded to a disqualifying foul.

If the review provides B1's foul was an unsportsmanlike foul, the foul shall remain an unsportsmanlike foul.

F-3.3.8 **举例** B1 被判一起侵人犯规。裁判员不确定该犯规是否应被升级为一起违反体育运动精神的犯规，还是究竟有没有发生身体接触。

解释 在比赛的任何时间，IRS 复审可用于确定一起侵人犯规是否应被升级为一起违反体育运动精神的犯规。然而，即便复审证实完全没有发生身体接触，也不能取消该侵人犯规。

F-3.3.9 **举例** A1 在快攻中朝向对方球篮运球，且在 A1 和对方球篮之间没有防守队员。B1 伸手断球时从 A1 的侧面触及了 A1。B1 被判一起违反体育运动精神的犯规。裁判员不确定是否正确地宣判了 B1 的违反体育运动精神的犯规。

解释 在比赛的任何时间，IRS 复审可用于确定一起违反体育运动精神的犯规是否应被降级为一起侵人犯规，还是应被升级为一起取消比赛资格的犯规。然而，如果复审证实 A1 应对击打 B1 手臂的接触负责，那么 B1 防守时的违反体育运动精神的犯规可以被降级为侵人犯规，但是，该犯规不能被取消或改判为 A1 的控制球队犯规。

F-3.3.10 **举例** B1 对运球队员 A1 犯规。裁判员不确定 B1 的犯规是否应被升级为一起违反体育运动精神的犯规。

解释 在比赛的任何时间，IRS 复审可用于确定一起侵人犯规是否应被升级为一起违反体育运动精神的犯规。然而，即便复审证实 A1 应对撞上 B1 的接触负责，B1 的防守犯规也不能被取消或改判为 A1 的控制球队犯规。

F-3.3.11 **举例** 运球队员 A1 发生带球走违例，接着发生了 B1 对 A1 的一起违反体育运动精神的犯规。裁判员不确定是否正确地宣判了 B1 的违反体育运动精神的犯规。

解释 在比赛的任何时间，IRS 复审可用于确定一起违反体育运动精神的犯规是否应被降级为一起侵人犯规，还是应被升级为一起取消比赛资格的犯规。

如果复审证实B1 的犯规是一起违反体育运动精神的犯规，那么该犯规应保留为违反体育运动精神的犯规。

If the review provides B1's foul was a personal foul, it shall be disregarded as it occurred after the travelling violation.

F-3.3.12 **Example:** B1 fouls A1 on an attempt for shot for a 2-point goal followed by B2's unsportsmanlike foul against A1 who is still in the act of shooting. The ball does not enter the basket. The referees become uncertain whether B2's foul was called correctly as an unsportsmanlike foul.

Interpretation: The IRS review can be used to decide, at any time during the game, whether an unsportsmanlike foul shall be downgraded to a personal foul or upgraded to a disqualifying foul.

If the review provides B2's foul was an unsportsmanlike foul, the foul shall remain an unsportsmanlike foul. A1 shall attempt 2 free throws with no line-up for B1's personal foul. A1 shall attempt another 2 free throws with no line-up for B2's unsportsmanlike foul. The game shall be resumed with a team A throw-in from the throw-in line in its frontcourt. Team A shall have 14 seconds on the shot clock.

If the review provides B2's foul was a personal foul, it shall be disregarded as it occurred after the first foul. A1 shall attempt 2 free throws for B1's personal foul. The game shall be resumed as after any last free throw.

F-3.3.13 **Example:** In the third quarter, B1 is charged with an unsportsmanlike foul against A2. In the fourth quarter, B1 fouls A1 on a successful goal. The referees become uncertain whether B1's foul shall be upgraded to an unsportsmanlike foul. During the IRS review, B1 is charged with a technical foul.

Interpretation: If the review provides B1's foul against A1 was an unsportsmanlike foul, B1 shall be game disqualified automatically for the second unsportsmanlike foul. B1's technical foul shall be disregarded and shall not be assessed either against B1 or against the team B head coach. A1 shall attempt 1 free throw with no line-up for B1's unsportsmanlike foul. The game shall be resumed with a team A throw-in from the throw-in line in its frontcourt. Team A shall have 14 seconds on the shot clock.

如果复审证实 B1 的犯规是一起侵人犯规，那么，由于该侵人犯规发生在带球走违例后，应被忽略。

F-3.3.12 **举例** B1 对正在做 2 分试投的 A1 犯规，接着发生了 B2 对仍在做投篮动作的 A1 的违反体育运动精神的犯规。球未进入球篮。裁判员不确定是否正确地宣判了 B2 的违反体育运动精神的犯规。

解释 在比赛的任何时间，IRS 复审可用于确定一起违反体育运动精神的犯规是否应被降级为一起侵人犯规，还是应被升级为一起取消比赛资格的犯规。

如果复审证实 B2 的犯规是一起违反体育运动精神的犯规，那么该犯规应保留为违反体育运动精神的犯规。应由 A1 执行 B1 侵人犯规导致的 2 次不占位的罚球。再由 A1 执行 B2 违反体育运动精神的犯规导致的 2 次不占位的罚球。应由 A 队在其前场的掷球入界线处执行掷球入界继续比赛。A 队应拥有 14 秒进攻时间。

如果复审证实 B2 的犯规是一起侵人犯规，那么，由于该侵人犯规发生在第一起犯规后，应被忽略。应由 A1 执行 B1 侵人犯规导致的 2 次罚球，应如同任何最后一次罚球后那样继续比赛。

F-3.3.13 **举例** 第 3 节，宣判了 B1 对 A2 的一起违反体育运动精神的犯规。第 4 节，B1 对中篮的 A1 犯规。裁判员不确定 B1 的犯规是否应被升级为一起违反体育运动精神的犯规。在 IRS 复审期间，B1 被判一起技术犯规。

解释 如果复审证实 B1 对 A1 的犯规是一起违反体育运动精神的犯规，B1 应被自动取消本场比赛资格，因为这是 B1 的第 2 次违反体育运动精神的犯规。B1 的技术犯规应被忽略且不应登记在 B1 或 B 队主教练的名下。应由 A1 执行 B1 违反体育运动精神的犯规导致的 1 次不占位的罚球。应由 A 队在其前场的掷球入界线处执行掷球入界继续比赛。A 队应拥有 14 秒进攻时间。

If the review provides B1's foul against A1 was a personal foul, A1's goal shall count. B1 shall be game disqualified automatically as B1 is charged with 1 technical foul and 1 unsportsmanlike foul. Any team A player shall attempt 1 free throw with no line-up. Then A1 shall attempt 1 free throw. The game shall be resumed as after any last free throw.

F-3.3.14 **Statement:** The IRS review can be used to decide at any time of the game, after a malfunction of the game clock or the shot clock, how much time shall be displayed on the game clock or shot clock.

In determining the correct time to be displayed on the shot clock the referees shall consider whether the ball touches or misses the ring on a shot for a goal and whether a new team control was established before the game was stopped.

F-3.3.15 **Example:** With 57.8 seconds on the game clock in the second quarter and 0.7 of a second on the shot clock A1 attempts a shot for a 3-point goal. The shot is unsuccessful after which

(a) A2 gains a new control of the ball close to the basket.

(b) B1 taps the ball out-of-bounds.

(c) A2 gains a new control of the ball close to the basket, immediately after which B1 taps the ball out-of-bounds.

The referees realise the shot clock has no display visible.

Interpretation: The IRS review can be used to decide, at any time of the game, how much time shall be shown on the shot clock, in the event of a malfunction of the shot clock.

In (a) the referees shall stop the game immediately.

In all cases, if the review provides that the ball missed the ring and the referees decide that the shot clock would have expired before the game was stopped, a shot clock violation has occurred. The game shall be resumed with a team B throw-in from behind its endline with 24 seconds on the shot clock.

如果复审证实 B1 对 A1 的犯规是侵人犯规，A1 的中篮应计得分。因为 B1 被登记了一起技术犯规和一起违反体育运动精神的犯规，B1 应被自动取消本场比赛资格。应由 A 队任一队员执行 1 次不占位的罚球。然后，应由 A1 执行 1 次罚球。应如同任何最后一次罚球后那样继续比赛。

F-3.3.14 陈述 在比赛的任何时间，在比赛计时钟或进攻计时钟发生故障后，IRS 复审可用于确定比赛计时钟或进攻计时钟应显示多少时间。

在将正确的时间显示在进攻计时钟上的判定过程中，裁判员应考虑投篮离手的球是否触及了篮圈，以及在比赛被停止之前是否有新的球队建立了控制球。

F-3.3.15 举例 第 2 节，比赛计时钟显示 57.8 秒，进攻计时钟显示 0.7 秒时，A1 尝试 3 分投篮。球未中篮，随后，

(a) A2 在靠近球篮处获得新的控制球。

(b) B1 将球拍出界。

(c) A2 在靠近球篮处获得新的控制球，随即球被 B1 拍出界。

裁判员察觉到进攻计时钟无显示。

解释 在比赛的任何时间，IRS 复审可在进攻计时钟发生故障的情况中用于确定进攻计时钟应显示多少时间。

在 (a) 中，裁判员应立即停止比赛。

在上述所有情况下，如果复审证实球未触及篮圈，并且裁判员认定在比赛被停止之前进攻时间应当已终了，则发生了一起进攻时间违例。应由 B 队在其端线后执行掷球入界继续比赛，B 队应拥有 24 秒进攻时间。

In all cases, if the review provides the ball touches the ring, a shot clock violation did not occur. The game shall be resumed with a team A throw-in from behind the endline in its frontcourt with 14 seconds on the shot clock.

F-3.3.16 **Example:** With 57.8 seconds on the game clock in the second quarter and 0.7 of a second on the shot clock A1 attempts a shot for a 3-point goal. The shot is unsuccessful after which

(a) B1 gains a new control of the ball close to the basket.

(b) B1 gains a new control of the ball close to the basket and immediately causes the ball to go out-of-bounds.

The referees realise the shot clock has no display visible.

Interpretation: The IRS review can be used to decide, at any time of the game, how much time shall be shown on the shot clock, in the event of a malfunction of the shot clock.

In (a) the referees shall stop the game immediately.

In both cases, if the review provides that the ball missed the ring and the referees decide that the shot clock would have expired before the game was stopped, a shot clock violation has occurred. The game shall be resumed with a team B throw-in from behind its endline with 24 seconds on the shot clock.

In (a) if the review provides that the ball touched the ring, the shot clock violation did not occur. The game shall be resumed with a team B throw-in from behind its endline with 24 seconds on the shot clock.

In (b) if the review provides that the ball touched the ring, the shot clock violation did not occur. The game shall be resumed with a team A throw-in from behind the endline in its frontcourt with 14 seconds on the shot clock.

F-3.3.17 **Example:** With 7 seconds on the shot clock, A1's shot for a goal misses the ring. A2 catches the ball and the shot clock operator erroneously resets the shot clock to 14 seconds. After few dribbles and passes, still with team A in control of the ball, A3 scores a goal. At this time, the error is recognised and the referees stop the game.

在上述所有情况下，如果复审证实球触及了篮圈，则未发生一起进攻时间违例。应由 A 队在其前场端线后执行掷球入界继续比赛，A 队应拥有 14 秒进攻时间。

F-3.3.16 **举例** 第 2 节，比赛计时钟显示 57.8 秒，进攻计时钟显示 0.7 秒时，A1 尝试 3 分投篮。球未中篮，随后，

（a）B1 在靠近球篮处获得新的控制球。

（b）B1 在靠近球篮处获得新的控制球，随即 B1 使球出界。

裁判员察觉到进攻计时钟无显示。

解释 在比赛的任何时间，IRS 复审可在进攻计时钟发生故障的情况中用于确定进攻计时钟应显示多少时间。

在（a）中，裁判员应立即停止比赛。

在这两种情况下，如果复审证实球未触及篮圈，并且裁判员认定在比赛被停止之前进攻时间应当已终了，则发生了一起进攻时间违例。应由 B 队在其端线后执行掷球入界继续比赛，B 队应拥有 24 秒进攻时间。

在（a）中，如果复审证实球触及了篮圈，则未发生一起进攻时间违例。应由 B 队在其端线后执行掷球入界继续比赛，B 队应拥有 24 秒进攻时间。

在（b）中，如果复审证实球触及了篮圈，则未发生一起进攻时间违例。应由 A 队在其前场端线后执行掷球入界继续比赛，A 队应拥有 14 秒进攻时间。

F-3.3.17 **举例** 进攻计时钟显示 7 秒，A1 的投篮未触及篮圈。A2 接到球，进攻计时员错误地将进攻计时钟复位到 14 秒。A 队仍然控制球，在几次运球和传球后，A3 中篮得分。此时，该失误被确认，并且裁判员停止比赛。

Interpretation:

If the review provides that the shot clock would have expired before A3 scored the goal, a shot clock violation has occurred and A3's goal shall not count. The game shall be resumed with a team B throw-in from the free-throw line extended, with 24 seconds on the shot clock.

If the review provides that the shot clock would not have expired before A3 scored the goal, a shot clock violation has not occurred and A3's goal shall count. The game shall be resumed with a team B throw-in from behind its endline, with 24 seconds on the shot clock.

F-3.3.18 **Example:** With 42.2 seconds on the game clock in the second quarter, A1 dribbles towards the frontcourt. At this time, the referees realise that the game clock and shot clock have no display visible.

Interpretation: The game shall be stopped immediately. The IRS review can be used to decide, at any time of the game, how much time shall be shown on both clocks. After the review, the game shall be resumed with a team A throw-in from the place nearest to where the ball was located when the game was stopped. Team A shall have the time remaining on the game clock and on the shot clock.

F-3.3.19 **Statement:** A2 attempts a second free throw. The ball enters the basket. At this time, the referees become uncertain whether A2 was the correct free-throw shooter.

Interpretation: The IRS review can be used to identify, at any time of the game, the correct free-throw shooter before the ball becomes live following the first dead ball after the game clock started following error.

If the review identifies a wrong free-throw shooter, a correctable error for permitting the wrong player to attempt the free throw(s) has occurred. A2's free throws, regardless of whether made or missed, shall be cancelled. The game shall be resumed with a team B throw-in from the free-throw line extended in its backcourt. Team B shall have 24 seconds on the shot clock.

解释 如果复审证实 A3 中篮得分之前进攻时间应当已终了，则发生了一起进攻时间违例且 A3 的中篮不应计得分。应由 B 队在罚球线延长线处执行掷球入界继续比赛，B 队应拥有 24 秒进攻时间。

如果复审证实 A3 中篮得分之前进攻时间应当未终了，则未发生一起进攻时间违例且 A3 的中篮应计得分。应由 B 队在其端线后执行掷球入界继续比赛，B 队应拥有 24 秒进攻时间。

F-3.3.18 **举例** 第 2 节，比赛计时钟显示 42.2 秒时，A1 向前场运球。此时，裁判员察觉到比赛计时钟和进攻计时钟均无显示。

解释 应立即停止比赛。在比赛的任何时间，IRS 复审可用于确定两个计时钟应显示多少时间。完成复审后，应由 A 队在最靠近比赛被停止时球所在位置的地点执行掷球入界继续比赛。A 队应拥有比赛计时钟和进攻计时钟显示的剩余时间。

F-3.3.19 **举例** A2 执行其第 2 次罚球。球进入球篮。此时，裁判员不确定 A2 是否是正确的罚球队员。

解释 在比赛的任何时间，在失误发生后且开动了比赛计时钟之后的第一个死球后，并在球成活球之前，IRS 复审可用于确认正确的罚球队员。

如果复审确认了一名错误的罚球队员，一起允许错误的队员执行罚球的可纠正的失误已发生。A2 的罚球，无论中篮与否，都应被取消。应由 B 队在其后场的罚球线延长线处执行掷球入界继续比赛。B 队应拥有 24 秒进攻时间。

F-3.3.20 **Example:** A1 and B1 start to throw punches at each other followed by more players and persons permitted to sit on the team benches entering the court, all getting involved in a fighting. After some minutes the referees restored order on the court.

Interpretation: After order is restored, the referees can use the IRS review to identify, at any time of the game, the involvement of other players and all persons permitted to sit on the team benches during any act of violence. After gathering clear and conclusive evidence of the fighting, the crew chief shall communicate the final decision in front of the scorer's table and to both head coaches.

F-3.3.21 **Example:** Two opponents start talking aggressively and slightly pushing each other. The referees stop the game. After order is restored on the court, the referees become uncertain of the players and persons involved.

Interpretation: After order is restored, the referees can use the IRS review to identify, at any time of the game, the involvement of players and persons permitted to sit on the team benches during any act of violence. After gathering clear and conclusive evidence of the fight, the crew chief shall communicate the final decision in front of the scorer's table and to both head coaches.

F-3.3.22 **Example:** The referees call a foul against B1. Before communicating the foul at the scorer's table, the referees become uncertain if after the foul was called an act of violence has occurred on the court.

Interpretation: The IRS review can be used to identify, at any time during the game, the involvement of the players in any act of violence. The referees may perform the review before they have communicated the foul to the scorer's table.

If the review provides that acts of violence have occurred, the referee communicates B1's foul followed by the act of violence and the game resumes with the penalties.

F-3.3.20 **举例** A1 和 B1 开始相互挥拳，随后，更多的队员和被允许坐在球队席上的人员都进入了比赛场地并参与了这起打架。几分钟后，裁判员恢复了比赛场地上的秩序。

解释 在恢复了秩序后，裁判员可（在比赛的任何时间）使用 IRS 复审确认所有参与暴力行为的其他队员和被允许坐在球队席的人员。在收集了这起打架的清晰和确凿的证据后，应由主裁判员在记录台前宣布最终决定，并将其决定通知双方主教练。

F-3.3.21 **举例** 两名互为对方的队员开始相互言语攻击并轻微推搡。裁判员停止了比赛。在恢复了比赛场地上的秩序后，裁判员不确定哪些队员和人员参与了其中。

解释 在恢复了秩序后，裁判员可（在比赛的任何时间）使用 IRS 复审确认所有参与暴力行为的队员和被允许坐在球队席的人员。在收集了这起打架的清晰和确凿的证据后，应由主裁判员在记录台前宣布最终决定，并将其决定通知双方主教练。

F-3.3.22 **举例** 裁判员宣判了 B1 一起犯规。在向记录台报告该犯规之前，裁判员不确定在宣判犯规后，场上是否发生了一起暴力行为。

解释 在比赛的任何时间，IRS 复审可用于确认所有参与暴力行为的队员。裁判员可以在向记录台报告犯规之前执行复审。

如果复审证实已发生了一起暴力行为，裁判员应在报告 B1 的犯规之后，报告该暴力行为，应在执行罚则后继续比赛。

F-3.3.23 **Statement:** In situations when an act of violence occurs which is not called immediately, referees are authorised to stop the game at any time to review any act of violence or potential act of violence. The referees must identify the need for the IRS review and the review must take place when the referees have stopped the game for the first time.

If the review provides there was an act of violence, the referees shall call the infraction and penalise all already called violations including the act of violence in the order the infractions occurred. Whatever occurred during the interval between the act of violence and the game being stopped shall remain valid.

If the review provides there was no act of violence, the original decision remains valid. The game shall be resumed from the place nearest to where the game was interrupted for the review.

An act of violence is an act of force that causes or is intended to cause harm, or an act that results or could result in a risk of injury. An act that does not meet the criteria of a disqualifying foul or an unsportsmanlike foul, a technical foul, or does not meet the criteria for a threatened violence is not an act of violence.

F-3.3.24 **Example:** A1 dribbles when A2 hits B2 with an elbow. The referees do not call a foul against A2 and after 15 seconds the referees stop the game when

(a) A1 continues to dribble.

(b) team B causes the ball to go out-of-bounds.

Interpretation: In both cases, the IRS review can be used to identify, at any time during the game, the involvement of the team members during any act of violence. The referees are authorised to stop the game immediately without placing either team at a disadvantage or may use the stoppage of the game for the review.

If the review provides A2 has hit B2 with an elbow the referees can charge A2 with an unsportsmanlike foul. B2 shall attempt 2 free throws with no line-up.

F-3.3.23 **陈述** 在已发生的暴力行为没有被立即宣判的情况中，裁判员有权在任何时间停止比赛并对任何这样的暴力行为或潜在的暴力行为执行复审。裁判员必须确认该复审的需求，并且该复审必须在裁判员首次停止比赛时执行。

如果复审证实已发生了一起暴力行为，裁判员应对包括暴力行为中所发生的规则违犯在内的所有规则违犯作出宣判，并根据这些规则违犯发生的顺序执行相应的罚则。从暴力行为的发生至停止比赛期间所发生的一切应保持有效。

如果复审证实未发生一起暴力行为，应维持最初决定。应在最靠近由于复审而中断比赛的地点执行掷球入界继续比赛。

暴力行为是一种会造成或意在造成伤害的行为，或是一种会导致或可能导致受伤的行为。没有达到一起取消比赛资格的犯规、违反体育运动精神的犯规或技术犯规的标准的行为，又或者没有达到暴力威胁的标准的行为，都不是一起暴力行为。

F-3.3.24 **举例** A1 运球时，A2 肘击 B2。裁判员没有宣判 A2 犯规，在 15 秒之后：

（a）A1 继续运球时，

（b）B 队使球出界时，

裁判员停止了比赛。

解释 在这两种情况下，IRS 复审可（在比赛的任何时间）用于确认参与暴力行为的球队成员。裁判员有权在不将任一队置于不利的情况下立即停止比赛，或者，裁判员可以利用一次比赛中断来执行复审。

如果复审证实 A2 肘击了 B2，裁判员可以登记 A2 一起违反体育运动精神的犯规。应由 B2 执行 2 次不占位的罚球。

If the review provides that A2 has committed a personal foul or a technical foul that does not constitute an act of violence or has done nothing, a personal foul or technical foul cannot be charged.

In all cases the game shall be resumed with a team A throw-in from the place nearest where the game was stopped. The right to possession for the unsportsmanlike foul penalty is lost as a result of further action after the foul by A2.

Team A shall have the time remaining on the shot clock and the game clock shall continue from the point it was stopped.

F-3.3.25 **Example:** B1 fouls A1 in the act of shooting for a 2-point goal. A1 hits B1 with an elbow

(a) before the shot is released.

(b) after the shot is released.

The referees do not call a foul against A1. The ball enters the basket.

Interpretation: In both cases, the IRS can be used to identify, at any time of the game, the involvement of team members during any act of violence. The IRS review provides that A1 has hit B1 with an elbow, before B1's foul.

The referees can charge A1 with an unsportsmanlike foul. B1's foul shall also be charged. In both cases A1's goal shall count.

The foul penalties shall be administered in the order they occurred. B1 shall attempt 2 free throws with no line-up for A1's unsportsmanlike foul. The right to possession as part of the unsportsmanlike foul penalty is lost as a result of the B1 foul.

A1 shall be awarded 1 free throw and the game shall continue as after any last free throw. The game clock shall continue from the point it was stopped.

F-3.3.26 **Example:** A1 dribbles when A2 hits B2 with an elbow. The referees do not call a foul against A2. After another 5 seconds B3 fouls dribbler A1.

(a) B3's foul is the third team foul in the quarter.

如果复审证实 A2 发生了一起未构成暴力行为的侵人犯规或技术犯规，又或者 A2 未发生规则违犯，则不能登记该起侵人犯规或技术犯规。

上述所有情况下，应由 A 队在最靠近比赛被停止的地点执行掷球入界。在 A2 犯规后发生的后续比赛情况，应导致该违反体育运动精神的犯规罚则中的球权被取消。

A 队应拥有进攻计时钟显示的剩余时间，且比赛计时钟应从比赛被停止处连续计算。

F-3.3.25 举例 B1 对正在做 2 分试投的 A1 犯规。A1 在：

（a）投篮球离手之前肘击 B1。

（b）投篮球离手之后肘击 B1。

裁判员没有宣判 A1 犯规。球进入球篮。

解释 在这两种情况下，IRS 可（在比赛的任何时间）用于确认参与暴力行为的球队成员。IRS 复审证实在 B1 犯规之前，A1 肘击了 B1。

裁判员可以登记 A1 一起违反体育运动精神的犯规。B1 的犯规也应被登记。在这两种情况下，A1 的中篮应计得分。

应根据这两起犯规发生的顺序执行罚则。应由 B1 执行 A1 违反体育运动精神的犯规导致的 2 次不占位的罚球。B1 的犯规，应导致该违反体育运动精神的犯规罚则中的球权被取消。

应判给 A1 执行 1 次罚球且应如同任何最后一次罚球后那样继续比赛，比赛计时钟应从比赛被停止处连续计算。

F-3.3.26 举例 A1 运球时，A2 肘击 B2。裁判员没有宣判 A2 犯规。又过了 5 秒，B3 对运球队员 A1 犯规。

（a）B3 的犯规是该节的第 3 次全队犯规。

(b) B3's foul is the fifth team foul in the quarter.

Interpretation: The IRS review can be used to identify, at any time during the game, the involvement of the team members during any act of violence.

If the review provides A2 has hit B2 with an elbow, the referees can charge A2 with an unsportsmanlike foul.

B3's foul shall also be charged. The foul penalties shall be administered in the order they occurred. B2 shall attempt 2 free throws with no line-up. The right to possession as part of the unsportsmanlike foul penalty is lost as a result of the B3 foul.

In (a) the game shall be resumed with a Team A throw-in nearest the place where the game was stopped.

In (b) A1 shall be awarded 2 free throws and the game shall continue as after any last free throw.

The game clock shall continue from the point it was stopped.

F-3.3.27 **Example:** A1 dribbles when A2 hits B2 with an elbow. The referees do not call a foul against A2. After another 5 seconds a personal foul is called against dribbler A1 in the team A

(a) frontcourt.

(b) backcourt.

Interpretation: The IRS review can be used to identify, at any time during the game, the involvement of the team members during any act of violence.

If the review provides A2 has hit B2 with an elbow, the referees can charge A2 with an unsportsmanlike foul. A1's foul shall also be charged.

The foul penalties shall be administered in the order they occurred. B2 shall attempt 2 free throws with no line-up. The right to possession as part of the unsportsmanlike foul penalty is lost as a result of the subsequent foul by dribbler A1.

（b）B3 的犯规是该节的第 5 次全队犯规。

解释 在比赛的任何时间，IRS 复审可用于确认参与暴力行为的球队成员。

如果复审证实 A2 肘击到了 B2，裁判员可以判给 A2 一起违反体育运动精神的犯规。

B3 的犯规也应被登记。应根据这两起犯规发生的顺序执行罚则。应由 B2 执行 2 次不占位的罚球。B3 的犯规，应导致该违反体育运动精神的犯规罚则中的球权被取消。

在（a）中，应由 A 队在最靠近比赛被停止的地点执行掷球入界继续比赛。

在（b）中，应判给 A1 执行 2 次罚球且应如同任何最后一次罚球后那样继续比赛。

比赛计时钟应从比赛被停止处连续计算。

F-3.3.27 **举例** A1 运球时，A2 肘击 B2。裁判员没有宣判 A2 犯规。又过了 5 秒，运球队员 A1 在 A 队的：

（a）前场被判一起侵人犯规。

（b）后场被判一起侵人犯规。

解释 在比赛的任何时间，IRS 复审可用于确认参与暴力行为的球队成员。

如果复审证实 A2 肘击到了 B2，裁判员可以登记 A2 一起违反体育运动精神的犯规。A1 的犯规也应被登记。

应根据这两起犯规发生的顺序执行罚则。应由 B2 执行 2 次不占位的罚球。运球队员 A1 后续的犯规，应导致该违反体育运动精神的犯规罚则中的球权被取消。

The game shall be resumed with a Team B throw-in at the point nearest where the game was stopped.

In (a) team B shall have 24 seconds on the shot clock.

In (b) team B shall have 14 seconds on the shot clock.

The game clock shall continue from the point it was stopped.

F-3.3.28 **Example:** A1 hits B1 with an elbow. The referees do not call a foul against A1. Four seconds later, B1 is charged with an unsportsmanlike foul against A1 in the act of shooting for a

(a) 2-point goal.

(b) 3-point goal.

The ball enters the basket.

Interpretation: The IRS review can be used to identify, at any time during the game, the involvement of the team members during any act of violence.

If the review provides A1 has hit B1 with an elbow, the referees can charge A1 with an unsportsmanlike foul.

A1's goal, shall count.

In both cases, the unequal unsportsmanlike foul penalties shall be administered in the order they occurred.

B1 shall attempt two free throws with no line-up. The right to possession as part of the unsportsmanlike foul penalty is lost as a result of the subsequent unsportsmanlike foul by B1.

A1 shall attempt one free throw and the game shall be resumed with a Team A throw-in at the frontcourt throw-in line. Team A shall have 14 seconds on the shot clock.

The game clock shall continue from the point it was stopped.

F-3.3.29 **Example:** A1 dribbles when A2 hits B2 with an elbow. The referees do not call a foul against A2. After another 5 seconds a technical foul is called against A1 or B1.

应由B队在最靠近比赛被停止的地点执行掷球入界继续比赛。

在（a）中，B队应拥有24秒进攻时间。

在（b）中，B队应拥有14秒进攻时间。

比赛计时钟应从比赛被停止处连续计算。

F-3.3.28 **举例** A1肘击B1。裁判员没有宣判A1犯规。4秒后，B1被判对正在做：

（a）2分试投的A1一起违反体育运动精神的犯规。

（b）3分试投的A1一起违反体育运动精神的犯规。

球进入球篮。

解释 在比赛的任何时间，IRS复审可用于确认参与暴力行为的球队成员。

如果复审证实A1肘击到了B1，裁判员可以登记A1一起违反体育运动精神的犯规。

A1的中篮应计得分。

在这两种情况下，应根据这两起违反体育运动精神的犯规发生的顺序执行它们不同的罚则。

应由B1执行2次不占位的罚球。B1后续的违反体育运动精神的犯规，应导致先前的违反体育运动精神的犯规罚则中的球权被取消。

应由A1执行1次罚球且应由A队在其前场的掷球入界线处执行掷球入界继续比赛。A队应拥有14秒进攻时间。

比赛计时钟应从比赛被停止处连续计算。

F-3.3.29 **举例** A1运球时，A2肘击B2。裁判员没有宣判A2犯规。又过了5秒，宣判了A1或B1一起技术犯规。

Interpretation: The IRS review can be used to identify, at any time during the game, the involvement of the team members during any act of violence.

If the review provides A2 has hit B2 with an elbow, the referees can charge A2 with an unsportsmanlike foul. The penalty for the technical foul shall be administered first. Any team B or team A player shall attempt 1 free throw with no line-up. B2 shall then attempt 2 free throws with no line-up. The right to possession for the unsportsmanlike foul penalty is lost as a result of further action after the foul by A2.

The game shall be resumed with a team A throw-in from the place nearest to where the game was stopped. Team A shall have time remaining on the shot clock.

In both cases the game clock shall continue from the point it was stopped.

F-4 Head coach's challenge (HCC)

F-4.1 **Statement:** The head coach requesting an HCC shall establish visual contact with the nearest referee. The head coach shall say loudly in English 'challenge' and show the HCC official signal, drawing a rectangle with the hands.

The head coach request for an HCC can be cancelled until the referee grants the request with the HCC signal.

A head coach can challenge only the game situations mentioned in the OBR, Appendix F.3.

An HCC may be requested at any time of the game for all IRS reviewable situations, including when the game clock shows 2:00 or less in the fourth quarter or overtime.

F-4.2 **Example:** The team B head coach requests an HCC. The head coach establishes visual contact with the nearest referee and says loudly in English 'challenge', and shows the signal for an HCC. Immediately thereafter, and before the referee grants the request with the HCC signal, the team B head coach asks to cancel the request.

解释 在比赛的任何时间，IRS 复审可用于确认参与暴力行为的球队成员。

如果复审证实 A2 肘击到了 B2，裁判员可以登记 A2 一起违反体育运动精神的犯规。应首先执行技术犯规的罚则。应由 B 队或 A 队的任一队员执行 1 次不占位的罚球。然后，应由 B2 执行 2 次不占位的罚球。在 A2 犯规后发生的后续比赛情况，应导致该违反体育运动精神的犯规罚则中的球权被取消。

应由 A 队在最靠近比赛被停止的地点执行掷球入界继续比赛。A 队应拥有进攻计时钟显示的剩余时间。

在这两种情况下，比赛计时钟应从比赛被停止处连续计算。

F-4 主教练挑战（HCC）

F-4.1 **陈述** 请求 HCC 的主教练应与最靠近的裁判员建立目光联系。该主教练应用英语大声说出“challenge”（挑战）并做出 HCC 手势，即用手画出一个长方形。

主教练请求的 HCC 可以在裁判员做出准予该请求的 HCC 手势之前被取消。

主教练只可以挑战《篮球规则》中附录 F.3 所述的比赛情况。

在比赛的任何时间，包括在第 4 节或决胜期比赛计时钟显示 2:00 或更少时，主教练可以对所有可执行 IRS 复审的情况请求一次 HCC。

F-4.2 **举例** B 队主教练请求一次 HCC。该主教练与最靠近的裁判员建立了目光联系，用英语大声说出了“challenge”（挑战）并做出了 HCC 的手势。紧接着，在裁判员做出准予该请求的 HCC 手势之前，B 队主教练提出取消该请求。

Interpretation: The team B head coach has asked to cancel the request for an HCC, prior to the referee granting the request by showing the HCC signal. The HCC request shall be cancelled. The team B head coach has not yet used the 1 HCC team B is entitled to.

F-4.3 **Example:** With 22 seconds on the game clock in the second quarter, A1 attempts a shot for a goal. The ball touches the backboard above the level of the ring and is then touched by B1. The referee decided that B1's touch is legal and therefore did not call a goaltending violation. The team A head coach believes the decision is not correct and requests an HCC, using the proper procedure.

Interpretation: The goaltending or interference can be challenged only when the referees have called a goaltending or an interference violation. The head coach's request to challenge the decision shall not be granted.

F-4.4 **Example:** With 4:16 on the game clock in the third quarter, A1 drives to the basket and scores a goal. The team B head coach believes that there was a clear travelling violation by A1 before the goal was scored. The team B head coach requests an HCC, using the proper procedure.

Interpretation: The team B HCC shall not be granted. Only the game situations as listed in the OBR, Appendix F.3 may be challenged. Travelling violations, regardless of whether called or not, cannot be challenged.

F-4.5 **Example:** With 9 seconds on the game clock in the fourth quarter A1 scores a 2-point goal. The score is now A 82 – B 80. After the team B throw-in from its endline, the team A head coach believes that A1's goal should count for 3 points and requests an HCC. The referees recognise the request while B1 dribbles in the frontcourt.

Interpretation: The team A HCC shall be granted. The referees shall stop the game immediately without placing either team at a disadvantage.

If the IRS review provides A1's shot was attempted from the 2-point goal area the game shall be resumed with the score A 82 – B 80,

解释 B 队主教练在裁判员做出准予该请求的 HCC 手势之前已提出取消 HCC 的请求。该 HCC 请求应被取消。B 队主教练的 1 次 B 队 HCC 权尚未被使用。

F-4.3 **举例** 第 2 节，比赛计时钟显示 22 秒时，A1 尝试投篮。球在篮圈水平面以上触及了篮板后被 B1 触及。裁判员判定 B1 的触球是合法的，因此未宣判干涉得分违例。A 队主教练认为该决定不正确，并依照正确的程序请求了一次 HCC。

解释 只有在裁判员宣判了一起干涉得分或干扰得分违例时，主教练才可以挑战干涉得分或干扰得分。不应准予该主教练挑战这次决定的请求。

F-4.4 **举例** 第 3 节，比赛计时钟显示 4:16 时，A1 突破上篮并中篮得分。B 队主教练认为 A1 在中篮得分前发生了一起明显的带球走违例。B 队主教练依照正确的程序请求了一次 HCC。

解释 不应准予 B 队的 HCC。主教练只可以挑战《篮球规则》中附录 F.3 所述的比赛情况。带球走违例，无论被裁判员宣判与否，都不可以被挑战。

F-4.5 **举例** 第 4 节，比赛计时钟显示 9 秒时，A1 中篮得 2 分。此时比分为 A 82 – B 80。在 B 队从其端线后执行掷球入界后，A 队主教练认为 A1 的中篮应计 3 分并请求了一次 HCC。B1 在前场运球时，裁判员注意到了该请求。

解释 应准予 A 队的 HCC。裁判员应在不将任一队置于不利的情况下立即停止比赛。

如果 IRS 复审证实 A1 从 2 分中篮区域试投，那么比分应是 A 82 – B 80。

If the review provides A1's shot was attempted from the 3-point goal area the game shall be resumed with the score A 83 – B 80,

and in both cases, with a team B frontcourt throw-in from the place nearest to where the game was stopped during B1's dribbling and with the remaining time on the game clock.

F-4.6 **Example:** With 8 seconds on the game clock in the fourth quarter A1 scores a 2-point goal. The score is now A 82 – B 80. After the team B throw-in from its endline, the team A head coach believes that A1's goal should count for 3 points and requests an HCC. The referees recognise the request after B1 scores a 2-point goal with 1 second on the game clock. The score is now A 82 – B 82.

Interpretation: The team A HCC shall be granted. The referees shall stop the game immediately.

If the IRS review provides A1's shot was attempted from the 2-point goal area the game shall be resumed with the score A 82 – B 82, with a team A throw-in from behind its endline and with 1 second on the game clock.

If the review provides A1's shot was attempted from the 3-point goal area the game shall be resumed with the score A 83 – B 82, with a team A throw-in from its endline and with 1 second on the game clock.

F-4.7 **Example:** With 7 seconds on the game clock in the fourth quarter A1 scores a 2-point goal. The score is now A 82 – B 80. After the team B throw-in from its endline, the team A head coach believes that A1's goal should count for 3 points and requests an HCC. The referees recognise the request after B1 scores a 2-point goal and the game clock sounds while the ball was in the air for the end of the game. The score is now A 82 – B 82.

Interpretation: The team A HCC shall be granted. The referees shall conduct the IRS review before signing the scoresheet.

If the review provides A1's shot was attempted from the 2-point goal area the game shall be resumed with an overtime according to the alternating possession procedure.

如果复审证实 A1 从 3 分中篮区域试投，那么比分应是 A 83 – B 80。

在这两种情况下，应由 B 队在其前场最靠近 B1 运球时比赛被停止的地点执行掷球入界继续比赛，比赛计时钟应显示剩余时间。

F-4.6 **举例** 第 4 节，比赛计时钟显示 8 秒时，A1 中篮得 2 分。此时比分为 A 82 – B 80。在 B 队从其端线后执行掷球入界后，A 队主教练认为 A1 的中篮应计 3 分并请求了一次 HCC。B1 在比赛计时钟显示 1 秒时中篮得 2 分后，裁判员注意到了该请求。此时比分为 A 82 – B 82。

解释 应准予 A 队的 HCC。裁判员应立即停止比赛。

如果 IRS 复审证实 A1 从 2 分中篮区域试投，那么比分应是 A 82 – B 82，并且应由 A 队在其端线后执行掷球入界继续比赛，比赛计时钟应显示 1 秒。

如果复审证实 A1 从 3 分中篮区域试投，那么比分应是 A 83 – B 82，并且应由 A 队在其端线处执行掷球入界继续比赛，比赛计时钟应显示 1 秒。

F-4.7 **举例** 第 4 节，比赛计时钟显示 7 秒时，A1 中篮得 2 分。此时比分为 A 82 – B 80。在 B 队从其端线后执行掷球入界后，A 队主教练认为 A1 的中篮应计 3 分并请求了一次 HCC。B1 离手的球在空中时，结束比赛的计时钟信号响起，随即该球中篮得 2 分后，裁判员注意到了该请求。此时比分为 A 82 – B 82。

解释 应准予 A 队的 HCC。裁判员应在于记录表上签字之前执行 IRS 复审。

如果复审证实 A1 从 2 分中篮区域试投，那么应进入决胜期并依照交替拥有程序继续比赛。

If the review provides A1's shot was attempted from the 3-point goal area the game has ended with the final score A 83 – B 82.

F-4.8 **Example:** With 6 seconds on the game clock in the fourth quarter A1 scores a 2-point goal. The score is now A 82 – B 80. Then B1 attempts a successful shot for a 2-point goal while the ball is in the air the game clock sounds for the end of the game. The score is now A 82 – B 82. The team A head coach believes that A1's goal should count for 3 points and immediately requests an HCC using the proper procedure.

Interpretation: The team A HCC shall be granted. The crew chief can use the IRS review for the HCC, at any time of the game, to decide whether the ball shall count for 2 or 3 points.

If the review provides A1's shot was attempted from the 2-point goal area the game shall be resumed with an overtime according to the alternation possession procedure.

If the review provides A1's shot was attempted from the 3-point goal area the game has ended with tho final score A 83 – B 82.

F-4.9 **Example:** With 6:36 on the game clock in the fourth quarter the ball goes out-of-bounds. The referees award the ball to team A. Team A is granted a time-out. The team B head coach believes the decision is not correct and requests a challenge, using the proper procedure.

Interpretation: The team B HCC shall be granted. The IRS review can be used to decide on an HCC, at any time of the game, whether the out-of-bounds violation was called correctly.

The time-out period shall not start until the review ends and the referee communicates the final decision. The team A time-out request may be withdrawn at any time during the review until after the referee communicates the final IRS decision.

F-4.10 **Example:** With 5:28 on the game clock in the second quarter, A1 dribbles close to the sideline and passes the ball to A2 who scores a goal. The team B head coach believes that team A has committed a clear 8-second violation before A2 scored the goal. The team B head coach requests an HCC, using the proper procedure.

如果复审证实 A1 从 3 分中篮区域试投，那么比赛已结束，最终比分为 A 83 – B 82。

F-4.8 **举例** 第 4 节，比赛计时钟显示 6 秒时，A1 中篮得 2 分。此时比分为 A 82 – B 80。随后 B1 试投 2 分，当球在空中时，结束比赛的计时钟信号响起，随即该球中篮，此时比分为 A 82 – B 82。A 队主教练认为 A1 的中篮应计 3 分并立即依照正确的程序请求了一次 HCC。

解释 应准予 A 队的 HCC。在比赛的任何时间，主裁判员都可以因 HCC 而使用 IRS 复审来确定球中篮应计 2 分还是 3 分。

如果复审证实 A1 从 2 分中篮区域试投，那么应进入决胜期并依照交替拥有程序继续比赛。

如果复审证实 A1 从 3 分中篮区域试投，那么比赛已结束，最终比分为 A 83 – B 82。

F-4.9 **举例** 第 4 节，比赛计时钟显示 6:36 时，球出界。裁判员将球判给 A 队。A 队此时被准予一次暂停。B 队主教练认为该决定不正确，并依照正确的程序请求了一次挑战。

解释 应准予 B 队的 HCC。在比赛的任何时间，IRS 复审可在一起 HCC 中用于确定是否正确地宣判了一起出界违例。

在裁判员完成复审并宣布最终决定后，该暂停时段才开始。A 队的暂停请求可以在复审期间的任何时间，以及在裁判员宣布 IRS 的最终决定后被取消。

F-4.10 **举例** 第 2 节，比赛计时钟显示 5:28 时，A1 在靠近边线处运球并传球给 A2，A2 随后中篮得分。B 队主教练认为在 A2 中篮得分之前，A 队发生了一起明显的 8 秒违例。B 队主教练依照正确的程序请求了一次 HCC。

Interpretation: The team B HCC shall not be granted. Only the game situations in the OBR, Appendix F.3 may be challenged. An 8-second violation can only be reviewed when it involves in a game situation at the end of the quarter or overtime.

The goal shall count. The team B head coach has not yet used the 1 HCC team B is entitled to.

F-4.11 **Example:** With 2:30 on the game clock in the third quarter B1 fouls A1. B1 is then charged with a technical foul, followed by a B1 disqualification for the further verbal abuse of the referees. The team A head coach believes that the personal foul against B1 should be upgraded to an unsportsmanlike foul and requests an HCC.

Interpretation: The team A HCC shall be granted. The IRS review can be used to decide, at any time during the game, whether a personal foul shall be upgraded to an unsportsmanlike foul.

If the review foul provides B1's personal foul was an unsportsmanlike foul, B1's technical foul shall lead to B1's automatic disqualification. B1's disqualification for the further abuse of the referees can no longer be penalised in the game and shall be reported to the governing body of the competition. Any team A player shall attempt 1 free throw with no line-up. Then A1 shall attempt 2 free throws with no line-up. The game shall be resumed with a team A throw-in from the throw-in line in its frontcourt.

F-4.12 **Example:** With 43.4 seconds on the game clock in the third quarter and 1.2 of a second on the shot clock A1 attempts a shot for a 3-point goal. The shot is unsuccessful and misses the ring after which B1 touches the ball close to the basket and the ball immediately goes out-of-bounds. The referees award the throw-in to team B when the referees realise the shot clock has no display visible.

The team A head coach believes that B1 caused the ball to go out-of-bounds and requests an HCC.

Interpretation: The IRS review can be used to decide, at any time of the game if an HCC is granted, which team caused an out-of-bounds violation. If so, the review can furthermore be used to decide how much time shall be shown on the shot clock, in the event of a malfunction of the shot clock.

解释 不应准予 B 队的 HCC。主教练只可以挑战《篮球规则》中附录 F.3 所述的比赛情况。8 秒违例只可以在一节或决胜期结束时发生在相关的比赛情况中时被复审。

中篮应计得分。B 队主教练的 1 次 B 队 HCC 权未被使用。

F-4.11 **举例** 第 3 节，比赛计时钟显示 2:30 时，B1 对 A1 犯规。然后 B1 被判一起技术犯规，接着 B1 又因为进一步辱骂裁判员被取消比赛资格。A 队主教练认为 B1 的侵人犯规应被升级为违反体育运动精神的犯规，并请求了一次 HCC。

解释 应准予 A 队的 HCC。在比赛的任何时间，IRS 复审可用于确定一起侵人犯规是否应被升级为一起违反体育运动精神的犯规。

如果复审证实 B1 的侵人犯规应当是一起违反体育运动精神的犯规，那么 B1 的技术犯规就应导致 B1 被自动取消比赛资格。B1 因为进一步辱骂裁判员而被判的取消比赛资格的犯规不能再被处罚，只应向竞赛的组织部门报告。应由 A 队任一队员执行 1 次不占位的罚球，然后应由 A1 执行 2 次不占位的罚球。应由 A 队在其前场的掷球入界线处执行掷球入界继续比赛。

F-4.12 **举例** 第 3 节，比赛计时钟显示 43.4 秒，进攻计时钟显示 1.2 秒时，A1 尝试 3 分投篮。球既没有进入球篮，也没有触及篮圈，随后，B1 在靠近球篮处触及球，球随即出界。裁判员判给 B 队掷球入界时，察觉到进攻计时钟无显示。

A 队主教练认为 B1 使球出界，并请求了一次 HCC。

解释 在比赛的任何时间，当准予 HCC 时，IRS 复审可用于确定发生出界违例的球队。如准予了 HCC，该复审还可以在进攻计时钟发生故障的情况中，进一步用来确定进攻计时钟应显示多少时间。

If the review provides that B1 has caused the ball to go out-of-bounds and the shot clock would have expired before the ball went out-of-bounds, there is no time remaining on the shot clock for team A, therefore this is a team A shot clock violation. The ball shall be awarded to team B for a throw-in from behind the endline with 24 seconds on the shot clock.

The team A head coach has not yet used the 1 HCC team A is entitled to.

If the review provides that A1 has caused the ball to go out-of-bounds, the ball shall be awarded to team B for a throw-in from behind the endline with 24 seconds on the shot clock.

The team A head coach has used the 1 HCC team A is entitled to.

If the review provides that B1 has caused the ball to go out-of-bounds and the shot clock did not expire before the ball went out-of-bounds, the game shall be resumed with a team A throw-in from behind the endline in its frontcourt with the remaining time on the shot clock.

The team A head coach has used the 1 HCC team A is entitled to.

F-4.13 **Statement:** When an HCC is requested after a time-out from either team has started, that time-out shall continue without any interruption. The HCC request cannot be cancelled, and the HCC review shall be administered after the time-out.

F-4.14 **Example:** A1 scores a 3-point goal. At this time, team B requests a time-out. During the time-out the team B head coach believes that A1 has stepped on the 3-point line before the shot was released and requests an HCC, using the proper procedure.

Interpretation: The team B HCC shall be granted. The IRS review can be used to decide whether a successful goal was released from the 2- or 3-point area. The time-out shall continue without any interruption. The HCC review shall be administered after the time-out.

F-4.15 **Statement:** In all games where the Instant Replay System (IRS) is used the head coach may be granted only one HCC. The time restrictions within OBR, Appendix F.3 do not apply.

如果复审证实 B1 使球出界，但在球出界之前进攻时间应当已终了，则 A 队已没有剩余的进攻时间，因此，这是 A 队的进攻时间违例。应判给 B 队在其端线后执行掷球入界，B 队应拥有 24 秒进攻时间。

A 队主教练的 1 次 A 队 HCC 权未被使用。

如果复审证实 A1 使球出界，应判给 B 队在其端线后执行掷球入界，B 队应拥有 24 秒进攻时间。

A 队主教练的 1 次 A 队 HCC 权已被使用。

如果复审证实 B1 使球出界，并且在球出界之前进攻时间未终了，应由 A 队在其前场端线后执行掷球入界继续比赛，A 队应拥有进攻计时钟显示的剩余时间。

A 队主教练的 1 次 A 队 HCC 权已被使用。

F-4.13 **陈述** 在任一队的暂停开始后请求一次 HCC 时，该暂停应继续，而非被中断。该 HCC 请求不能被取消，该 HCC 复审应在暂停结束后执行。

F-4.14 **举例** A1 中篮得 3 分。此时，B 队请求一次暂停。在暂停期间，B 队主教练认为 A1 在投篮球离手之前脚踩 3 分线，并依照正确的程序请求了一次 HCC。

解释 应准予 B 队的 HCC。在比赛的任何时间，IRS 复审可用于确定球中篮是从 2 分中篮区域还是 3 分中篮区域离手的。该暂停应继续，而非被中断。该 HCC 复审应在暂停结束后执行。

F-4.15 **陈述** 在所有使用即时回放系统（IRS）的比赛中，每名主教练只可以被准予一次 HCC。《篮球规则》中附录 F.3 对时间的限制不适用。

F-4.16 **Example:** With 3:23 on the game clock in the second quarter the ball goes out-of-bounds. The referees award the ball to team A. The team B head coach believes the decision is not correct and requests an HCC, using the proper procedure. This is

(a) the first team B HCC requested in the game.

(b) the second team B HCC requested in the game.

Interpretation:

(a) The HCC shall be granted. The crew chief shall use the IRS review, at any time of the game, to decide whether the out-of-bounds violation was called correctly.

If the review provides the decision is correct, the game shall be resumed with a team A throw-in.

If the review provides the decision is not correct, the decision shall be corrected. The game shall be resumed with a team B throw-in.

In both cases, the team B head coach has used the 1 HCC team B is entitled to.

(b) The team B head coach has already used the 1 HCC team B is entitled to. The request shall not be granted.

F-4.17 **Example:** With 3:21 on the game clock in the second quarter the ball goes out-of-bounds. The referees award the ball to team A. The team B head coach believes the decision is not correct and requests an HCC, using the proper procedure. The HCC is granted. Immediately after the team B head coach changes the mind and asks the request to be withdrawn.

Interpretation: Once the HCC is granted, the challenge request shall be final and irreversible.

F-4.18 **Example:** With 2:35 on the game clock in the second quarter, A1 scores a goal close to the end of the shot clock period and the game continues.

The team B head coach believes that the shot clock signal had sounded before the shot was released. B1 dribbles when the team B head coach requests an HCC, using the proper procedure.

F-4.16 **举例** 第 2 节，比赛计时钟显示 3:23 时，球出界。裁判员将球判给 A 队。B 队主教练认为该决定不正确，并依照正确的程序请求了一次 HCC。这是：

（a）B 队主教练在本场比赛中请求的第 1 次 HCC。

（b）B 队主教练在本场比赛中请求的第 2 次 HCC。

解释

（a）应准予 B 队的 HCC。在比赛的任何时间，应由主裁判员使用 IRS 复审来确定是否正确地宣判了一起出界违例。

如果复审证实裁判员的决定是正确的，应由 A 队执行掷球入界继续比赛。

如果复审证实裁判员的决定是不正确的，应纠正该决定。应由 B 队执行掷球入界继续比赛。

B 队主教练的 1 次 B 队 HCC 权在这两种情况下都已被使用。

（b）B 队主教练已经使用过了 1 次 B 队 HCC 权。不应准予该请求。

F-4.17 **举例** 第 2 节，比赛计时钟显示 3:21 时，球出界。裁判员将球判给 A 队。B 队主教练认为该决定不正确，并依照正确的程序请求了一次 HCC。该 HCC 被准予后，B 队主教练改变了想法并立即提出要取消该请求。

解释 一旦准予了 HCC，该请求就应是最终且不可取消的。

F-4.18 **举例** 第 2 节，比赛计时钟显示 2:35 时，A1 在临近进攻时间结束时中篮得分，比赛继续。

B 队主教练认为进攻计时钟的信号在投篮球离手之前已响。B1 运球时，B 队主教练依照正确的程序请求了一次 HCC。

Interpretation: The team B HCC shall be granted. The IRS review can be used to decide, at any time of the game, whether the ball had left A1's hands on a shot for a goal before the shot clock signal sounded. An HCC may be requested at any time in the game.

The referees are authorized to stop the game immediately and conduct a review.

If the review provides the ball was released before the shot clock signal sounded, the goal shall count. The game shall be resumed with a team B throw-in from the place nearest to where the ball was located when the game was stopped. Team B shall have the time remaining on the shot clock.

If the review provides the ball was released after the shot clock signal sounded, the goal shall not count. The game shall be resumed with a team B throw-in from the place nearest to where the ball was located when the game was stopped. Team B shall have the time remaining on the shot clock.

In both cases, the team B head coach has used the 1 HCC team B is entitled to.

F-4.19 **Example:** With 2:29 on the game clock in the second quarter, A1 scores a goal close to the end of the shot clock period and the game continues.

The referees stop the game in the team B frontcourt when A2 causes the ball to go out-of-bounds. At this time, the team B head coach believes that the shot clock signal had sounded before the shot was released and requests an HCC, using the proper procedure.

Interpretation: An HCC may be requested, at any time of the game, at the latest when the referees have stopped the game for the first time after the decision. The team B HCC shall be granted. The IRS review can be used to decide, whether the ball had left A1's hands on a shot for a goal before the shot clock signal sounded.

If the review provides the ball was released before the shot clock signal sounded, the goal shall count.

解释 应准予 B 队的 HCC。在比赛的任何时间，IRS 复审可用于确定 A1 的投篮是否在进攻计时钟信号响之前球离手。一名主教练可以在比赛的任何时间请求一次 HCC。

裁判员有权立即停止比赛并执行一次复审。

如果复审证实进攻计时钟信号响之前球已离手，中篮应计得分。应由 B 队在最靠近比赛被停止时球所在位置的地点执行掷球入界继续比赛。B 队应拥有进攻计时钟显示的剩余时间。

如果复审证实进攻计时钟信号响之后球才离手，中篮不应计得分。应由 B 队在最靠近比赛被停止时球所在位置的地点执行掷球入界继续比赛。B 队应拥有进攻计时钟显示的剩余时间。

B 队主教练的 1 次 B 队 HCC 权在这两种情况下都已被使用。

F-4.19 **举例** 第 2 节，比赛计时钟显示 2:29 时，A1 在临近进攻时间结束时中篮得分，比赛继续。

A2 在 B 队前场使球出界时，裁判员停止了比赛。此时，B 队主教练认为进攻计时钟的信号在投篮球离手之前已响，并依照正确的程序请求了一次 HCC。

解释 一名主教练可以在比赛的任何时间请求一次 HCC，但该请求最迟必须在裁判员对有待复审的情况作出决定后首次停止比赛时提出。应准予 B 队的 HCC。IRS 复审可用于确定 A1 的投篮是否在进攻计时钟信号响之前球离手。

如果复审证实进攻计时钟信号响之前球已离手，中篮应计得分。

If the review provides the ball was released after the shot clock signal sounded, the goal shall not count.

In both cases, the game shall be resumed with a team B throw-in from the place nearest where the ball went out-of-bounds. Team B shall have the time remaining on the shot clock. The team B head coach has used the 1 HCC team B is entitled to.

F-4.20 **Example:** With 7:22 on the game clock in the third quarter, B1 fouls dribbler A1. This is the second team B foul in the quarter.

The team A head coach believes that there was no legitimate attempt to play the ball and that B1's personal foul should be upgraded to an unsportsmanlike foul. The team A head coach requests an HCC, using the proper procedure.

Interpretation: The team A HCC shall be granted. The IRS review can be used to decide, at any time of the game, whether a personal foul, an unsportsmanlike foul or a disqualifying foul shall be upgraded or downgraded or shall be considered as a technical foul.

If the review provides the foul was a personal foul, the game shall be resumed with a team A throw-in from the place nearest to where the ball was located when the personal foul was called.

If the review provides the personal foul was an unsportsmanlike foul, the personal foul shall be upgraded. The game shall be resumed as after any other unsportsmanlike foul.

In both cases, the team A head coach has used the 1 HCC team A is entitled to.

F-4.21 **Example:** With 7:16 on the game clock in the third quarter

(a) B1 fouls dribbler A1. This is the second team B foul in the quarter. The game is resumed with a team A throw-in. A2 then scores a 2-point goal.

(b) B1 fouls A1 in the act of shooting. The ball does not enter the basket. A1 has the ball at the disposal for the first free throw.

如果复审证实进攻计时钟信号响之后球才离手，中篮不应计得分。

在这两种情况下，应由B队在最靠近球出界的地点执行掷球入界继续比赛。B队应拥有进攻计时钟显示的剩余时间。B队主教练的1次B队HCC权已被使用。

F-4.20 **举例** 第3节，比赛计时钟显示7:22时，B1对运球队员A1犯规，这是该节B队的第2次全队犯规。

A队主教练认为该犯规动作不是合理的篮球动作，并应将B1的侵人犯规升级为违反体育运动精神的犯规。A队主教练依照正确的程序请求了一次HCC。

解释 应准予A队的HCC。在比赛的任何时间，IRS复审可用于确定一起侵人犯规、违反体育运动精神的犯规或取消比赛资格的犯规是否应被升级或降级，还是应被视为一起技术犯规。

如果复审证实该犯规是一起侵人犯规，应由A队在最靠近宣判该侵人犯规时球所在位置的地点执行掷球入界继续比赛。

如果复审证实该侵人犯规应当是一起违反体育运动精神的犯规，就应将该侵人犯规升级。应如同发生任何其他的违反体育运动精神的犯规后那样继续比赛。

A队主教练的1次A队HCC权在这两种情况下都已被使用。

F-4.21 **举例** 第3节，比赛计时钟显示7:16时，

(a) B1对运球队员A1犯规，这是该节B队的第2次全队犯规。由A队执行掷球入界继续比赛。然后，A2中篮得2分。

(b) B1对正在做投篮动作的A1犯规。球未进入球篮。此时A1在执行第1次罚球时已可处理球。

The team A head coach now believes that there was no legitimate attempt to play the ball and that B1's personal foul should be upgraded to an unsportsmanlike foul. The team A head coach requests an HCC, using the proper procedure.

Interpretation: The team A HCC shall not be granted. After the ball is at the team A player's disposal for the

(a) throw-in,

(b) first free throw,

it is too late for the HCC to be granted. The head coach must request the HCC and the IRS review must take place at the latest when the referees have stopped the game for the first time after the decision and before the ball becomes live again.

The team A head coach has not yet used the 1 HCC team A is entitled to.

F-4.22 **Example:** A1 scores a goal close to the end of the shot clock period and the game continues.

The team B first assistant coach believes that the shot clock signal had sounded before the shot was released and requests a challenge, using the correct procedure.

Interpretation: The team B first assistant coach request shall not be granted. The IRS review can be requested only by the team B head coach.

F-4.23 **Example:** The scorer shall enter all requested team HCCs on the scoresheet.

Interpretation: Only the granted HCC shall be entered on the scoresheet in the 2 boxes, next to the HCC. In the first box the scorer shall enter the quarter or overtime and in the second box the minute of the playing time in the quarter or overtime.

此时，A 队主教练认为该犯规动作不是合理的篮球动作，并应将 B1 的侵人犯规升级为违反体育运动精神的犯规。A 队主教练依照正确的程序请求了一次 HCC。

解释 不应准予 A 队的 HCC。在 A 队队员的：

（a）掷球入界可处理球后，

（b）第 1 次罚球可处理球后，

要准予该 HCC 已经太晚。一名主教练最迟必须在裁判员对有待复审的情况作出决定后首次停止比赛且球再次成为活球之前提出 HCC 请求。

A 队主教练的 1 次 A 队 HCC 权尚未被使用。

F-4.22 **举例** A1 在临近进攻时间结束时中篮得分，比赛继续。

B 队第一助理教练认为进攻计时钟的信号在投篮球离手之前已响，并依照正确的程序请求了一次挑战。

解释 不应准予 B 队第一助理教练请求的挑战。只有 B 队主教练才可以请求 IRS 复审。

F-4.23 **举例** 记录员应在记录表上登记所有球队请求的 HCC。

解释 应只将被准予的 HCC 登记在记录表上“HCC”旁的两个空格内。记录员应在第一个空格内填入某节或决胜期，并在第二个空格内填入该节或决胜期此时的比赛时间（分）。

NOTE